Python Web Scra
Cookbook

Over 90 proven recipes to get you scraping with Python, microservices, Docker, and AWS

Michael Heydt

Packt

BIRMINGHAM - MUMBAI

Python Web Scraping Cookbook

Commissioning Editor: Veena Pagare
Acquisition Editor: Tushar Gupta
Content Development Editor: Tejas Limkar
Technical Editor: Danish Shaikh
Copy Editor: Safis Editing
Project Coordinator: Manthan Patel
Proofreader: Safis Editing
Indexer: Rekha Nair
Graphics: Tania Dutta
Production Coordinator: Shraddha Falebhai

First published: February 2018

Production reference: 1070218

Published by Packt Publishing Ltd.
Livery Place
35 Livery Street
Birmingham
B3 2PB, UK.

ISBN 978-1-78728-521-7

www.packtpub.com

Contributors

About the author

Michael Heydt is an independent consultant specializing in social, mobile, analytics, and cloud technologies, with an emphasis on cloud native 12-factor applications. Michael has been a software developer and trainer for over 30 years and is the author of books such as D3.js By Example, Learning Pandas, Mastering Pandas for Finance, and Instant Lucene.NET. You can find more information about him on LinkedIn at `michaelheydt`.

I would like to greatly thank my family for putting up with me disappearing for months on end and sacrificing my sparse free time to indulge in creation of content and books like this one. They are my true inspiration and enablers.

About the reviewers

Dimitrios Kouzis-Loukas has over 15 years of experience providing software systems to small and big organisations. His most recent projects are typically distributed systems with ultra-low latency and high availability. He is language agnostic but has a slight preference for C++ and Python. A firm believer in open source, he hopes that his contributions will benefit individual communities as well as all of humanity.

Lazar Telebak is a freelance web developer specializing in web scraping, crawling, and indexing web pages using Python libraries/frameworks.
He has worked mostly on projects of automation, website scraping, crawling, and exporting data in various formats (CSV, JSON, XML, and TXT) and databases such as (MongoDB, SQLAlchemy, and Postgres). Lazar also has experience of fronted technologies and languages such as HTML, CSS, JavaScript, and jQuery.

Packt is searching for authors like you

If you're interested in becoming an author for Packt, please visit `authors.packtpub.com` and apply today. We have worked with thousands of developers and tech professionals, just like you, to help them share their insight with the global tech community. You can make a general application, apply for a specific hot topic that we are recruiting an author for, or submit your own idea.

Table of Contents

Preface 1

Chapter 1: Getting Started with Scraping 7

- **Introduction** 7
- **Setting up a Python development environment** 8
  - Getting ready 8
  - How to do it... 8
- **Scraping Python.org with Requests and Beautiful Soup** 13
  - Getting ready... 13
  - How to do it... 14
  - How it works... 17
- **Scraping Python.org in urllib3 and Beautiful Soup** 19
  - Getting ready... 19
  - How to do it... 19
  - How it works 20
  - There's more... 20
- **Scraping Python.org with Scrapy** 21
  - Getting ready... 21
  - How to do it... 22
  - How it works 23
- **Scraping Python.org with Selenium and PhantomJS** 25
  - Getting ready 25
  - How to do it... 26
  - How it works 28
  - There's more... 28

Chapter 2: Data Acquisition and Extraction 29

- **Introduction** 29
- **How to parse websites and navigate the DOM using BeautifulSoup** 30
  - Getting ready 30
  - How to do it... 32
  - How it works 35
  - There's more... 35
- **Searching the DOM with Beautiful Soup's find methods** 35
  - Getting ready 35

How to do it... 36
Querying the DOM with XPath and lxml 38
Getting ready 39
How to do it... 39
How it works 45
There's more... 45
Querying data with XPath and CSS selectors 46
Getting ready 46
How to do it... 47
How it works 47
There's more... 48
Using Scrapy selectors 48
Getting ready 48
How to do it... 48
How it works 50
There's more... 50
Loading data in unicode / UTF-8 50
Getting ready 51
How to do it... 52
How it works 53
There's more... 53
Chapter 3: Processing Data 55
Introduction 55
Working with CSV and JSON data 56
Getting ready 56
How to do it 58
How it works 64
There's more... 64
Storing data using AWS S3 65
Getting ready 65
How to do it 66
How it works 69
There's more... 70
Storing data using MySQL 70
Getting ready 70
How to do it 71
How it works 75
There's more... 75

Storing data using PostgreSQL 76
Getting ready 76
How to do it 77
How it works 80
There's more... 80
Storing data in Elasticsearch 81
Getting ready 81
How to do it 81
How it works 84
There's more... 84
How to build robust ETL pipelines with AWS SQS 85
Getting ready 85
How to do it - posting messages to an AWS queue 86
How it works 87
How to do it - reading and processing messages 88
How it works 90
There's more... 90
Chapter 4: Working with Images, Audio, and other Assets 91
Introduction 92
Downloading media content from the web 92
Getting ready 92
How to do it 93
How it works 93
There's more... 94
Parsing a URL with urllib to get the filename 94
Getting ready 94
How to do it 94
How it works 95
There's more... 95
Determining the type of content for a URL 96
Getting ready 96
How to do it 96
How it works 96
There's more... 97
Determining the file extension from a content type 98
Getting ready 98
How to do it 98
How it works 98

There's more... 99
Downloading and saving images to the local file system 99
How to do it 100
How it works 100
There's more... 101
Downloading and saving images to S3 101
Getting ready 101
How to do it 101
How it works 102
There's more... 103
Generating thumbnails for images 103
Getting ready 104
How to do it 104
How it works 105
Taking a screenshot of a website 106
Getting ready 106
How to do it 106
How it works 108
Taking a screenshot of a website with an external service 109
Getting ready 110
How to do it 111
How it works 113
There's more... 115
Performing OCR on an image with pytesseract 115
Getting ready 115
How to do it 116
How it works 117
There's more... 117
Creating a Video Thumbnail 117
Getting ready 117
How to do it 117
How it works 119
There's more.. 120
Ripping an MP4 video to an MP3 120
Getting ready 120
How to do it 121
There's more... 121
Chapter 5: Scraping - Code of Conduct 123

Introduction 123
Scraping legality and scraping politely 123
Getting ready 124
How to do it 125
Respecting robots.txt 125
Getting ready 127
How to do it 127
How it works 128
There's more... 129
Crawling using the sitemap 129
Getting ready 131
How to do it 132
How it works 133
There's more... 135
Crawling with delays 137
Getting ready 137
How to do it 137
How it works 139
There's more... 139
Using identifiable user agents 140
How to do it 140
How it works 140
There's more... 141
Setting the number of concurrent requests per domain 141
How it works 141
Using auto throttling 142
How to do it 142
How it works 142
There's more... 143
Using an HTTP cache for development 143
How to do it 143
How it works 143
There's more... 144
Chapter 6: Scraping Challenges and Solutions 145
Introduction 146
Retrying failed page downloads 146
How to do it 146
How it works 147

Supporting page redirects 147
How to do it 147
How it works 148
Waiting for content to be available in Selenium 149
How to do it 150
How it works 151
Limiting crawling to a single domain 152
How to do it 152
How it works 153
Processing infinitely scrolling pages 153
Getting ready 154
How to do it 156
How it works 157
There's more... 158
Controlling the depth of a crawl 159
How to do it 159
How it works 160
Controlling the length of a crawl 162
How to do it 162
How it works 162
Handling paginated websites 163
Getting ready 163
How to do it 164
How it works 164
There's more... 166
Handling forms and forms-based authorization 166
Getting ready 166
How to do it 167
How it works 169
There's more... 169
Handling basic authorization 170
How to do it 170
How it works 170
There's more... 170
Preventing bans by scraping via proxies 171
Getting ready 171
How to do it 171
How it works 172
Randomizing user agents 172

How to do it 173
Caching responses 174
How to do it 174
There's more... 175
Chapter 7: Text Wrangling and Analysis 177
Introduction 178
Installing NLTK 178
How to do it 178
Performing sentence splitting 179
How to do it 180
There's more... 181
Performing tokenization 181
How to do it 182
Performing stemming 183
How to do it 183
Performing lemmatization 184
How to do it 185
Determining and removing stop words 186
How to do it 186
There's more... 188
Calculating the frequency distributions of words 188
How to do it 189
There's more... 190
Identifying and removing rare words 190
How to do it 190
Identifying and removing rare words 192
How to do it 192
Removing punctuation marks 193
How to do it 193
There's more... 194
Piecing together n-grams 194
How to do it 195
There's more... 198
Scraping a job listing from StackOverflow 198
Getting ready 199
How to do it 201
There's more... 202
Reading and cleaning the description in the job listing 203

Getting ready 203
How to do it... 203
Chapter 8: Searching, Mining and Visualizing Data 209
Introduction 209
Geocoding an IP address 210
Getting ready 210
How to do it 212
How to collect IP addresses of Wikipedia edits 213
Getting ready 214
How to do it 215
How it works 216
There's more... 217
Visualizing contributor location frequency on Wikipedia 217
How to do it 218
Creating a word cloud from a StackOverflow job listing 220
Getting ready 221
How to do it 221
Crawling links on Wikipedia 222
Getting ready 222
How to do it 223
How it works 224
Theres more... 227
Visualizing page relationships on Wikipedia 227
Getting ready 227
How to do it 228
How it works 229
There's more... 230
Calculating degrees of separation 232
How to do it 232
How it works 232
There's more... 233
Chapter 9: Creating a Simple Data API 235
Introduction 235
Creating a REST API with Flask-RESTful 236
Getting ready 236
How to do it 236
How it works 237
There's more... 238

Integrating the REST API with scraping code 239
Getting ready 239
How to do it 241
Adding an API to find the skills for a job listing 242
Getting ready 242
How to do it 243
Storing data in Elasticsearch as the result of a scraping request 244
Getting ready 244
How to do it 245
How it works 248
There's more... 248
Checking Elasticsearch for a listing before scraping 250
How to do it 250
There's more... 251
Chapter 10: Creating Scraper Microservices with Docker 253
Introduction 253
Installing Docker 254
Getting ready 254
How to do it 255
Installing a RabbitMQ container from Docker Hub 256
Getting ready 257
How to do it 257
Running a Docker container (RabbitMQ) 259
Getting ready 259
How to do it 260
There's more... 262
Creating and running an Elasticsearch container 262
How to do it 262
Stopping/restarting a container and removing the image 264
How to do it 264
There's more... 267
Creating a generic microservice with Nameko 267
Getting ready 267
How to do it 268
How it works 270
There's more... 271
Creating a scraping microservice 271
How to do it 271

There's more... 273
Creating a scraper container 273
Getting ready 273
How to do it 275
How it works 277
Creating an API container 279
Getting ready 279
How to do it 279
There's more... 282
Composing and running the scraper locally with docker-compose 282
Getting ready 282
How to do it 283
There's more... 288
Chapter 11: Making the Scraper as a Service Real 289
Introduction 290
Creating and configuring an Elastic Cloud trial account 290
How to do it 291
Accessing the Elastic Cloud cluster with curl 294
How to do it 294
Connecting to the Elastic Cloud cluster with Python 295
Getting ready 295
How to do it 295
There's more... 297
Performing an Elasticsearch query with the Python API 299
Getting ready 300
How to do it 300
There's more... 303
Using Elasticsearch to query for jobs with specific skills 303
Getting ready 303
How to do it 303
Modifying the API to search for jobs by skill 307
How to do it 308
How it works 309
There's more... 310
Storing configuration in the environment 310
How to do it 311
Creating an AWS IAM user and a key pair for ECS 312
Getting ready 312

How to do it 312
Configuring Docker to authenticate with ECR 314
Getting ready 314
How to do it 314
Pushing containers into ECR 316
Getting ready 316
How to do it 318
Creating an ECS cluster 322
How to do it 322
Creating a task to run our containers 325
Getting ready 325
How to do it 325
How it works 328
Starting and accessing the containers in AWS 331
Getting ready 331
How to do it 332
There's more... 335
Other Books You May Enjoy 337
Index 341

Preface

The internet contains a wealth of data. This data is both provided through structured APIs as well as by content delivered directly through websites. While the data in APIs is highly structured, information found in web pages is often unstructured and requires collection, extraction, and processing to be of value. And collecting data is just the start of the journey, as that data must also be stored, mined, and then exposed to others in a value-added form.

With this book, you will learn many of the core tasks needed in collecting various forms of information from websites. We will cover how to collect it, how to perform several common data operations (including storage in local and remote databases), how to perform common media-based tasks such as converting images an videos to thumbnails, how to clean unstructured data with NTLK, how to examine several data mining and visualization tools, and finally core skills in building a microservices-based scraper and API that can, and will, be run on the cloud.

Through a recipe-based approach, we will learn independent techniques to solve specific tasks involved in not only scraping but also data manipulation and management, data mining, visualization, microservices, containers, and cloud operations. These recipes will build skills in a progressive and holistic manner, not only teaching how to perform the fundamentals of scraping but also taking you from the results of scraping to a service offered to others through the cloud. We will be building an actual web-scraper-as-a-service using common tools in the Python, container, and cloud ecosystems.

Who this book is for

This book is for those who want to learn to extract data from websites using the process of scraping and also how to work with various data management tools and cloud services. The coding will require basic skills in the Python programming language.

The book is also for those who wish to learn about a larger ecosystem of tools for retrieving, storing, and searching data, as well as using modern tools and Pythonic libraries to create data APIs and cloud services. You may also be using Docker and Amazon Web Services to package and deploy a scraper on the cloud.

What this book covers

`Chapter 1`, *Getting Started with Scraping*, introduces several concepts and tools for web scraping. We will examine how to install and do basic tasks with tools such as requests, urllib, BeautifulSoup, Scrapy, PhantomJS and Selenium.

`Chapter 2`, *Data Acquisition and Extraction*, is based on an understanding of the structure of HTML and how to find and extract embedded data. We will cover many of the concepts in the DOM and how to find and extract data using BeautifulSoup, XPath, LXML, and CSS selectors. We also briefly examine working with Unicode / UTF8.

`Chapter 3`, *Processing Data*, teaches you to load and manipulate data in many formats, and then how to store that data in various data stores (S3, MySQL, PostgreSQL, and ElasticSearch). Data in web pages is represented in various formats, the most common being HTML, JSON, CSV, and XML We will also examine the use of message queue systems, primarily AWS SQS, to help build robust data processing pipelines.

`Chapter 4`, *Working with Images, Audio and other Assets*, examines the means of retrieving multimedia items, storing them locally, and also performing several tasks such as OCR, generating thumbnails, making web page screenshots, audio extraction from videos, and finding all video URLs in a YouTube playlist.

`Chapter 5`, *Scraping – Code of Conduct*, covers several concepts involved in the legality of scraping, and practices for performing polite scraping. We will examine tools for processing robots.txt and sitemaps to respect the web host's desire for acceptable behavior. We will also examine the control of several facets of crawling, such as using delays, containing the depth and length of crawls, using user agents, and implementing caching to prevent repeated requests.

`Chapter 6`, *Scraping Challenges and Solutions*, covers many of the challenges that writing a robust scraper is rife with, and how to handle many scenarios. These scenarios are pagination, redirects, login forms, keeping the crawler within the same domain, retrying requests upon failure, and handling captchas.

`Chapter 7`, *Text Wrangling and Analysis*, examines various tools such as using NLTK for natural language processing and how to remove common noise words and punctuation. We often need to process the textual content of a web page to find information on the page that is part of the text and neither structured/embedded data nor multimedia. This requires knowledge of using various concepts and tools to clean and understand text.

`Chapter 8`, *Searching, Mining, and Visualizing Data*, covers several means of searching for data on the Web, storing and organizing data, and deriving results from the identified relationships. We will see how to understand the geographic locations of contributors to Wikipedia, finding relationships between actors on IMDB, and finding jobs on Stack Overflow that match specific technologies.

`Chapter 9`, *Creating a Simple Data API*, teaches us how to create a scraper as a service. We will create a REST API for a scraper using Flask. We will run the scraper as a service behind this API and be able to submit requests to scrape specific pages, in order to dynamically query data from a scrape as well as a local ElasticSearch instance.

`Chapter 10`, *Creating Scraper Microservices with Docker*, continues the growth of our scraper as a service by packaging the service and API in a Docker swarm and distributing requests across scrapers via a message queuing system (AWS SQS). We will also cover scaling of scraper instances up and down using Docker swarm tools.

`Chapter 11`, *Making the Scraper as a Service Real*, concludes by fleshing out the services crated in the previous chapter to add a scraper that pulls together various concepts covered earlier. This scraper can assist in analyzing job posts on StackOverflow to find and compare employers using specified technologies. The service will collect posts and allow a query to find and compare those companies.

To get the most out of this book

The primary tool required for the recipes in this book is a Python 3 interpreter. The recipes have been written using the free version of the Anaconda Python distribution, specifically version 3.6.1. Other Python version 3 distributions should work well but have not been tested.

The code in the recipes will often require the use of various Python libraries. These are all available for installation using `pip` and accessible using `pip install`. Wherever required, these installations will be elaborated in the recipes.

Several recipes require an Amazon AWS account. AWS accounts are available for the first year for free-tier access. The recipes will not require anything more than free-tier services. A new account can be created at `https://portal.aws.amazon.com/billing/signup`.

Several recipes will utilize Elasticsearch. There is a free, open source version available on GitHub at `https://github.com/elastic/elasticsearch`, with installation instructions on that page. Elastic.co also offers a fully capable version (also with Kibana and Logstash) hosted on the cloud with a 14-day free trial available at `http://info.elastic.co` (which we will utilize). There is a version for docker-compose with all x-pack features available at `https://github.com/elastic/stack-docker`, all of which can be started with a simple `docker-compose up` command.

Finally, several of the recipes use MySQL and PostgreSQL as database examples and several common clients for those databases. For those recipes, these will need to be installed locally. MySQL Community Server is available at `https://dev.mysql.com/downloads/mysql/`, and PostgreSQL can be found at `https://www.postgresql.org/`.

We will also look at creating and using docker containers for several of the recipes. Docker CE is free and is available at `https://www.docker.com/community-edition`.

Download the example code files

You can download the example code files for this book from your account at `www.packtpub.com`. If you purchased this book elsewhere, you can visit `www.packtpub.com/support` and register to have the files emailed directly to you.

You can download the code files by following these steps:

1. Log in or register at `www.packtpub.com`.
2. Select the **SUPPORT** tab.
3. Click on **Code Downloads & Errata**.
4. Enter the name of the book in the **Search** box and follow the onscreen instructions.

Once the file is downloaded, please make sure that you unzip or extract the folder using the latest version of:

- WinRAR/7-Zip for Windows
- Zipeg/iZip/UnRarX for Mac
- 7-Zip/PeaZip for Linux

The code bundle for the book is also hosted on GitHub at `https://github.com/PacktPublishing/Python-Web-Scraping-Cookbook`. We also have other code bundles from our rich catalog of books and videos available at `https://github.com/PacktPublishing/`. Check them out!

Conventions used

There are a number of text conventions used throughout this book.

`CodeInText`: Indicates code words in text, database table names, folder names, filenames, file extensions, pathnames, dummy URLs, user input, and Twitter handles. Here is an example: "This will loop through up to 20 characters and drop them into the `sw` index with a document type of `people`"

A block of code is set as follows:

```
from elasticsearch import Elasticsearch
import requests
import json

if __name__ == '__main__':
    es = Elasticsearch(
        [
```

Any command-line input or output is written as follows:

```
$ curl
https://elastic:tduhdExunhEWPjSuH73O6yLS@7dc72d3327076cc4daf5528103
c46a27.us-west-2.aws.found.io:9243
```

Bold: Indicates a new term, an important word, or words that you see onscreen. For example, words in menus or dialog boxes appear in the text like this. Here is an example: "Select **System info** from the **Administration** panel."

Warnings or important notes appear like this.

Tips and tricks appear like this.

Get in touch

Feedback from our readers is always welcome.

General feedback: Email `feedback@packtpub.com` and mention the book title in the subject of your message. If you have questions about any aspect of this book, please email us at `questions@packtpub.com`.

Errata: Although we have taken every care to ensure the accuracy of our content, mistakes do happen. If you have found a mistake in this book, we would be grateful if you would report this to us. Please visit `www.packtpub.com/submit-errata`, selecting your book, clicking on the Errata Submission Form link, and entering the details.

Piracy: If you come across any illegal copies of our works in any form on the internet, we would be grateful if you would provide us with the location address or website name. Please contact us at `copyright@packtpub.com` with a link to the material.

If you are interested in becoming an author: If there is a topic that you have expertise in and you are interested in either writing or contributing to a book, please visit `authors.packtpub.com`.

Reviews

Please leave a review. Once you have read and used this book, why not leave a review on the site that you purchased it from? Potential readers can then see and use your unbiased opinion to make purchase decisions, we at Packt can understand what you think about our products, and our authors can see your feedback on their book. Thank you!

For more information about Packt, please visit `packtpub.com`.

1
Getting Started with Scraping

In this chapter, we will cover the following topics:

- Setting up a Python development environment
- Scraping Python.org with Requests and Beautiful Soup
- Scraping Python.org with urllib3 and Beautiful Soup
- Scraping Python.org with Scrapy
- Scraping Python.org with Selenium and PhantomJs

Introduction

The amount of data available on the web is consistently growing both in quantity and in form. Businesses require this data to make decisions, particularly with the explosive growth of machine learning tools which require large amounts of data for training. Much of this data is available via Application Programming Interfaces, but at the same time a lot of valuable data is still only available through the process of web scraping.

This chapter will focus on several fundamentals of setting up a scraping environment and performing basic requests for data with several of the tools of the trade. Python is the programing language of choice for this book, as well as amongst many who build systems to perform scraping. It is an easy to use programming language which has a very rich ecosystem of tools for many tasks. If you program in other languages, you will find it easy to pick up and you may never go back!

Setting up a Python development environment

If you have not used Python before, it is important to have a working development environment. The recipes in this book will be all in Python and be a mix of interactive examples, but primarily implemented as scripts to be interpreted by the Python interpreter. This recipe will show you how to set up an isolated development environment with `virtualenv` and manage project dependencies with `pip` . We also get the code for the book and install it into the Python virtual environment.

Getting ready

We will exclusively be using Python 3.x, and specifically in my case 3.6.1. While Mac and Linux normally have Python version 2 installed, and Windows systems do not. So it is likely that in any case that Python 3 will need to be installed. You can find references for Python installers at www.python.org.

You can check Python's version with `python --version`

```
~ $ python --version
Python 3.6.1 :: Anaconda custom (x86_64)
~ $
```

> `pip` comes installed with Python 3.x, so we will omit instructions on its installation. Additionally, all command line examples in this book are run on a Mac. For Linux users the commands should be identical. On Windows, there are alternate commands (like dir instead of ls), but these alternatives will not be covered.

How to do it...

We will be installing a number of packages with `pip`. These packages are installed into a Python environment. There often can be version conflicts with other packages, so a good practice for following along with the recipes in the book will be to create a new virtual Python environment where the packages we will use will be ensured to work properly.

Virtual Python environments are managed with the `virtualenv` tool. This can be installed with the following command:

```
~ $ pip install virtualenv
Collecting virtualenv
 Using cached virtualenv-15.1.0-py2.py3-none-any.whl
Installing collected packages: virtualenv
Successfully installed virtualenv-15.1.0
```

Now we can use `virtualenv`. But before that let's briefly look at `pip`. This command installs Python packages from PyPI, a package repository with literally 10's of thousands of packages. We just saw using the install subcommand to pip, which ensures a package is installed. We can also see all currently installed packages with `pip list`:

```
~ $ pip list
alabaster (0.7.9)
amqp (1.4.9)
anaconda-client (1.6.0)
anaconda-navigator (1.5.3)
anaconda-project (0.4.1)
aniso8601 (1.3.0)
```

I've truncated to the first few lines as there are quite a few. For me there are 222 packages installed.

Packages can also be uninstalled using `pip uninstall` followed by the package name. I'll leave it to you to give it a try.

Now back to `virtualenv`. Using `virtualenv` is very simple. Let's use it to create an environment and install the code from github. Let's walk through the steps:

1. Create a directory to represent the project and enter the directory.

```
~ $ mkdir pywscb
~ $ cd pywscb
```

2. Initialize a virtual environment folder named env:

```
pywscb $ virtualenv env
Using base prefix '/Users/michaelheydt/anaconda'
New python executable in /Users/michaelheydt/pywscb/env/bin/python
copying /Users/michaelheydt/anaconda/bin/python =>
/Users/michaelheydt/pywscb/env/bin/python
copying /Users/michaelheydt/anaconda/bin/../lib/libpython3.6m.dylib
=> /Users/michaelheydt/pywscb/env/lib/libpython3.6m.dylib
Installing setuptools, pip, wheel...done.
```

3. This creates an env folder. Let's take a look at what was installed.

```
pywscb $ ls -la env
total 8
drwxr-xr-x 6  michaelheydt staff 204 Jan 18 15:38 .
drwxr-xr-x 3  michaelheydt staff 102 Jan 18 15:35 ..
drwxr-xr-x 16 michaelheydt staff 544 Jan 18 15:38 bin
drwxr-xr-x 3  michaelheydt staff 102 Jan 18 15:35 include
drwxr-xr-x 4  michaelheydt staff 136 Jan 18 15:38 lib
-rw-r--r-- 1  michaelheydt staff 60 Jan 18 15:38  pip-
selfcheck.json
```

4. New we activate the virtual environment. This command uses the content in the `env` folder to configure Python. After this all python activities are relative to this virtual environment.

```
pywscb $ source env/bin/activate
(env) pywscb $
```

5. We can check that python is indeed using this virtual environment with the following command:

```
(env) pywscb $ which python
/Users/michaelheydt/pywscb/env/bin/python
```

With our virtual environment created, let's clone the books sample code and take a look at its structure.

```
(env) pywscb $ git clone
https://github.com/PacktBooks/PythonWebScrapingCookbook.git
 Cloning into 'PythonWebScrapingCookbook'...
 remote: Counting objects: 420, done.
 remote: Compressing objects: 100% (316/316), done.
 remote: Total 420 (delta 164), reused 344 (delta 88), pack-reused 0
 Receiving objects: 100% (420/420), 1.15 MiB | 250.00 KiB/s, done.
 Resolving deltas: 100% (164/164), done.
 Checking connectivity... done.
```

This created a `PythonWebScrapingCookbook` directory.

```
(env) pywscb $ ls -l
 total 0
 drwxr-xr-x 9 michaelheydt staff 306 Jan 18 16:21 PythonWebScrapingCookbook
 drwxr-xr-x 6 michaelheydt staff 204 Jan 18 15:38 env
```

Let's change into it and examine the content.

```
(env) PythonWebScrapingCookbook $ ls -l
 total 0
 drwxr-xr-x 15 michaelheydt staff 510 Jan 18 16:21 py
 drwxr-xr-x 14 michaelheydt staff 476 Jan 18 16:21 www
```

There are two directories. Most the the Python code is is the `py` directory. `www` contains some web content that we will use from time-to-time using a local web server. Let's look at the contents of the `py` directory:

```
(env) py $ ls -l
 total 0
 drwxr-xr-x 9  michaelheydt staff 306 Jan 18 16:21 01
 drwxr-xr-x 25 michaelheydt staff 850 Jan 18 16:21 03
 drwxr-xr-x 21 michaelheydt staff 714 Jan 18 16:21 04
 drwxr-xr-x 10 michaelheydt staff 340 Jan 18 16:21 05
 drwxr-xr-x 14 michaelheydt staff 476 Jan 18 16:21 06
 drwxr-xr-x 25 michaelheydt staff 850 Jan 18 16:21 07
 drwxr-xr-x 14 michaelheydt staff 476 Jan 18 16:21 08
 drwxr-xr-x 7  michaelheydt staff 238 Jan 18 16:21 09
 drwxr-xr-x 7  michaelheydt staff 238 Jan 18 16:21 10
 drwxr-xr-x 9  michaelheydt staff 306 Jan 18 16:21 11
 drwxr-xr-x 8  michaelheydt staff 272 Jan 18 16:21 modules
```

Code for each chapter is in the numbered folder matching the chapter (there is no code for chapter 2 as it is all interactive Python).

Note that there is a `modules` folder. Some of the recipes throughout the book use code in those modules. Make sure that your Python path points to this folder. On Mac and Linux you can sets this in your `.bash_profile` file (and environments variables dialog on Windows):

```
export
PYTHONPATH="/users/michaelheydt/dropbox/packt/books/pywebscrcookbook/code/p
y/modules"
export PYTHONPATH
```

The contents in each folder generally follows a numbering scheme matching the sequence of the recipe in the chapter. The following is the contents of the chapter 6 folder:

```
(env) py $ ls -la 06
 total 96
 drwxr-xr-x 14 michaelheydt staff 476 Jan 18 16:21 .
 drwxr-xr-x 14 michaelheydt staff 476 Jan 18 16:26 ..
 -rw-r--r-- 1  michaelheydt staff 902 Jan 18 16:21  01_scrapy_retry.py
 -rw-r--r-- 1  michaelheydt staff 656 Jan 18 16:21  02_scrapy_redirects.py
```

```
-rw-r--r-- 1  michaelheydt staff 1129 Jan 18 16:21 03_scrapy_pagination.py
-rw-r--r-- 1  michaelheydt staff 488 Jan 18 16:21  04_press_and_wait.py
-rw-r--r-- 1  michaelheydt staff 580 Jan 18 16:21  05_allowed_domains.py
-rw-r--r-- 1  michaelheydt staff 826 Jan 18 16:21  06_scrapy_continuous.py
-rw-r--r-- 1  michaelheydt staff 704 Jan 18 16:21
07_scrape_continuous_twitter.py
-rw-r--r-- 1  michaelheydt staff 1409 Jan 18 16:21 08_limit_depth.py
-rw-r--r-- 1  michaelheydt staff 526 Jan 18 16:21  09_limit_length.py
-rw-r--r-- 1  michaelheydt staff 1537 Jan 18 16:21 10_forms_auth.py
-rw-r--r-- 1  michaelheydt staff 597 Jan 18 16:21  11_file_cache.py
-rw-r--r-- 1  michaelheydt staff 1279 Jan 18 16:21
12_parse_differently_based_on_rules.py
```

In the recipes I'll state that we'll be using the script in <chapter directory>/<recipe filename>.

Congratulations, you've now got a Python environment configured with the books code!

Now just the be complete, if you want to get out of the Python virtual environment, you can exit using the following command:

```
(env) py $ deactivate
py $
```

And checking which python we can see it has switched back:

```
py $ which python
/Users/michaelheydt/anaconda/bin/python
```

I won't be using the virtual environment for the rest of the book. When you see command prompts they will be either of the form "<directory> $" or simply "$".

Now let's move onto doing some scraping.

Scraping Python.org with Requests and Beautiful Soup

In this recipe we will install Requests and Beautiful Soup and scrape some content from www.python.org. We'll install both of the libraries and get some basic familiarity with them. We'll come back to them both in subsequent chapters and dive deeper into each.

Getting ready...

In this recipe, we will scrape the upcoming Python events from `https://www.python.org/events/pythonevents`. The following is an an example of `The Python.org Events Page` (it changes frequently, so your experience will differ):

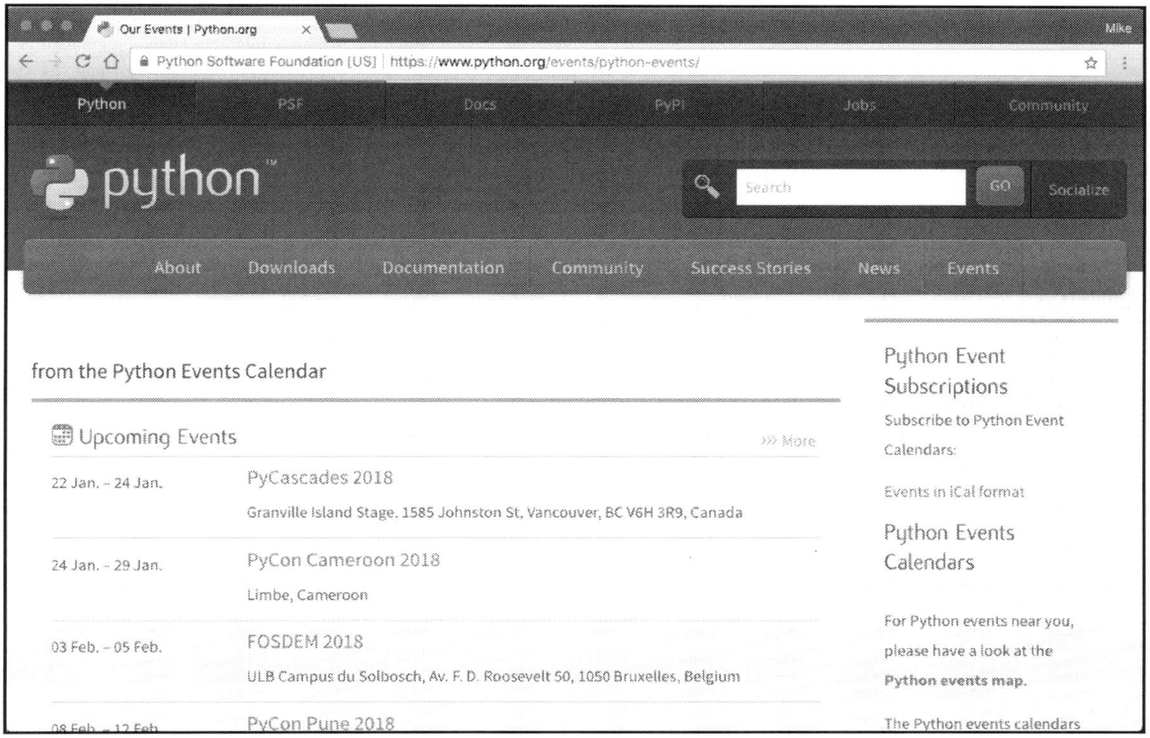

We will need to ensure that Requests and Beautiful Soup are installed. We can do that with the following:

```
pywscb $ pip install requests
Downloading/unpacking requests
 Downloading requests-2.18.4-py2.py3-none-any.whl (88kB): 88kB downloaded
Downloading/unpacking certifi>=2017.4.17 (from requests)
 Downloading certifi-2018.1.18-py2.py3-none-any.whl (151kB): 151kB
downloaded
Downloading/unpacking idna>=2.5,<2.7 (from requests)
 Downloading idna-2.6-py2.py3-none-any.whl (56kB): 56kB downloaded
Downloading/unpacking chardet>=3.0.2,<3.1.0 (from requests)
 Downloading chardet-3.0.4-py2.py3-none-any.whl (133kB): 133kB downloaded
Downloading/unpacking urllib3>=1.21.1,<1.23 (from requests)
 Downloading urllib3-1.22-py2.py3-none-any.whl (132kB): 132kB downloaded
Installing collected packages: requests, certifi, idna, chardet, urllib3
Successfully installed requests certifi idna chardet urllib3
Cleaning up...
pywscb $ pip install bs4
Downloading/unpacking bs4
 Downloading bs4-0.0.1.tar.gz
 Running setup.py (path:/Users/michaelheydt/pywscb/env/build/bs4/setup.py)
egg_info for package bs4
```

How to do it...

Now let's go and learn to scrape a couple events. For this recipe we will start by using interactive python.

1. Start it with the `ipython` command:

```
$ ipython
Python 3.6.1 |Anaconda custom (x86_64)| (default, Mar 22 2017,
19:25:17)
Type "copyright", "credits" or "license" for more information.
IPython 5.1.0 -- An enhanced Interactive Python.
? -> Introduction and overview of IPython's features.
%quickref -> Quick reference.
help -> Python's own help system.
object? -> Details about 'object', use 'object??' for extra
details.
In [1]:
```

2. Next we import Requests

```
In [1]: import requests
```

3. We now use requests to make a GET HTTP request for the following url: `https://www.python.org/events/python-events/` by making a `GET` request:

```
In [2]: url = 'https://www.python.org/events/python-events/'
In [3]: req = requests.get(url)
```

4. That downloaded the page content but it is stored in our requests object req. We can retrieve the content using the `.text` property. This prints the first 200 characters.

```
req.text[:200]
Out[4]: '<!doctype html>\n<!--[if lt IE 7]> <html class="no-js ie6
lt-ie7 lt-ie8 lt-ie9"> <![endif]-->\n<!--[if IE 7]> <html
class="no-js ie7 lt-ie8 lt-ie9"> <![endif]-->\n<!--[if IE 8]> <h'
```

We now have the raw HTML of the page. We can now use beautiful soup to parse the HTML and retrieve the event data.

1. First import Beautiful Soup

```
In [5]: from bs4 import BeautifulSoup
```

2. Now we create a `BeautifulSoup` object and pass it the HTML.

```
In [6]: soup = BeautifulSoup(req.text, 'lxml')
```

3. Now we tell Beautiful Soup to find the main `<ul>` tag for the recent events, and then to get all the `<li>` tags below it.

```
In [7]: events = soup.find('ul', {'class': 'list-recent-
events'}).findAll('li')
```

4. And finally we can loop through each of the `<li>` elements, extracting the event details, and print each to the console:

```
In [13]: for event in events:
  ...: event_details = dict()
  ...: event_details['name'] = event_details['name'] =
event.find('h3').find("a").text
  ...: event_details['location'] = event.find('span', {'class',
'event-location'}).text
  ...: event_details['time'] = event.find('time').text
```

```
    ...: print(event_details)
    ...:
{'name': 'PyCascades 2018', 'location': 'Granville Island Stage,
1585 Johnston St, Vancouver, BC V6H 3R9, Canada', 'time': '22 Jan.
- 24 Jan. 2018'}
{'name': 'PyCon Cameroon 2018', 'location': 'Limbe, Cameroon',
'time': '24 Jan. - 29 Jan. 2018'}
{'name': 'FOSDEM 2018', 'location': 'ULB Campus du Solbosch, Av. F.
D. Roosevelt 50, 1050 Bruxelles, Belgium', 'time': '03 Feb. - 05
Feb. 2018'}
{'name': 'PyCon Pune 2018', 'location': 'Pune, India', 'time': '08
Feb. - 12 Feb. 2018'}
{'name': 'PyCon Colombia 2018', 'location': 'Medellin, Colombia',
'time': '09 Feb. - 12 Feb. 2018'}
{'name': 'PyTennessee 2018', 'location': 'Nashville, TN, USA',
'time': '10 Feb. - 12 Feb. 2018'}
```

This entire example is available in the `01/01_events_with_requests.py` script file. The following is its content and it pulls together all of what we just did step by step:

```
import requests
from bs4 import BeautifulSoup

def get_upcoming_events(url):
    req = requests.get(url)

    soup = BeautifulSoup(req.text, 'lxml')

    events = soup.find('ul', {'class': 'list-recent-events'}).findAll('li')

    for event in events:
        event_details = dict()
        event_details['name'] = event.find('h3').find("a").text
        event_details['location'] = event.find('span', {'class', 'event-
location'}).text
        event_details['time'] = event.find('time').text
        print(event_details)

get_upcoming_events('https://www.python.org/events/python-events/')
```

You can run this using the following command from the terminal:

```
$ python 01_events_with_requests.py
{'name': 'PyCascades 2018', 'location': 'Granville Island Stage, 1585
Johnston St, Vancouver, BC V6H 3R9, Canada', 'time': '22 Jan. - 24 Jan.
2018'}
{'name': 'PyCon Cameroon 2018', 'location': 'Limbe, Cameroon', 'time': '24
Jan. - 29 Jan. 2018'}
{'name': 'FOSDEM 2018', 'location': 'ULB Campus du Solbosch, Av. F. D.
Roosevelt 50, 1050 Bruxelles, Belgium', 'time': '03 Feb. - 05 Feb. 2018'}
{'name': 'PyCon Pune 2018', 'location': 'Pune, India', 'time': '08 Feb. - 12
Feb. 2018'}
{'name': 'PyCon Colombia 2018', 'location': 'Medellin, Colombia', 'time':
'09 Feb. - 12 Feb. 2018'}
{'name': 'PyTennessee 2018', 'location': 'Nashville, TN, USA', 'time': '10
Feb. - 12 Feb. 2018'}
```

How it works...

We will dive into details of both Requests and Beautiful Soup in the next chapter, but for now let's just summarize a few key points about how this works. The following important points about Requests:

- Requests is used to execute HTTP requests. We used it to make a GET verb request of the URL for the events page.
- The Requests object holds the results of the request. This is not only the page content, but also many other items about the result such as HTTP status codes and headers.
- Requests is used only to get the page, it does not do an parsing.

We use Beautiful Soup to do the parsing of the HTML and also the finding of content within the HTML.

To understand how this worked, the content of the page has the following HTML to start the **Upcoming Events** section:

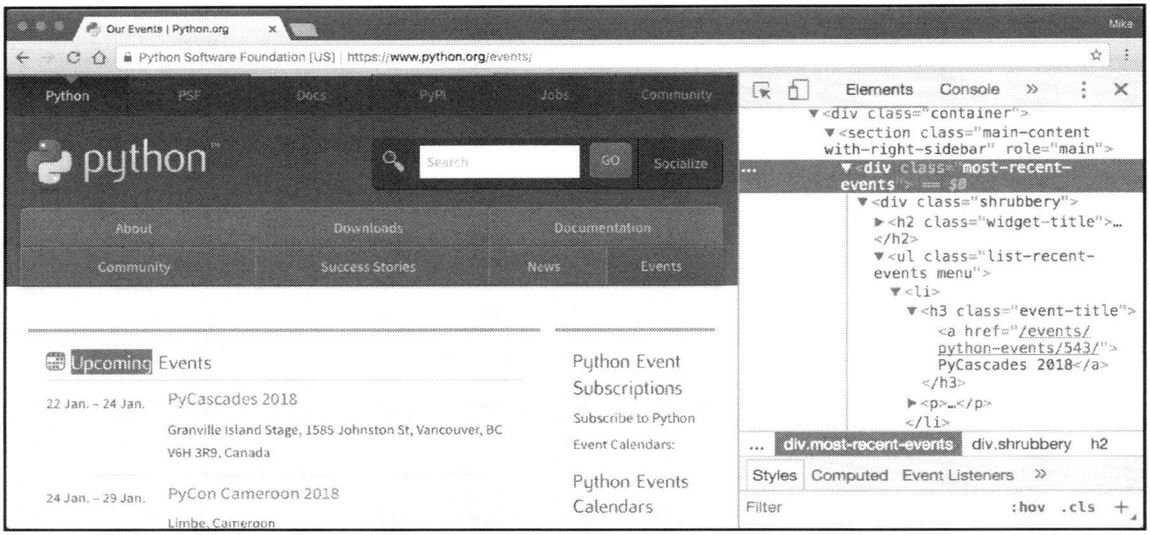

We used the power of Beautiful Soup to:

- Find the `<ul>` element representing the section, which is found by looking for a `<ul>` with the a `class` attribute that has a value of `list-recent-events`.
- From that object, we find all the `<li>` elements.

Each of these `<li>` tags represent a different event. We iterate over each of those making a dictionary from the event data found in child HTML tags:

- The name is extracted from the `<a>` tag that is a child of the `<h3>` tag
- The location is the text content of the `<span>` with a class of `event-location`
- And the time is extracted from the `datetime` attribute of the <time> tag.

Scraping Python.org in urllib3 and Beautiful Soup

In this recipe we swap out the use of requests for another library `urllib3`. This is another common library for retrieving data from URLs and for other functions involving URLs such as parsing of the parts of the actual URL and handling various encodings.

Getting ready...

This recipe requires `urllib3` installed. So install it with `pip`:

```
$ pip install urllib3
Collecting urllib3
 Using cached urllib3-1.22-py2.py3-none-any.whl
Installing collected packages: urllib3
Successfully installed urllib3-1.22
```

How to do it...

The recipe is implemented in `01/02_events_with_urllib3.py`. The code is the following:

```
import urllib3
from bs4 import BeautifulSoup

def get_upcoming_events(url):
    req = urllib3.PoolManager()
    res = req.request('GET', url)

    soup = BeautifulSoup(res.data, 'html.parser')

    events = soup.find('ul', {'class': 'list-recent-events'}).findAll('li')

    for event in events:
        event_details = dict()
        event_details['name'] = event.find('h3').find("a").text
        event_details['location'] = event.find('span', {'class', 'event-
location'}).text
        event_details['time'] = event.find('time').text
        print(event_details)

get_upcoming_events('https://www.python.org/events/python-events/')
```

The run it with the python interpreter. You will get identical output to the previous recipe.

How it works

The only difference in this recipe is how we fetch the resource:

```
req = urllib3.PoolManager()
res = req.request('GET', url)
```

Unlike `Requests`, `urllib3` doesn't apply header encoding automatically. The reason why the code snippet works in the preceding example is because BS4 handles encoding beautifully. But you should keep in mind that encoding is an important part of scraping. If you decide to use your own framework or use other libraries, make sure encoding is well handled.

There's more...

Requests and urllib3 are very similar in terms of capabilities. it is generally recommended to use Requests when it comes to making HTTP requests. The following code example illustrates a few advanced features:

```
import requests

# builds on top of urllib3's connection pooling
# session reuses the same TCP connection if
# requests are made to the same host
# see https://en.wikipedia.org/wiki/HTTP_persistent_connection for details
session = requests.Session()

# You may pass in custom cookie
r = session.get('http://httpbin.org/get', cookies={'my-cookie': 'browser'})
print(r.text)
# '{"cookies": {"my-cookie": "test cookie"}}'

# Streaming is another nifty feature
# From
http://docs.python-requests.org/en/master/user/advanced/#streaming-requests
# copyright belongs to reques.org
r = requests.get('http://httpbin.org/stream/20', stream=True)
```

```
for line in r.iter_lines():
  # filter out keep-alive new lines
  if line:
     decoded_line = line.decode('utf-8')
     print(json.loads(decoded_line))
```

Scraping Python.org with Scrapy

Scrapy is a very popular open source Python scraping framework for extracting data. It was originally designed for only scraping, but it is has also evolved into a powerful web crawling solution.

In our previous recipes, we used Requests and urllib2 to fetch data and Beautiful Soup to extract data. Scrapy offers all of these functionalities with many other built-in modules and extensions. It is also our tool of choice when it comes to scraping with Python.

Scrapy offers a number of powerful features that are worth mentioning:

- Built-in extensions to make HTTP requests and handle compression, authentication, caching, manipulate user-agents, and HTTP headers
- Built-in support for selecting and extracting data with selector languages such as CSS and XPath, as well as support for utilizing regular expressions for selection of content and links
- Encoding support to deal with languages and non-standard encoding declarations
- Flexible APIs to reuse and write custom middleware and pipelines, which provide a clean and easy way to implement tasks such as automatically downloading assets (for example, images or media) and storing data in storage such as file systems, S3, databases, and others

Getting ready...

There are several means of creating a scraper with Scrapy. One is a programmatic pattern where we create the crawler and spider in our code. It is also possible to configure a Scrapy project from templates or generators and then run the scraper from the command line using the `scrapy` command. This book will follow the programmatic pattern as it contains the code in a single file more effectively. This will help when we are putting together specific, targeted, recipes with Scrapy.

This isn't necessarily a better way of running a Scrapy scraper than using the command line execution, just one that is a design decision for this book. Ultimately this book is not about Scrapy (there are other books on just Scrapy), but more of an exposition on various things you may need to do when scraping, and in the ultimate creation of a functional scraper as a service in the cloud.

How to do it...

The script for this recipe is `01/03_events_with_scrapy.py`. The following is the code:

```
import scrapy
from scrapy.crawler import CrawlerProcess

class PythonEventsSpider(scrapy.Spider):
    name = 'pythoneventsspider'

    start_urls = ['https://www.python.org/events/python-events/',]
    found_events = []

    def parse(self, response):
        for event in response.xpath('//ul[contains(@class, "list-recent-
events")]/li'):
            event_details = dict()
            event_details['name'] = event.xpath('h3[@class="event-
title"]/a/text()').extract_first()
            event_details['location'] = event.xpath('p/span[@class="event-
location"]/text()').extract_first()
            event_details['time'] =
event.xpath('p/time/text()').extract_first()
            self.found_events.append(event_details)

if __name__ == "__main__":
    process = CrawlerProcess({ 'LOG_LEVEL': 'ERROR'})
    process.crawl(PythonEventsSpider)
    spider = next(iter(process.crawlers)).spider
    process.start()

    for event in spider.found_events: print(event)
```

The following runs the script and shows the output:

```
~ $ python 03_events_with_scrapy.py
{'name': 'PyCascades 2018', 'location': 'Granville Island Stage, 1585
Johnston St, Vancouver, BC V6H 3R9, Canada', 'time': '22 Jan. - 24 Jan. '}
{'name': 'PyCon Cameroon 2018', 'location': 'Limbe, Cameroon', 'time': '24
Jan. - 29 Jan. '}
{'name': 'FOSDEM 2018', 'location': 'ULB Campus du Solbosch, Av. F. D.
Roosevelt 50, 1050 Bruxelles, Belgium', 'time': '03 Feb. - 05 Feb. '}
{'name': 'PyCon Pune 2018', 'location': 'Pune, India', 'time': '08 Feb. - 12
Feb. '}
{'name': 'PyCon Colombia 2018', 'location': 'Medellin, Colombia', 'time':
'09 Feb. - 12 Feb. '}
{'name': 'PyTennessee 2018', 'location': 'Nashville, TN, USA', 'time': '10
Feb. - 12 Feb. '}
{'name': 'PyCon Pakistan', 'location': 'Lahore, Pakistan', 'time': '16 Dec.
- 17 Dec. '}
{'name': 'PyCon Indonesia 2017', 'location': 'Surabaya, Indonesia', 'time':
'09 Dec. - 10 Dec. '}
```

The same result but with another tool. Let's go take a quick review of how this works.

How it works

We will get into some details about Scrapy in later chapters, but let's just go through this code quick to get a feel how it is accomplishing this scrape. Everything in Scrapy revolves around creating a **spider**. Spiders crawl through pages on the Internet based upon rules that we provide. This spider only processes one single page, so it's not really much of a spider. But it shows the pattern we will use through later Scrapy examples.

The spider is created with a class definition that derives from one of the Scrapy spider classes. Ours derives from the `scrapy.Spider` class.

```
class PythonEventsSpider(scrapy.Spider):
    name = 'pythoneventsspider'

    start_urls = ['https://www.python.org/events/python-events/',]
```

Every spider is given a `name`, and also one or more `start_urls` which tell it where to start the crawling.

This spider has a field to store all the events that we find:

```
    found_events = []
```

The spider then has a method names parse which will be called for every page the spider collects.

```
def parse(self, response):
        for event in response.xpath('//ul[contains(@class, "list-recent-
events")]/li'):
            event_details = dict()
            event_details['name'] = event.xpath('h3[@class="event-
title"]/a/text()').extract_first()
            event_details['location'] = event.xpath('p/span[@class="event-
location"]/text()').extract_first()
            event_details['time'] =
event.xpath('p/time/text()').extract_first()
            self.found_events.append(event_details)
```

The implementation of this method uses and XPath selection to get the events from the page (XPath is the built in means of navigating HTML in Scrapy). It them builds the `event_details` dictionary object similarly to the other examples, and then adds it to the `found_events` list.

The remaining code does the programmatic execution of the Scrapy crawler.

```
process = CrawlerProcess({ 'LOG_LEVEL': 'ERROR'})
process.crawl(PythonEventsSpider)
spider = next(iter(process.crawlers)).spider
process.start()
```

It starts with the creation of a CrawlerProcess which does the actual crawling and a lot of other tasks. We pass it a LOG_LEVEL of ERROR to prevent the voluminous Scrapy output. Change this to DEBUG and re-run it to see the difference.

Next we tell the crawler process to use our Spider implementation. We get the actual spider object from that crawler so that we can get the items when the crawl is complete. And then we kick of the whole thing by calling `process.start()`.

When the crawl is completed we can then iterate and print out the items that were found.

```
for event in spider.found_events: print(event)
```

This example really didn't touch any of the power of Scrapy. We will look more into some of the more advanced features later in the book.

Scraping Python.org with Selenium and PhantomJS

This recipe will introduce Selenium and PhantomJS, two frameworks that are very different from the frameworks in the previous recipes. In fact, Selenium and PhantomJS are often used in functional/acceptance testing. We want to demonstrate these tools as they offer unique benefits from the scraping perspective. Several that we will look at later in the book are the ability to fill out forms, press buttons, and wait for dynamic JavaScript to be downloaded and executed.

Selenium itself is a programming language neutral framework. It offers a number of programming language bindings, such as Python, Java, C#, and PHP (amongst others). The framework also provides many components that focus on testing. Three commonly used components are:

- IDE for recording and replaying tests
- Webdriver, which actually launches a web browser (such as Firefox, Chrome, or Internet Explorer) by sending commands and sending the results to the selected browser
- A grid server executes tests with a web browser on a remote server. It can run multiple test cases in parallel.

Getting ready

First we need to install Selenium. We do this with our trusty `pip`:

```
~ $ pip install selenium
Collecting selenium
 Downloading selenium-3.8.1-py2.py3-none-any.whl (942kB)
 100% |████████████████████████████████| 952kB 236kB/s
Installing collected packages: selenium
Successfully installed selenium-3.8.1
```

This installs the Selenium Client Driver for Python (the language bindings). You can find more information on it at `https://github.com/SeleniumHQ/selenium/blob/master/py/docs/source/index.rst` if you want to in the future.

For this recipe we also need to have the driver for Firefox in the directory (it's named `geckodriver`). This file is operating system specific. I've included the file for Mac in the folder. To get other versions, visit `https://github.com/mozilla/geckodriver/releases`.

Still, when running this sample you may get the following error:

```
FileNotFoundError: [Errno 2] No such file or directory: 'geckodriver'
```

If you do, put the geckodriver file somewhere on your systems PATH, or add the `01` folder to your path. Oh, and you will need to have Firefox installed.

Finally, it is required to have PhantomJS installed. You can download and find installation instructions at: `http://phantomjs.org/`

How to do it...

The script for this recipe is `01/04_events_with_selenium.py`.

1. The following is the code:

```
from selenium import webdriver

def get_upcoming_events(url):
    driver = webdriver.Firefox()
    driver.get(url)

    events = driver.find_elements_by_xpath('//ul[contains(@class, "list-
recent-events")]/li')

    for event in events:
        event_details = dict()
        event_details['name'] =
event.find_element_by_xpath('h3[@class="event-title"]/a').text
        event_details['location'] =
event.find_element_by_xpath('p/span[@class="event-location"]').text
        event_details['time'] = event.find_element_by_xpath('p/time').text
        print(event_details)

    driver.close()

get_upcoming_events('https://www.python.org/events/python-events/')
```

2. And run the script with Python. You will see familiar output:

```
~ $ python 04_events_with_selenium.py
{'name': 'PyCascades 2018', 'location': 'Granville Island Stage, 1585
Johnston St, Vancouver, BC V6H 3R9, Canada', 'time': '22 Jan. - 24 Jan.'}
{'name': 'PyCon Cameroon 2018', 'location': 'Limbe, Cameroon', 'time': '24
Jan. - 29 Jan.'}
{'name': 'FOSDEM 2018', 'location': 'ULB Campus du Solbosch, Av. F. D.
Roosevelt 50, 1050 Bruxelles, Belgium', 'time': '03 Feb. - 05 Feb.'}
{'name': 'PyCon Pune 2018', 'location': 'Pune, India', 'time': '08 Feb. - 12
Feb.'}
{'name': 'PyCon Colombia 2018', 'location': 'Medellin, Colombia', 'time':
'09 Feb. - 12 Feb.'}
{'name': 'PyTennessee 2018', 'location': 'Nashville, TN, USA', 'time': '10
Feb. - 12 Feb.'}
```

During this process, Firefox will pop up and open the page. We have reused the previous recipe and adopted Selenium.

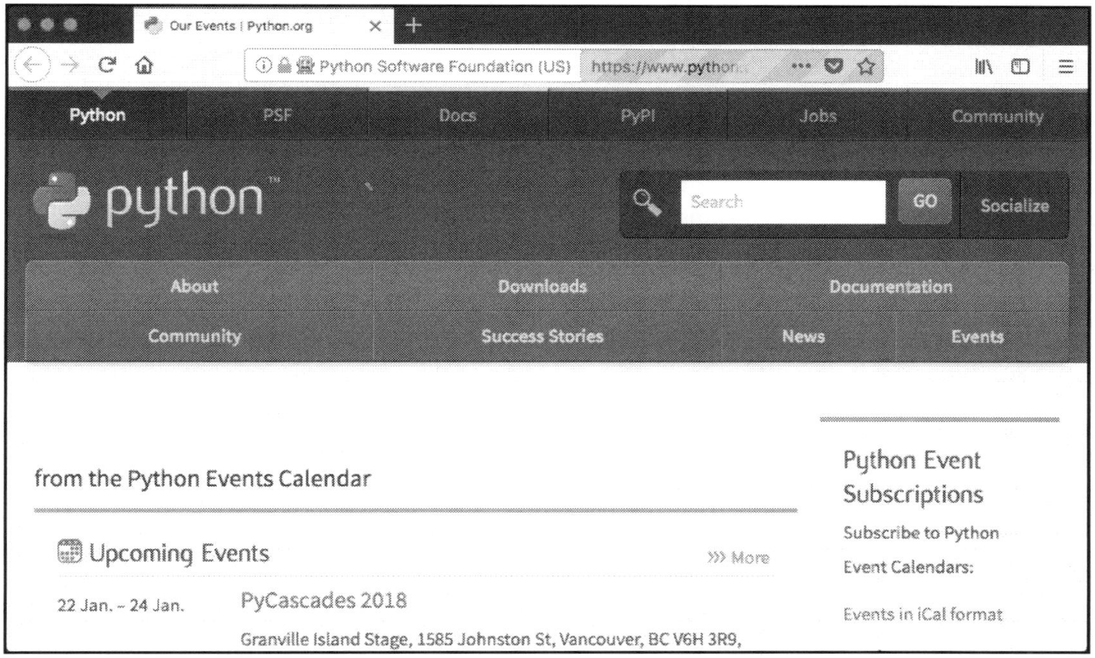

The Window Popped up by Firefox

How it works

The primary difference in this recipe is the following code:

```
driver = webdriver.Firefox()
driver.get(url)
```

This gets the Firefox driver and uses it to get the content of the specified URL. This works by starting Firefox and automating it to go the the page, and then Firefox returns the page content to our app. This is why Firefox popped up. The other difference is that to find things we need to call `find_element_by_xpath` to search the resulting HTML.

There's more...

PhantomJS, in many ways, is very similar to Selenium. It has fast and native support for various web standards, with features such as DOM handling, CSS selector, JSON, Canvas, and SVG. It is often used in web testing, page automation, screen capturing, and network monitoring.

There is one key difference between Selenium and PhantomJS: PhantomJS is **headless** and uses WebKit. As we saw, Selenium opens and automates a browser. This is not very good if we are in a continuous integration or testing environment where the browser is not installed, and where we also don't want thousands of browser windows or tabs being opened. Being headless, makes this faster and more efficient.

The example for PhantomJS is in the `01/05_events_with_phantomjs.py` file. There is a single one line change:

```
driver = webdriver.PhantomJS('phantomjs')
```

And running the script results in similar output to the Selenium / Firefox example, but without a browser popping up and also it takes less time to complete.

2
Data Acquisition and Extraction

In this chapter, we will cover:

- How to parse websites and navigate the DOM using BeautifulSoup
- Searching the DOM with Beautiful Soup's find methods
- Querying the DOM with XPath and lxml
- Querying data with XPath and CSS Selectors
- Using Scrapy selectors
- Loading data in Unicode / UTF-8 format

Introduction

The key aspects for effective scraping are understanding how content and data are stored on web servers, identifying the data you want to retrieve, and understanding how the tools support this extraction. In this chapter, we will discuss website structures and the DOM, introduce techniques to parse, and query websites with lxml, XPath, and CSS. We will also look at how to work with websites developed in other languages and different encoding types such as Unicode.

Ultimately, understanding how to find and extract data within an HTML document comes down to understanding the structure of the HTML page, its representation in the DOM, the process of querying the DOM for specific elements, and how to specify which elements you want to retrieve based upon how the data is represented.

How to parse websites and navigate the DOM using BeautifulSoup

When the browser displays a web page it builds a model of the content of the page in a representation known as the **document object model** (**DOM**). The DOM is a hierarchical representation of the page's entire content, as well as structural information, style information, scripts, and links to other content.

It is critical to understand this structure to be able to effectively scrape data from web pages. We will look at an example web page, its DOM, and examine how to navigate the DOM with Beautiful Soup.

Getting ready

We will use a small web site that is included in the `www` folder of the sample code. To follow along, start a web server from within the `www` folder. This can be done with Python 3 as follows:

```
www $ python3 -m http.server 8080
Serving HTTP on 0.0.0.0 port 8080 (http://0.0.0.0:8080/) ...
```

The DOM of a web page can be examined in Chrome by right-clicking the page and selecting **Inspect**. This opens the Chrome Developer Tools. Open a browser page to `http://localhost:8080/planets.html`. Within chrome you can right click and select 'inspect' to open developer tools (other browsers have similar tools).

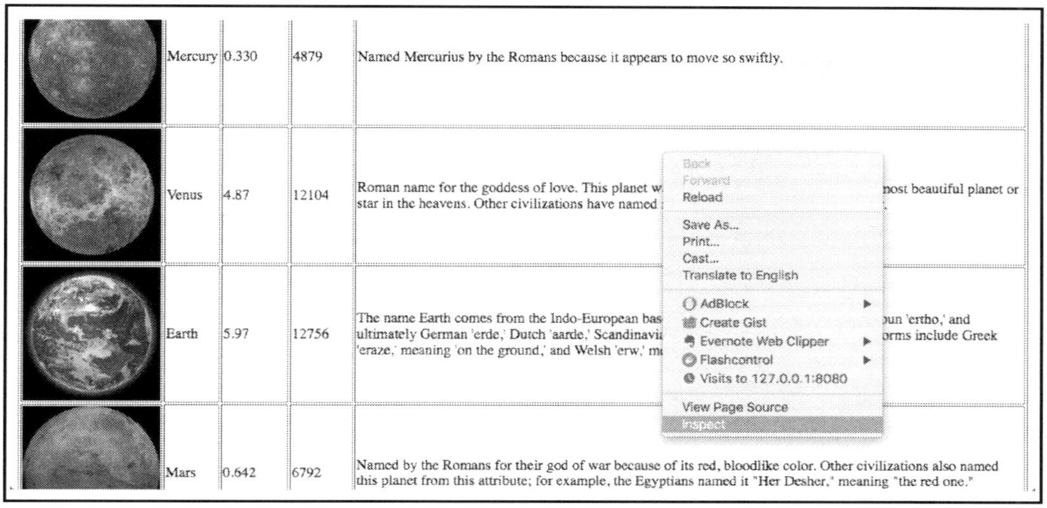

Selecting Inspect on the Page

This opens the developer tools and the inspector. The DOM can be examined in the Elements tab.

The following shows the selection of the first row in the table:

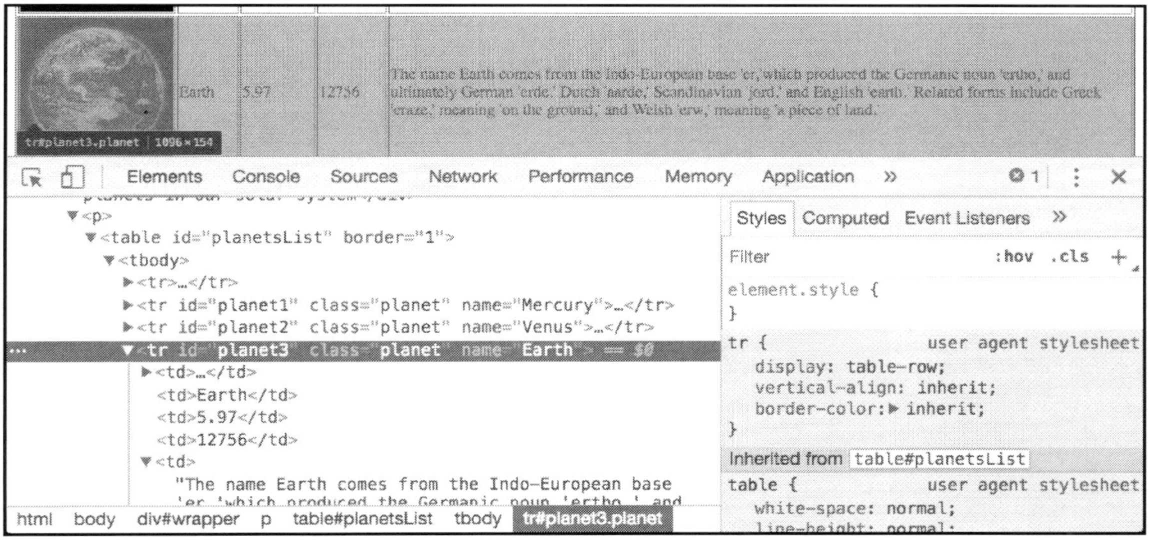

Inspecting the First Row

Each row of planets is within a <tr> element. There are several characteristics of this element and its neighboring elements that we will examine because they are designed to model common web pages.

Firstly, this element has three attributes: id, planet, and name. Attributes are often important in scraping as they are commonly used to identify and locate data embedded in the HTML.

Secondly, the <tr> element has children, and in this case, five <td> elements. We will often need to look into the children of a specific element to find the actual data that is desired.

This element also has a parent element, <tbody>. There are also sibling elements, and the a set of <tr> child elements. From any planet, we can go up to the parent and find the other planets. And as we will see, we can use various constructs in the various tools, such as the **find** family of functions in Beautiful Soup, and also XPath queries, to easily navigate these relationships.

How to do it...

This recipe, and most of the others in this chapter, will be presented with iPython in an interactive manner. But all of the code for each is available in a script file. The code for this recipe is in 02/01_parsing_html_wtih_bs.py. You can type the following in, or cut and paste from the script file.

Now let's walk through parsing HTML with Beautiful Soup. We start by loading this page into a BeautifulSoup object using the following code, which creates a BeautifulSoup object, loads the content of the page using with requests.get, and loads it into a variable named soup.

```
In [1]: import requests
   ...: from bs4 import BeautifulSoup
   ...: html =
requests.get("http://localhost:8080/planets.html").text
   ...: soup = BeautifulSoup(html, "lxml")
   ...:
```

The HTML in the soup object can be retrieved by converting it to a string (most BeautifulSoup objects have this characteristic). This following shows the first 1000 characters of the HTML in the document:

```
In [2]: str(soup)[:1000]
Out[2]: '<html>\n<head>\n</head>\n<body>\n<div
id="planets">\n<h1>Planetary data</h1>\n<div id="content">Here are
```

```
some interesting facts about the planets in our solar
system</div>\n<p></p>\n<table border="1" id="planetsTable">\n<tr
id="planetHeader">\n<th>\n</th>\n<th>\r\n Name\r\n </th>\n<th>\r\n
Mass (10^24kg)\r\n </th>\n<th>\r\n Diameter (km)\r\n
</th>\n<th>\r\n How it got its Name\r\n </th>\n<th>\r\n More
Info\r\n </th>\n</tr>\n<tr class="planet" id="planet1"
name="Mercury">\n<td>\n<img
src="img/mercury-150x150.png"/>\n</td>\n<td>\r\n Mercury\r\n
</td>\n<td>\r\n 0.330\r\n </td>\n<td>\r\n 4879\r\n </td>\n<td>Named
Mercurius by the Romans because it appears to move so
swiftly.</td>\n<td>\n<a
href="https://en.wikipedia.org/wiki/Mercury_(planet)">Wikipedia</a>
\n</td>\n</tr>\n<tr class="p'
```

We can navigate the elements in the DOM using properties of `soup`. `soup` represents the overall document and we can drill into the document by chaining the tag names. The following navigates to the `<table>` containing the data:

```
In [3]: str(soup.html.body.div.table)[:200]
Out[3]: '<table border="1" id="planetsTable">\n<tr
id="planetHeader">\n<th>\n</th>\n<th>\r\n Name\r\n </th>\n<th>\r\n Mass
(10^24kg)\r\n </th>\n<th>\r\n '
```

The following retrieves the the first child `<tr>` of the table:

```
In [6]: soup.html.body.div.table.tr
Out[6]: <tr id="planetHeader">
<th>
</th>
<th>
                    Name
                </th>
<th>
                    Mass (10^24kg)
                </th>
<th>
                    Diameter (km)
                </th>
<th>
                    How it got its Name
                </th>
<th>
                    More Info
                </th>
</tr>
```

Note this type of notation retrieves only the first child of that type. Finding more requires iterations of all the children, which we will do next, or using the find methods (the next recipe).

Each node has both children and descendants. Descendants are all the nodes underneath a given node (event at further levels than the immediate children), while children are those that are a first level descendant. The following retrieves the children of the table, which is actually a `list_iterator` object:

```
In [4]: soup.html.body.div.table.children
Out[4]: <list_iterator at 0x10eb11cc0>
```

We can examine each child element in the iterator using a `for` loop or a Python generator. The following uses a generator to get all the children of the and return the first few characters of their constituent HTML as a list:

```
In [5]: [str(c)[:45] for c in soup.html.body.div.table.children]
Out[5]:
['\n',
 '<tr id="planetHeader">\n<th>\n</th>\n<th>\r\n ',
 '\n',
 '<tr class="planet" id="planet1" name="Mercury',
 '\n',
 '<tr class="planet" id="planet2" name="Venus">',
 '\n',
 '<tr class="planet" id="planet3" name="Earth">',
 '\n',
 '<tr class="planet" id="planet4" name="Mars">\n',
 '\n',
 '<tr class="planet" id="planet5" name="Jupiter',
 '\n',
 '<tr class="planet" id="planet6" name="Saturn"',
 '\n',
 '<tr class="planet" id="planet7" name="Uranus"',
 '\n',
 '<tr class="planet" id="planet8" name="Neptune',
 '\n',
 '<tr class="planet" id="planet9" name="Pluto">',
 '\n']
```

Last but not least, the parent of a node can be found using the `.parent` property:

```
In [7]: str(soup.html.body.div.table.tr.parent)[:200]
Out[7]: '<table border="1" id="planetsTable">\n<tr
id="planetHeader">\n<th>\n</th>\n<th>\r\n Name\r\n </th>\n<th>\r\n
Mass (10^24kg)\r\n </th>\n<th>\r\n '
```

How it works

Beautiful Soup converts the HTML from the page into its own internal representation. This model has an identical representation to the DOM that would be created by a browser. But Beautiful Soup also provides many powerful capabilities for navigating the elements in the DOM, such as what we have seen when using the tag names as properties. These are great for finding things when we know a fixed path through the HTML with the tag names.

There's more...

This manner of navigating the DOM is relatively inflexible and is highly dependent upon the structure. It is possible that this structure can change over time as web pages are updated by their creator(s). The pages could even look identical, but have a completely different structure that breaks your scraping code.

So how can we deal with this? As we will see, there are several ways of searching for elements that are much better than defining explicit paths. In general, we can do this using XPath and by using the find methods of beautiful soup. We will examine both in recipes later in this chapter.

Searching the DOM with Beautiful Soup's find methods

We can perform simple searches of the DOM using Beautiful Soup's find methods. These methods give us a much more flexible and powerful construct for finding elements that are not dependent upon the hierarchy of those elements. In this recipe we will examine several common uses of these functions to locate various elements in the DOM.

Getting ready

ff you want to cut and paste the following into ipython, you can find the samples in `02/02_bs4_find.py`.

How to do it...

We will start with a fresh iPython session and start by loading the planets page:

```
In [1]: import requests
   ...: from bs4 import BeautifulSoup
   ...: html = requests.get("http://localhost:8080/planets.html").text
   ...: soup = BeautifulSoup(html, "lxml")
   ...:
```

In the previous recipe, to access all of the <tr> in the table, we used a chained property syntax to get the table, and then needed to get the children and iterator over them. This does have a problem as the children could be elements other than <tr>. A more preferred method of getting just the <tr> child elements is to use findAll.

Lets start by first finding the <table>:

```
In [4]: table = soup.find("table")
   ...: str(table)[:100]
   ...:
Out[4]: '<table border="1" id="planetsTable">\n<tr
id="planetHeader">\n<th>\n</th>\n<th>\r\n Nam'
```

This tells the soup object to find the first <table> element in the document. From this element we can find all of the <tr> elements that are descendants of the table with findAll:

```
In [8]: [str(tr)[:50] for tr in table.findAll("tr")]
Out[8]:
['<tr id="planetHeader">\n<th>\n</th>\n<th>\r\n ',
 '<tr class="planet" id="planet1" name="Mercury">\n<t',
 '<tr class="planet" id="planet2" name="Venus">\n<td>',
 '<tr class="planet" id="planet3" name="Earth">\n<td>',
 '<tr class="planet" id="planet4" name="Mars">\n<td>\n',
 '<tr class="planet" id="planet5" name="Jupiter">\n<t',
 '<tr class="planet" id="planet6" name="Saturn">\n<td',
 '<tr class="planet" id="planet7" name="Uranus">\n<td',
 '<tr class="planet" id="planet8" name="Neptune">\n<t',
 '<tr class="planet" id="planet9" name="Pluto">\n<td>']
```

Note that these are the descendants and not immediate children. Change the query to "td" to see the difference. The are no direct children that are <td>, but each row has multiple <td> elements. In all, there would be 54 <td> elements found.

There is a small issue here if we want only rows that contain data for planets. The table header is also included. We can fix this by utilizing the `id` attribute of the target rows. The following finds the row where the value of `id` is `"planet3"`.

```
In [14]: table.find("tr", {"id": "planet3"})
    ...:
Out[14]:
<tr class="planet" id="planet3" name="Earth">
<td>
<img src="img/earth-150x150.png"/>
</td>
<td>
                   Earth
               </td>
<td>
                   5.97
               </td>
<td>
                   12756
               </td>
<td>
                   The name Earth comes from the Indo-European base
'er,'which produced the Germanic noun 'ertho,' and ultimately German
'erde,'
                   Dutch 'aarde,' Scandinavian 'jord,' and English
'earth.' Related forms include Greek 'eraze,' meaning
                   'on the ground,' and Welsh 'erw,' meaning 'a piece of
land.'
               </td>
<td>
<a href="https://en.wikipedia.org/wiki/Earth">Wikipedia</a>
</td>
</tr>
```

Awesome! We used the fact that this page uses this attribute to represent table rows with actual data.

Now let's go one step further and collect the masses for each planet and put the name and mass in a dictionary:

```
In [18]: items = dict()
    ...: planet_rows = table.findAll("tr", {"class": "planet"})
    ...: for i in planet_rows:
    ...: tds = i.findAll("td")
    ...: items[tds[1].text.strip()] = tds[2].text.strip()
    ...:
```

```
In [19]: items
Out[19]:
{'Earth': '5.97',
 'Jupiter': '1898',
 'Mars': '0.642',
 'Mercury': '0.330',
 'Neptune': '102',
 'Pluto': '0.0146',
 'Saturn': '568',
 'Uranus': '86.8',
 'Venus': '4.87'}
```

And just like that we have made a nice data structure from the content embedded within the page.

Querying the DOM with XPath and lxml

XPath is a query language for selecting nodes from an XML document and is a must-learn query language for anyone performing web scraping. XPath offers a number of benefits to its user over other model-based tools:

- Can easily navigate through the DOM tree
- More sophisticated and powerful than other selectors like CSS selectors and regular expressions
- It has a great set (200+) of built-in functions and is extensible with custom functions
- It is widely supported by parsing libraries and scraping platforms

XPath contains seven data models (we have seen some of them previously):

- root node (top level parent node)
- element nodes (`<a>..</a>`)
- attribute nodes (`href="example.html"`)
- text nodes (`"this is a text"`)
- comment nodes (`<!-- a comment -->`)
- namespace nodes
- processing instruction nodes

XPath expressions can return different data types:

- strings
- booleans
- numbers
- node-sets (probably the most common case)

An (XPath) **axis** defines a node-set relative to the current node. A total of 13 axes are defined in XPath to enable easy searching for different node parts, from the current context node, or the root node.

lxml is a Python wrapper on top of the libxml2 XML parsing library, which is written in C. The implementation in C helps make it faster than Beautiful Soup, but also harder to install on some computers. The latest installation instructions are available at: `http://lxml.de/installation.html`.

lxml supports XPath, which makes it considerably easy to manage complex XML and HTML documents. We will examine several techniques of using lxml and XPath together, and how to use lxml and XPath to navigate the DOM and access data.

Getting ready

The code for these snippets is in `02/03_lxml_and_xpath.py` in case you want to save some typing. We will start by importing `html` from `lxml`, as well as `requests`, and then load the page.

```
In [1]: from lxml import html
   ...: import requests
   ...: page_html = requests.get("http://localhost:8080/planets.html").text
```

By this point, lxml should be installed as a dependency of other installs. If you get errors, install it with `pip install lxml`.

How to do it...

The first thing that we do is to load the HTML into an lxml "etree". This is lxml's representation of the DOM.

```
in [2]: tree = html.fromstring(page_html)
```

The `tree` variable is now an lxml representation of the DOM which models the HTML content. Let's now examine how to use it and XPath to select various elements from the document.

Out first XPath example will be to find all the the `<tr>` elements below the `<table>` element.

```
In [3]: [tr for tr in tree.xpath("/html/body/div/table/tr")]
Out[3]:
[<Element tr at 0x10cfd1408>,
 <Element tr at 0x10cfd12c8>,
 <Element tr at 0x10cfd1728>,
 <Element tr at 0x10cfd16d8>,
 <Element tr at 0x10cfd1458>,
 <Element tr at 0x10cfd1868>,
 <Element tr at 0x10cfd1318>,
 <Element tr at 0x10cfd14a8>,
 <Element tr at 0x10cfd10e8>,
 <Element tr at 0x10cfd1778>,
 <Element tr at 0x10cfd1638>]
```

This XPath navigates by tag name from the root of the document down to the `<tr>` element. This example looks similar to the property notation from Beautiful Soup, but ultimately it is significantly more expressive. And notice one difference in the result. All the the `<tr>` elements were returned and not just the first. As a matter of fact, the tags at each level of this path with return multiple items if they are available. If there was multiple `<div>` elements just below `<body>`, then the search for `table/tr` would be executed on all of those `<div>`.

The actual result was an `lxml` element object. The following gets the HTML associated with the elements but using `etree.tostring()` (albeit they have encoding applied):

```
In [4]: from lxml import etree
   ...: [etree.tostring(tr)[:50] for tr in
tree.xpath("/html/body/div/table/tr")]
Out[4]:
[b'<tr id="planetHeader">
\n <th>&#',
 b'<tr id="planet1" class="planet" name="Mercury">&#1',
 b'<tr id="planet2" class="planet" name="Venus">
',
 b'<tr id="planet3" class="planet" name="Earth">
',
 b'<tr id="planet4" class="planet" name="Mars">
\n',
 b'<tr id="planet5" class="planet" name="Jupiter">&#1',
```

```
 b'<tr id="planet6" class="planet" name="Saturn">&#13',
 b'<tr id="planet7" class="planet" name="Uranus">&#13',
 b'<tr id="planet8" class="planet" name="Neptune">&#1',
 b'<tr id="planet9" class="planet" name="Pluto">
',
 b'<tr id="footerRow">
\n <td>
']
```

Now let's look at using XPath to select only the <tr> elements that are planets.

```
In [5]: [etree.tostring(tr)[:50] for tr in
tree.xpath("/html/body/div/table/tr[@class='planet']")]
Out[5]:
[b'<tr id="planet1" class="planet" name="Mercury">&#1',
 b'<tr id="planet2" class="planet" name="Venus">
',
 b'<tr id="planet3" class="planet" name="Earth">
',
 b'<tr id="planet4" class="planet" name="Mars">
\n',
 b'<tr id="planet5" class="planet" name="Jupiter">&#1',
 b'<tr id="planet6" class="planet" name="Saturn">&#13',
 b'<tr id="planet7" class="planet" name="Uranus">&#13',
 b'<tr id="planet8" class="planet" name="Neptune">&#1',
 b'<tr id="planet9" class="planet" name="Pluto">
']
```

The use of the `[]` next to a tag states that we want to do a selection based on some criteria upon the current element. The `@` states that we want to examine an attribute of the tag, and in this cast we want to select tags where the attribute is equal to `"planet"`.

There is also another point to be made out of the query that had 11 <tr> rows. As stated earlier, the XPath runs the navigation on all the nodes found at each level. There are two tables in this document, both children of a different <div> that are both a child or the <body> element. The row with `id="planetHeader"` came from our desired target table, the other, with `id="footerRow"`, came from the second table.

Previously we solved this by selecting <tr> with `class="row"`, but there are also other ways worth a brief mention. The first is that we can also use `[]` to specify a specific element at each section of the XPath like they are arrays. Take the following:

```
In [6]: [etree.tostring(tr)[:50] for tr in
tree.xpath("/html/body/div[1]/table/tr")]
Out[6]:
[b'<tr id="planetHeader">
```

```
\n <th>&#',
 b'<tr id="planet1" class="planet" name="Mercury">&#1',
 b'<tr id="planet2" class="planet" name="Venus">
',
 b'<tr id="planet3" class="planet" name="Earth">
',
 b'<tr id="planet4" class="planet" name="Mars">
\n',
 b'<tr id="planet5" class="planet" name="Jupiter">&#1',
 b'<tr id="planet6" class="planet" name="Saturn">&#13',
 b'<tr id="planet7" class="planet" name="Uranus">&#13',
 b'<tr id="planet8" class="planet" name="Neptune">&#1',
 b'<tr id="planet9" class="planet" name="Pluto">
']
```

Arrays in XPath start at 1 instead of 0 (a common source of error). This selected the first `<div>`. A change to `[2]` selects the second `<div>` and hence only the second `<table>`.

```
In [7]: [etree.tostring(tr)[:50] for tr in
tree.xpath("/html/body/div[2]/table/tr")]
Out[7]: [b'<tr id="footerRow">
\n <td>
']
```

The first `<div>` in this document also has an id attribute:

```
<div id="planets">
```

This can be used to select this `<div>`:

```
In [8]: [etree.tostring(tr)[:50] for tr in
tree.xpath("/html/body/div[@id='planets']/table/tr")]
Out[8]:
[b'<tr id="planetHeader">
\n <th>&#',
 b'<tr id="planet1" class="planet" name="Mercury">&#1',
 b'<tr id="planet2" class="planet" name="Venus">
',
 b'<tr id="planet3" class="planet" name="Earth">
',
 b'<tr id="planet4" class="planet" name="Mars">
\n',
 b'<tr id="planet5" class="planet" name="Jupiter">&#1',
 b'<tr id="planet6" class="planet" name="Saturn">&#13',
 b'<tr id="planet7" class="planet" name="Uranus">&#13',
 b'<tr id="planet8" class="planet" name="Neptune">&#1',
 b'<tr id="planet9" class="planet" name="Pluto">
']
```

Earlier we selected the planet rows based upon the value of the class attribute. We can also exclude rows:

```
In [9]: [etree.tostring(tr)[:50] for tr in
tree.xpath("/html/body/div[@id='planets']/table/tr[@id!='planetHeader']")]
Out[9]:
[b'<tr id="planet1" class="planet" name="Mercury">&#1',
 b'<tr id="planet2" class="planet" name="Venus">
',
 b'<tr id="planet3" class="planet" name="Earth">
',
 b'<tr id="planet4" class="planet" name="Mars">
\n',
 b'<tr id="planet5" class="planet" name="Jupiter">&#1',
 b'<tr id="planet6" class="planet" name="Saturn">&#13',
 b'<tr id="planet7" class="planet" name="Uranus">&#13',
 b'<tr id="planet8" class="planet" name="Neptune">&#1',
 b'<tr id="planet9" class="planet" name="Pluto">
']
```

Suppose that the planet rows did not have attributes (nor the header row), then we could do this by position, skipping the first row:

```
In [10]: [etree.tostring(tr)[:50] for tr in
tree.xpath("/html/body/div[@id='planets']/table/tr[position() > 1]")]
Out[10]:
[b'<tr id="planet1" class="planet" name="Mercury">&#1',
 b'<tr id="planet2" class="planet" name="Venus">
',
 b'<tr id="planet3" class="planet" name="Earth">
',
 b'<tr id="planet4" class="planet" name="Mars">
\n',
 b'<tr id="planet5" class="planet" name="Jupiter">&#1',
 b'<tr id="planet6" class="planet" name="Saturn">&#13',
 b'<tr id="planet7" class="planet" name="Uranus">&#13',
 b'<tr id="planet8" class="planet" name="Neptune">&#1',
 b'<tr id="planet9" class="planet" name="Pluto">
']
```

It is possible to navigate to the parent of a node using `parent::*`:

```
In [11]: [etree.tostring(tr)[:50] for tr in
tree.xpath("/html/body/div/table/tr/parent::*")]
Out[11]:
[b'<table id="planetsTable" border="1">
\n ',
 b'<table id="footerTable">
\n <tr id="']
```

This returned two parents as, remember, this XPath returns the rows from two tables, so the parents of all those rows are found. The `*` is a wild card that represents any parent tags with any name. In this case, the two parents are both tables, but in general the result can be any number of HTML element types. The following has the same result, but if the two parents where different HTML tags then it would only return the `<table>` elements.

```
In [12]: [etree.tostring(tr)[:50] for tr in
tree.xpath("/html/body/div/table/tr/parent::table")]
Out[12]:
[b'<table id="planetsTable" border="1">
\n ',
 b'<table id="footerTable">
\n <tr id="']
```

It is also possible to specify a specific parent by position or attribute. The following selects the parent with `id="footerTable"`:

```
In [13]: [etree.tostring(tr)[:50] for tr in
tree.xpath("/html/body/div/table/tr/parent::table[@id='footerTable']")]
Out[13]: [b'<table id="footerTable">
\n <tr id="']
```

A shortcut for parent is `..` (and `.` also represents the current node):

```
In [14]: [etree.tostring(tr)[:50] for tr in
tree.xpath("/html/body/div/table/tr/..")]
Out[14]:
[b'<table id="planetsTable" border="1">
\n ',
 b'<table id="footerTable">
\n <tr id="']
```

And the last example finds the mass of Earth:

```
In [15]: mass =
tree.xpath("/html/body/div[1]/table/tr[@name='Earth']/td[3]/text()[1]")
[0].strip()
    ...: mass
Out[15]: '5.97'
```

The trailing portion of this XPath,`/td[3]/text()[1]`, selects the third <td> element in the row, then the text of that element (which is an array of all the text in the element), and the first of those which is the mass.

How it works

XPath is a element of the **XSLT** (**eXtensible Stylesheet Language Transformation**) standard and provides the ability to select nodes in an XML document. HTML is a variant of XML, and hence XPath can work on on HTML document (although HTML can be improperly formed and mess up XPath parsing in those cases).

XPath itself is designed to model the structure of XML nodes, attributes, and properties. The syntax provides means of finding items in the XML that match the expression. This can include matching or logical comparison of any of the nodes, attributes, values, or text in the XML document.

TIP

XPath expressions can be combined to form very complex paths within the document. It is also possible to navigate the document based upon relative positions, which helps greatly in finding data based upon relative positions instead of absolute positions within the DOM.

Understanding XPath is essential for knowing how to parse HTML and perform web scraping. And as we will see, it underlies, and provides an implementation for, many of the higher level libraries such as lxml.

There's more...

XPath is actually an amazing tool for working with XML and HTML documents. It is quite rich in its capabilities, and we have barely touched the surface of its capabilities for demonstrating a few examples that are common to scraping data in HTML documents.

To learn much more, please visit the following links:

- https://www.w3schools.com/xml/xml_xpath.asp
- https://www.w3.org/TR/xpath/

Querying data with XPath and CSS selectors

CSS selectors are patterns used for selecting elements and are often used to define the elements that styles should be applied to. They can also be used with lxml to select nodes in the DOM. CSS selectors are commonly used as they are more compact than XPath and generally can be more reusable in code. Examples of common selectors which may be used are as follows:

What you are looking for	Example
All tags	*
A specific tag (that is, tr)	.planet
A class name (that is, "planet")	tr.planet
A tag with an ID "planet3"	tr#planet3
A child tr of a table	table tr
A descendant tr of a table	table tr
A tag with an attribute (that is, tr with id="planet4")	a[id=Mars]

Getting ready

Let's start examining CSS selectors using the same start up code we used in the last recipe. These code snippets are also in the 02/04_css_selectors.py.

```
In [1]: from lxml import html
   ...: import requests
   ...: page_html = requests.get("http://localhost:8080/planets.html").text
   ...: tree = html.fromstring(page_html)
   ...:
```

How to do it...

Now let's start playing with XPath and CSS selectors. The following selects all <tr> elements with a class equal to "planet":

```
In [2]: [(v, v.xpath("@name")) for v in tree.cssselect('tr.planet')]
Out[2]:
[(<Element tr at 0x10d3a2278>, ['Mercury']),
 (<Element tr at 0x10c16ed18>, ['Venus']),
 (<Element tr at 0x10e445688>, ['Earth']),
 (<Element tr at 0x10e477228>, ['Mars']),
 (<Element tr at 0x10e477408>, ['Jupiter']),
 (<Element tr at 0x10e477458>, ['Saturn']),
 (<Element tr at 0x10e4774a8>, ['Uranus']),
 (<Element tr at 0x10e4774f8>, ['Neptune']),
 (<Element tr at 0x10e477548>, ['Pluto'])]
```

Data for the Earth can be found in several ways. The following gets the row based on `id`:

```
In [3]: tr = tree.cssselect("tr#planet3")
   ...: tr[0], tr[0].xpath("./td[2]/text()")[0].strip()
   ...:
Out[3]: (<Element tr at 0x10e445688>, 'Earth')
```

The following uses an attribute with a specific value:

```
In [4]: tr = tree.cssselect("tr[name='Pluto']")
   ...: tr[0], tr[0].xpath("td[2]/text()")[0].strip()
   ...:
Out[5]: (<Element tr at 0x10e477548>, 'Pluto')
```

Note that unlike XPath, the `@` symbol need not be used to specify an attribute.

How it works

lxml converts the CSS selector you provide to XPath, and then performs that XPath expression against the underlying document. In essence, CSS selectors in lxml provide a shorthand to XPath, which makes finding nodes that fit certain patterns simpler than with XPath.

There's more...

Because CSS selectors utilize XPath under the covers, there is overhead to its use as compared to using XPath directly. This difference is, however, almost a non-issue, and hence in certain scenarios it is easier to just use cssselect.

A full description of CSS selectors can be found at: `https://www.w3.org/TR/2011/REC-css3-selectors-20110929/`

Using Scrapy selectors

Scrapy is a Python web spider framework that is used to extract data from websites. It provides many powerful features for navigating entire websites, such as the ability to follow links. One feature it provides is the ability to find data within a document using the DOM, and using the now, quite familiar, XPath.

In this recipe we will load the list of current questions on StackOverflow, and then parse this using a scrapy selector. Using that selector, we will extract the text of each question.

Getting ready

The code for this recipe is in `02/05_scrapy_selectors.py`.

How to do it...

We start by importing `Selector` from `scrapy`, and also `requests` so that we can retrieve the page:

```
In [1]: from scrapy.selector import Selector
   ...: import requests
   ...:
```

Next we load the page. For this example we are going to retrieve the most recent questions on StackOverflow and extract their titles. We can make this query with the the following:

```
In [2]: response = requests.get("http://stackoverflow.com/questions")
```

Now create a `Selector` and pass it the response object:

```
In [3]: selector = Selector(response)
   ...: selector
   ...:
Out[3]: <Selector xpath=None data='<html>\r\n\r\n <head>\r\n\r\n
<title>N'>
```

Examining the content of this page we can see that questions have the following structure to their HTML:

<div class="summary"> == $0
<h3>
<a href="/questions/48353062/can-not-delete-unselected-dates-from-array-in-material-calendar-view-android" class="question-hyperlink">Can not delete unSelected dates from array in material calendar view android</a>
</h3>
<div class="excerpt">…</div>
<div class="tags t-android t-arrays t-calendar t-material">…</div>
<div class="started fr">…</div>
</div>
</div>

The HTML of a StackOverflow Question

With the selector we can find these using XPath:

```
In [4]: summaries = selector.xpath('//div[@class="summary"]/h3')
   ...: summaries[0:5]
   ...:
Out[4]:
[<Selector xpath='//div[@class="summary"]/h3' data='<h3><a
href="/questions/48353091/how-to-'>,
 <Selector xpath='//div[@class="summary"]/h3' data='<h3><a
href="/questions/48353090/move-fi'>,
 <Selector xpath='//div[@class="summary"]/h3' data='<h3><a
href="/questions/48353089/java-la'>,
 <Selector xpath='//div[@class="summary"]/h3' data='<h3><a
href="/questions/48353086/how-do-'>,
 <Selector xpath='//div[@class="summary"]/h3' data='<h3><a
href="/questions/48353085/running'>]
```

And now we drill a little further into each to get the title of the question.

```
In [5]: [x.extract() for x in summaries.xpath('a[@class="question-
hyperlink"]/text()')][:10]
Out[5]:
['How to convert stdout binary file to a data URL?',
 'Move first letter from sentence to the end',
 'Java launch program and interact with it programmatically',
 'How do I build vala from scratch',
 'Running Sql Script',
 'Mysql - Auto create, update, delete table 2 from table 1',
 'how to map meeting data corresponding calendar time in java',
 'Range of L*a* b* in Matlab',
 'set maximum and minimum number input box in js,html',
 'I created generic array and tried to store the value but it is
showing ArrayStoreException']
```

How it works

Underneath the covers, Scrapy builds its selectors on top of lxml. It offers a smaller and slightly simpler API, which is similar in performance to lxml.

There's more...

To learn more about Scrapy Selectors see: `https://doc.scrapy.org/en/latest/topics/selectors.html`.

Loading data in unicode / UTF-8

A document's encoding tells an application how the characters in the document are represented as bytes in the file. Essentially, the encoding specifies how many bits there are per character. In a standard ASCII document, all characters are 8 bits. HTML files are often encoded as 8 bits per character, but with the globalization of the internet, this is not always the case. Many HTML documents are encoded as 16-bit characters, or use a combination of 8- and 16-bit characters.

A particularly common form HTML document encoding is referred to as UTF-8. This is the encoding form that we will examine.

Getting ready

We will read a file named `unicode.html` from our local web server, located at `http://localhost:8080/unicode.html`. This file is UTF-8 encoded and contains several sets of characters in different parts of the encoding space. For example, the page looks as follows in your browser:

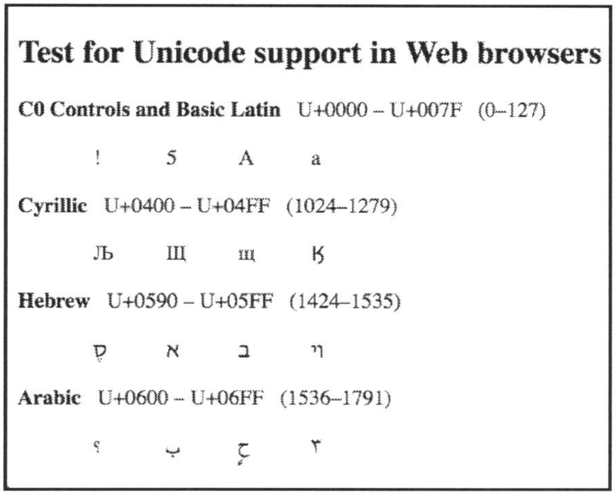
Test for Unicode support in Web browsers
C0 Controls and Basic Latin U+0000 – U+007F (0–127)
! 5 A a
Cyrillic U+0400 – U+04FF (1024–1279)
Љ Щ щ
Hebrew U+0590 – U+05FF (1424–1535)
ק א ב
Arabic U+0600 – U+06FF (1536–1791)
؟ ب

The Page in the Browser

Using an editor that supports UTF-8, we can see how the Cyrillic characters are rendered in the editor:

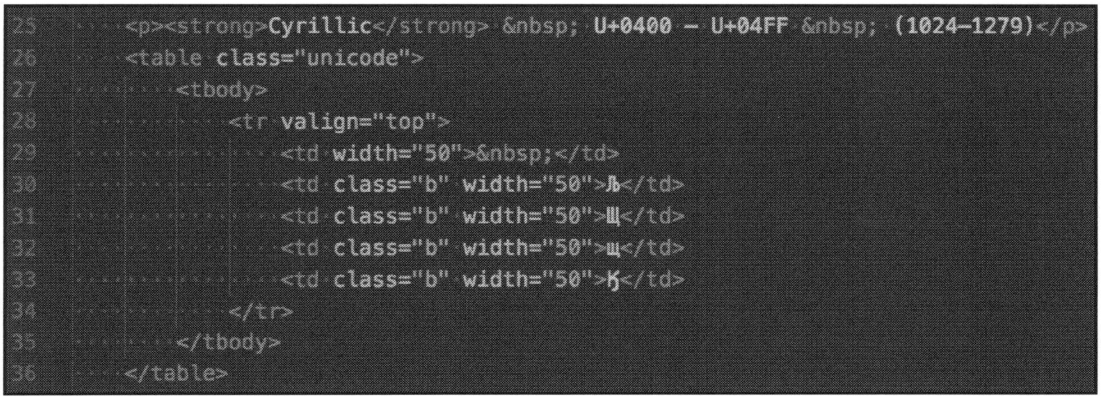

The HTML in an Editor

Code for the sample is in `02/06_unicode.py`.

How to do it...

We will look at using `urlopen` and `requests` to handle HTML in UTF-8. These two libraries handle this differently, so let's examine this. Let's start importing `urllib`, loading the page, and examining some of the content.

```
In [8]: from urllib.request import urlopen
   ...: page = urlopen("http://localhost:8080/unicode.html")
   ...: content = page.read()
   ...: content[840:1280]
   ...:
Out[8]: b'><strong>Cyrillic</strong>   U+0400 \xe2\x80\x93
U+04FF   (1024\xe2\x80\x931279)</p>\n <table
class="unicode">\n <tbody>\n <tr valign="top">\n <td
width="50"> </td>\n <td class="b" width="50">\xd0\x89</td>\n
<td class="b" width="50">\xd0\xa9</td>\n <td class="b"
width="50">\xd1\x89</td>\n <td class="b" width="50">\xd3\x83</td>\n
</tr>\n </tbody>\n </table>\n\n '
```

Note how the Cyrillic characters were read in as multi-byte codes using \ notation, such as `\xd0\x89`.

To rectify this, we can convert the content to UTF-8 format using the Python `str` statement:

```
In [9]: str(content, "utf-8")[837:1270]
Out[9]: '<strong>Cyrillic</strong>   U+0400 – U+04FF  
(1024–1279)</p>\n <table class="unicode">\n <tbody>\n <tr
valign="top">\n <td width="50"> </td>\n <td class="b"
width="50">Љ</td>\n <td class="b" width="50">Щ</td>\n <td
class="b" width="50">щ</td>\n <td class="b" width="50">Ӄ</td>\n
</tr>\n </tbody>\n </table>\n\n '
```

Note that the output now has the characters encoded properly.

We can exclude this extra step by using `requests`.

```
In [9]: import requests
   ...: response =
requests.get("http://localhost:8080/unicode.html").text
   ...: response.text[837:1270]
   ...:
'<strong>Cyrillic</strong>   U+0400 – U+04FF  
(1024–1279)</p>\n <table class="unicode">\n <tbody>\n <tr
valign="top">\n <td width="50"> </td>\n <td class="b"
width="50">Љ</td>\n <td class="b" width="50">Щ</td>\n <td
class="b" width="50">щ</td>\n <td class="b" width="50">Ӄ</td>\n
</tr>\n </tbody>\n </table>\n\n '
```

How it works

In the case of using `urlopen`, the conversion was explicitly performed by using the str statement and specifying that the content should be converted to UTF-8. For `requests`, the library was able to determine from the content within the HTML that it was in UTF-8 format by seeing the following tag in the document:

```
<meta http-equiv="Content-Type" content="text/html; charset=UTF-8">
```

There's more...

There are a number of resources available on the internet for learning about Unicode and UTF-8 encoding techniques. Perhaps the best is the following Wikipedia article, which has an excellent summary and a great table describing the encoding technique: `https://en.wikipedia.org/wiki/UTF-8`

3
Processing Data

In this chapter, we will cover:

- Working with CSV and JSON data
- Storing data using AWS S3
- Storing data using MySQL
- Storing data using PostgreSQL
- Storing store data using Elasticsearch
- How to build robust ETL pipelines with AWS SQS

Introduction

In this chapter, we will introduce the use of data in JSON, CSV, and XML formats. This will include the means of parsing and converting this data to other formats, including storing that data in relational databases, search engines such as Elasticsearch, and cloud storage including AWS S3. We will also discuss the creation of distributed and large-scale scraping tasks through the use of messaging systems including AWS Simple Queue Service (SQS). The goal is to provide both an understanding of the various forms of data you may retrieve and need to parse, and an instruction the the various backends where you can store the data you have scraped. Finally, we get a first introduction to one and Amazon Web Service (AWS) offerings. By the end of the book we will be getting quite heavy into AWS and this gives a gentle introduction.

Working with CSV and JSON data

Extracting data from HTML pages is done using the techniques in the previous chapter, primarily using XPath through various tools and also with Beautiful Soup. While we will focus primarily on HTML, HTML is a variant of XML (eXtensible Markup Language). XML one was the most popular for of expressing data on the web, but other have become popular, and even exceeded XML in popularity.

Two common formats that you will see are JSON (JavaScript Object Notation) and CSV (Comma Separated Values). CSV is easy to create and a common form for many spreadsheet applications, so many web sites provide data in that for, or you will need to convert scraped data to that format for further storage or collaboration. JSON really has become the preferred format, due to its easy within programming languages such as JavaScript (and Python), and many database now support it as a native data format.

In this recipe let's examine converting scraped data to CSV and JSON, as well as writing the data to files and also reading those data files from remote servers. The tools we will examine are the Python CSV and JSON libraries. We will also examine using `pandas` for these techniques.

Also implicit in these examples is the conversion of XML data to CSV and JSON, so we won't have a dedicated section for those examples.

Getting ready

We will be using the planets data page and converting that data into CSV and JSON files. Let's start by loading the planets data from the page into a list of python dictionary objects. The following code (found in (`03/get_planet_data.py`) provides a function that performs this task, which will be reused throughout the chapter:

```
import requests
from bs4 import BeautifulSoup

def get_planet_data():
   html = requests.get("http://localhost:8080/planets.html").text
   soup = BeautifulSoup(html, "lxml")

   planet_trs = soup.html.body.div.table.findAll("tr", {"class": "planet"})

   def to_dict(tr):
```

```
        tds = tr.findAll("td")
        planet_data = dict()
        planet_data['Name'] = tds[1].text.strip()
        planet_data['Mass'] = tds[2].text.strip()
        planet_data['Radius'] = tds[3].text.strip()
        planet_data['Description'] = tds[4].text.strip()
        planet_data['MoreInfo'] = tds[5].findAll("a")[0]["href"].strip()
        return planet_data

    planets = [to_dict(tr) for tr in planet_trs]

    return planets

if __name__ == "__main__":
    print(get_planet_data())
```

Running the script gives the following output (briefly truncated):

```
03 $python get_planet_data.py
[{'Name': 'Mercury', 'Mass': '0.330', 'Radius': '4879', 'Description':
'Named Mercurius by the Romans because it appears to move so swiftly.',
'MoreInfo': 'https://en.wikipedia.org/wiki/Mercury_(planet)'}, {'Name':
'Venus', 'Mass': '4.87', 'Radius': '12104', 'Description': 'Roman name for
the goddess of love. This planet was considered to be the brightest and
most beautiful planet or star in the\r\n heavens. Other civilizations have
named it for their god or goddess of love/war.', 'MoreInfo':
'https://en.wikipedia.org/wiki/Venus'}, {'Name': 'Earth', 'Mass': '5.97',
'Radius': '12756', 'Description': "The name Earth comes from the Indo-
European base 'er,'which produced the Germanic noun 'ertho,' and ultimately
German 'erde,'\r\n Dutch 'aarde,' Scandinavian 'jord,' and English 'earth.'
Related forms include Greek 'eraze,' meaning\r\n 'on the ground,' and Welsh
'erw,' meaning 'a piece of land.'", 'MoreInfo':
'https://en.wikipedia.org/wiki/Earth'}, {'Name': 'Mars', 'Mass': '0.642',
'Radius': '6792', 'Description': 'Named by the Romans for their god of war
because of its red, bloodlike color. Other civilizations also named this
planet\r\n from this attribute; for example, the Egyptians named it "Her
Desher," meaning "the red one."', 'MoreInfo':
...
```

It may be required to install csv, json and pandas. You can do that with the following three commands:

```
pip install csv
pip install json
pip install pandas
```

How to do it

We will start by converting the planets data into a CSV file.

1. This will be performed using `csv`. The following code writes the planets data to a CSV file (the code is in`03/create_csv.py`):

```
import csv
from get_planet_data import get_planet_data

planets = get_planet_data()

with open('../../www/planets.csv', 'w+', newline='') as csvFile:
    writer = csv.writer(csvFile)
    writer.writerow(['Name', 'Mass', 'Radius', 'Description',
'MoreInfo'])
for planet in planets:
        writer.writerow([planet['Name'],
planet['Mass'],planet['Radius'], planet['Description'],
planet['MoreInfo']])
```

2. The output file is put into the www folder of our project. Examining it we see the following content::

```
Name,Mass,Radius,Description,MoreInfo
Mercury,0.330,4879,Named Mercurius by the Romans because it appears
to move so swiftly.,https://en.wikipedia.org/wiki/Mercury_(planet)
Venus,4.87,12104,Roman name for the goddess of love. This planet
was considered to be the brightest and most beautiful planet or
star in the heavens. Other civilizations have named it for their
god or goddess of love/war.,https://en.wikipedia.org/wiki/Venus
Earth,5.97,12756,"The name Earth comes from the Indo-European base
'er,'which produced the Germanic noun 'ertho,' and ultimately
German 'erde,' Dutch 'aarde,' Scandinavian 'jord,' and English
'earth.' Related forms include Greek 'eraze,' meaning 'on the
ground,' and Welsh 'erw,' meaning 'a piece of
land.'",https://en.wikipedia.org/wiki/Earth
Mars,0.642,6792,"Named by the Romans for their god of war because
of its red, bloodlike color. Other civilizations also named this
planet from this attribute; for example, the Egyptians named it
""Her Desher,"" meaning ""the red
one.""",https://en.wikipedia.org/wiki/Mars
Jupiter,1898,142984,The largest and most massive of the planets was
named Zeus by the Greeks and Jupiter by the Romans; he was the most
important deity in both
pantheons.,https://en.wikipedia.org/wiki/Jupiter
Saturn,568,120536,"Roman name for the Greek Cronos, father of
```

```
Zeus/Jupiter. Other civilizations have given different names to
Saturn, which is the farthest planet from Earth that can be
observed by the naked human eye. Most of its satellites were named
for Titans who, according to Greek mythology, were brothers and
sisters of Saturn.",https://en.wikipedia.org/wiki/Saturn
Uranus,86.8,51118,"Several astronomers, including Flamsteed and Le
Monnier, had observed Uranus earlier but had recorded it as a fixed
star. Herschel tried unsuccessfully to name his discovery
""Georgian Sidus"" after George III; the planet was named by Johann
Bode in 1781 after the ancient Greek deity of the sky Uranus, the
father of Kronos (Saturn) and grandfather of Zeus
(Jupiter).",https://en.wikipedia.org/wiki/Uranus
Neptune,102,49528,"Neptune was ""predicted"" by John Couch Adams
and Urbain Le Verrier who, independently, were able to account for
the irregularities in the motion of Uranus by correctly predicting
the orbital elements of a trans- Uranian body. Using the predicted
parameters of Le Verrier (Adams never published his predictions),
Johann Galle observed the planet in 1846. Galle wanted to name the
planet for Le Verrier, but that was not acceptable to the
international astronomical community. Instead, this planet is named
for the Roman god of the
sea.",https://en.wikipedia.org/wiki/Neptune
Pluto,0.0146,2370,"Pluto was discovered at Lowell Observatory in
Flagstaff, AZ during a systematic search for a trans-Neptune planet
predicted by Percival Lowell and William H. Pickering. Named after
the Roman god of the underworld who was able to render himself
invisible.",https://en.wikipedia.org/wiki/Pluto
```

We wrote this file into the www directory so that we can download it with our web server.

3. This data can now be used in applications that support CSV content, such as Excel:

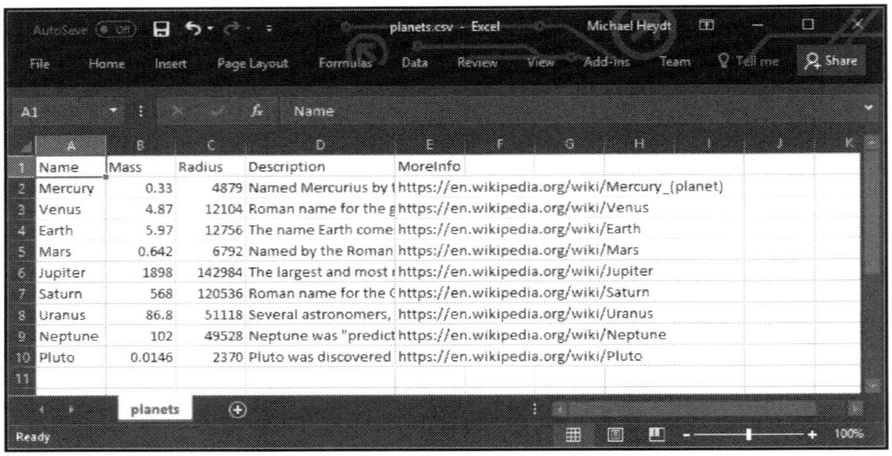

Name	Mass	Radius	Description	MoreInfo
Mercury	0.33	4879	Named Mercurius by t	https://en.wikipedia.org/wiki/Mercury_(planet)
Venus	4.87	12104	Roman name for the g	https://en.wikipedia.org/wiki/Venus
Earth	5.97	12756	The name Earth come	https://en.wikipedia.org/wiki/Earth
Mars	0.642	6792	Named by the Roman	https://en.wikipedia.org/wiki/Mars
Jupiter	1898	142984	The largest and most	https://en.wikipedia.org/wiki/Jupiter
Saturn	568	120536	Roman name for the (	https://en.wikipedia.org/wiki/Saturn
Uranus	86.8	51118	Several astronomers,	https://en.wikipedia.org/wiki/Uranus
Neptune	102	49528	Neptune was "predict	https://en.wikipedia.org/wiki/Neptune
Pluto	0.0146	2370	Pluto was discovered	https://en.wikipedia.org/wiki/Pluto

The File Opened in Excel

4. CSV data can also be read from a web server using the `csv` library and by first retrieving the content with `requests` . The following code is in the `03/read_csv_from_web.py`):

```
import requests
import csv

planets_data =
requests.get("http://localhost:8080/planets.csv").text
planets = planets_data.split('\n!)
reader = csv.reader(planets, delimiter=',', quotechar='"')
lines = [line for line in reader][:-1]
for line in lines: print(line)
```

The following is a portion of the output

```
['Name', 'Mass', 'Radius', 'Description', 'MoreInfo']
['Mercury', '0.330', '4879', 'Named Mercurius by the Romans because
it appears to move so swiftly.',
'https://en.wikipedia.org/wiki/Mercury_(planet)']
['Venus', '4.87', '12104', 'Roman name for the goddess of love.
This planet was considered to be the brightest and most beautiful
planet or star in the heavens. Other civilizations have named it
for their god or goddess of love/war.',
'https://en.wikipedia.org/wiki/Venus']
```

```
['Earth', '5.97', '12756', "The name Earth comes from the Indo-
European base 'er,'which produced the Germanic noun 'ertho,' and
ultimately German 'erde,' Dutch 'aarde,' Scandinavian 'jord,' and
English 'earth.' Related forms include Greek 'eraze,' meaning 'on
the ground,' and Welsh 'erw,' meaning 'a piece of land.'",
'https://en.wikipedia.org/wiki/Earth']
```

One thing to point our is that the CSV writer left a trailing blank like would add an empty list item if not handled. This was handled by slicing the rows: This following statement returned all lines except the last one:

```
lines = [line for line in reader][:-1]
```

5. This can also be done quite easily using pandas. The following constructs a DataFrame from the scraped data. The code is in `03/create_df_planets.py`:

```
import pandas as pd
planets_df =
pd.read_csv("http://localhost:8080/planets_pandas.csv",
index_col='Name')
print(planets_df)
```

Running this gives the following output:

```
                                               Description Mass
Radius
Name
Mercury Named Mercurius by the Romans because it appea...  0.330
4879
Venus   Roman name for the goddess of love. This plane...   4.87
12104
Earth   The name Earth comes from the Indo-European ba...   5.97
12756
Mars    Named by the Romans for their god of war becau...  0.642
6792
Jupiter The largest and most massive of the planets wa...   1898
142984
Saturn  Roman name for the Greek Cronos, father of Zeu...    568
120536
Uranus  Several astronomers, including Flamsteed and L...   86.8
51118
Neptune Neptune was "predicted" by John Couch Adams an...    102
49528
Pluto   Pluto was discovered at Lowell Observatory in ... 0.0146
2370
```

6. And the `DataFrame` can be saved to a CSV file with a simple call to `.to_csv()` (code is in `03/save_csv_pandas.py`):

```
import pandas as pd
from get_planet_data import get_planet_data

# construct a data from from the list
planets = get_planet_data()
planets_df = pd.DataFrame(planets).set_index('Name')
planets_df.to_csv("../../www/planets_pandas.csv")
```

7. A CSV file can be read in from a `URL` very easily with `pd.read_csv()` - no need for other libraries. You can use the code in`03/read_csv_via_pandas.py`):

```
import pandas as pd
planets_df =
pd.read_csv("http://localhost:8080/planets_pandas.csv",
index_col='Name')
print(planets_df)
```

8. Converting data to JSON is also quite easy. Manipulation of JSON with Python can be done with the Python `json` library. This library can be used to convert Python objects to and from JSON. The following converts the list of planets into JSON and prints it to the console:prints the planets data as JSON (code in `03/convert_to_json.py`):

```
import json
from get_planet_data import get_planet_data
planets=get_planet_data()
print(json.dumps(planets, indent=4))
```

Executing this script produces the following output (some of the output is omitted):

```
[
    {
        "Name": "Mercury",
        "Mass": "0.330",
        "Radius": "4879",
        "Description": "Named Mercurius by the Romans because it
appears to move so swiftly.",
        "MoreInfo":
"https://en.wikipedia.org/wiki/Mercury_(planet)"
    },
    {
        "Name": "Venus",
```

```
        "Mass": "4.87",
        "Radius": "12104",
        "Description": "Roman name for the goddess of love. This
planet was considered to be the brightest and most beautiful planet
or star in the heavens. Other civilizations have named it for their
god or goddess of love/war.",
        "MoreInfo": "https://en.wikipedia.org/wiki/Venus"
    },
```

9. And this can also be used to easily save JSON to a file (`03/save_as_json.py`):

```
import json
from get_planet_data import get_planet_data
planets=get_planet_data()
with open('../../www/planets.json', 'w+') as jsonFile:
   json.dump(planets, jsonFile, indent=4)
```

10. Checking the output using `!head -n 13 ../../www/planets.json` shows:

```
[
    {
        "Name": "Mercury",
        "Mass": "0.330",
        "Radius": "4879",
        "Description": "Named Mercurius by the Romans because it
appears to move so swiftly.",
        "MoreInfo":
"https://en.wikipedia.org/wiki/Mercury_(planet)"
    },
    {
        "Name": "Venus",
        "Mass": "4.87",
        "Radius": "12104",
        "Description": "Roman name for the goddess of love. This
planet was considered to be the brightest and most beautiful planet
or star in the heavens. Other civilizations have named it for their
god or goddess of love/war.",
```

11. JSON can be read from a web server with `requests` and converted to a Python object (`03/read_http_json_requests.py`):

```
import requests
import json

planets_request =
requests.get("http://localhost:8080/planets.json")
print(json.loads(planets_request.text))
```

12. pandas also provides JSON capabilities to save to CSV (03/save_json_pandas.py):

```
import pandas as pd
from get_planet_data import get_planet_data

planets = get_planet_data()
planets_df = pd.DataFrame(planets).set_index('Name')
planets_df.reset_index().to_json("../../www/planets_pandas.json",
orient='records')
```

Unfortunately, there is not currently a way to pretty-print the JSON that is output from `.to_json()`. Also note the use of `orient='records'` and the use of `rest_index()`. This is necessary for reproducing an identical JSON structure to the JSON written using the JSON library example.

13. JSON can be read into a DataFrame using `.read_json()`, as well as from HTTP and files (03/read_json_http_pandas.py):

```
import pandas as pd
planets_df =
pd.read_json("http://localhost:8080/planets_pandas.json").set_index
('Name')
print(planets_df)
```

How it works

The `csv` and `json` libraries are a standard part of Python, and provide a straightforward means of reading and writing data in both formats.

pandas does not come as standard in some Python distributions and you will likely need to install it. The pandas functions for both CSV and JSON are also a much higher level in operation, with many powerful data operations available, and also with support for accessing data from remote servers.

There's more...

The choice of csv, json, or pandas libraries is yours to make but I tend to like pandas and we will examine its use in scraping more throughout the book, although we won't get too deep into its usage.

For an in-depth understanding of pandas, check out `pandas.pydata.org`, or pick up my other book From Packt, Learning pandas, 2ed.

For more info on the csv library, see `https://docs.python.org/3/library/csv.html`

For more on the json library, see `https://docs.python.org/3/library/json.html`

Storing data using AWS S3

There are many cases where we just want to save content that we scrape into a local copy for archive purposes, backup, or later bulk analysis. We also might want to save media from those sites for later use. I've built scrapers for advertisement compliance companies, where we would track and download advertisement based media on web sites to ensure proper usage, and also to store for later analysis, compliance and transcoding.

The storage required for these types of systems can be immense, but with the advent of cloud storage services such as AWS S3 (Simple Storage Service), this becomes much easier and more cost effective than managing a large SAN (Storage Area Network) in your own IT department. Plus, S3 can also automatically move data from hot to cold storage, and then to long-term storage, such as a glacier, which can save you much more money.

We won't get into all of those details, but simply look at storing our `planets.html` file into an S3 bucket. Once you can do this, you can save any content you want to year hearts desire.

Getting ready

To perform the following example, you will need an AWS account and have access to secret keys for use in your Python code. They will be unique to your account. We will use the `boto3` library for S3 access. You can install this using `pip install boto3`. Also, you will need to have environment variables set to authenticate. These will look like the following:

```
AWS_ACCESS_KEY_ID=AKIAIDCQ5PH3UMWKZEWA
AWS_SECRET_ACCESS_KEY=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
```

These are available in the AWS portal under IAM (Identity Access Management) portion of the portal.

It's a good practice to put these keys in environment variables. Having them in code can lead to their theft. During the writing of this book, I had this hard coded and accidentally checked them in to GitHub. The next morning I woke up to critical messages from AWS that I had thousands of servers running! There are GitHub scrapers looking for these keys and they will get found and use for nefarious purposes. By the time I had them all turned off, my bill was up to $6000, all accrued overnight. Thankfully, AWS waived these fees!

How to do it

We won't parse the data in the `planets.html` file, but simply retrieve it from the local web server using requests:

1. The following code, (found in `03/S3.py`), reads the planets web page and stores it in S3:

```
import requests
import boto3

data = requests.get("http://localhost:8080/planets.html").text

# create S3 client, use environment variables for keys
s3 = boto3.client('s3')

# the bucket
bucket_name = "planets-content"

# create bucket, set
s3.create_bucket(Bucket=bucket_name, ACL='public-read')
s3.put_object(Bucket=bucket_name, Key='planet.html',
              Body=data, ACL="public-read")
```

2. This app will give you output similar to the following, which is S3 info telling you various facts about the new item.

```
{'ETag': '"3ada9dcd8933470221936534abbf7f3e"',
 'ResponseMetadata': {'HTTPHeaders': {'content-length': '0',
   'date': 'Sun, 27 Aug 2017 19:25:54 GMT',
   'etag': '"3ada9dcd8933470221936534abbf7f3e"',
   'server': 'AmazonS3',
```

```
    'x-amz-id-2':
'57BkfScql637op1dIXqJ7TeTmMyjVPk07cAMNVqE7C8jKsb7nRO+0GSbkkLWUBWh81
k+q2nMQnE=',
    'x-amz-request-id': 'D8446EDC6CBA4416'},
   'HTTPStatusCode': 200,
   'HostId':
'57BkfScql637op1dIXqJ7TeTmMyjVPk07cAMNVqE7C8jKsb7nRO+0GSbkkLWUBWh81
k+q2nMQnE=',
   'RequestId': 'D8446EDC6CBA4416',
   'RetryAttempts': 0}}
```

3. This output shows us that the object was successfully created in the bucket. At this point, you can navigate to the S3 console and see your bucket:

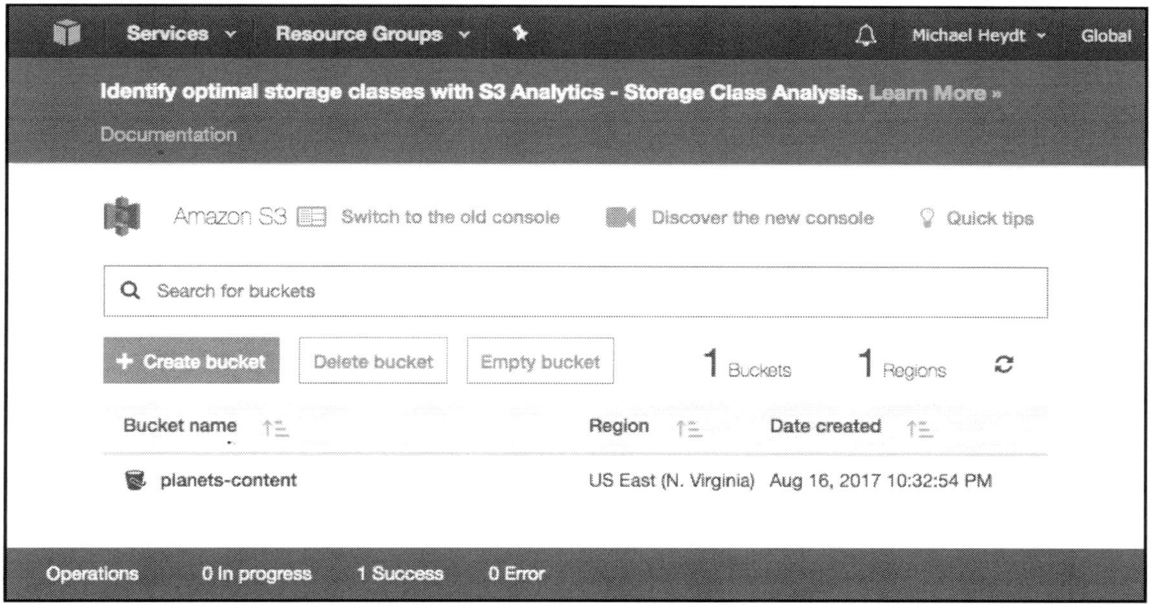

The Bucket in S3

4. Inside the bucket you will see the `planet.html` file:

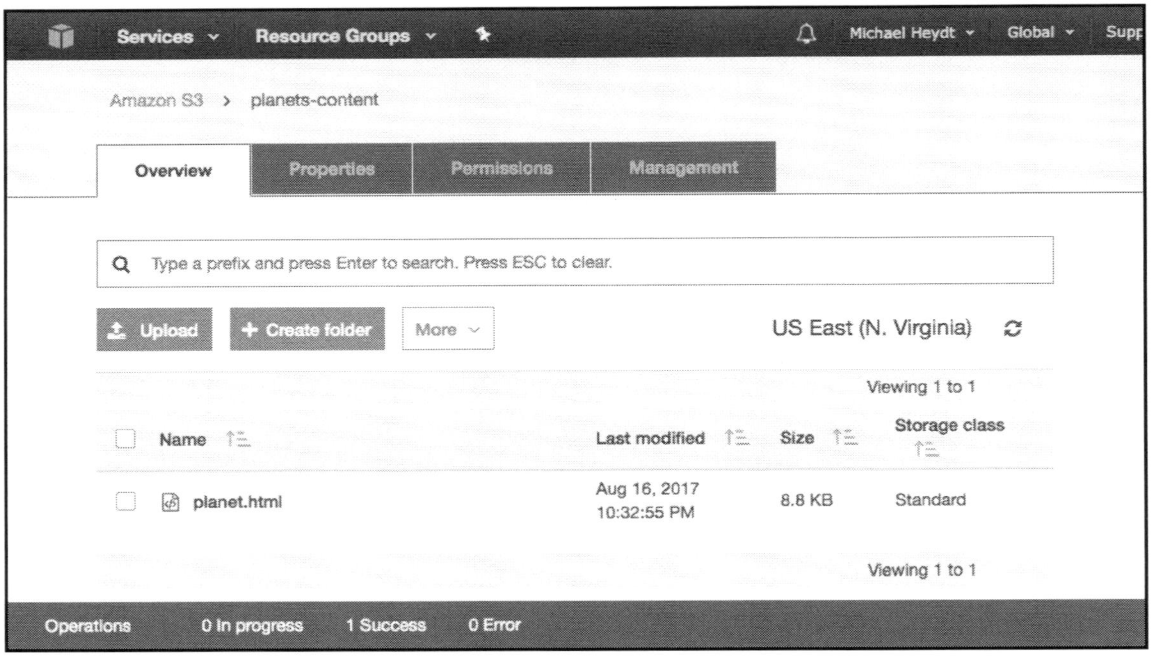

The File in the Bucket

5. By clicking on the file you can see the property and URL to the file within S3:

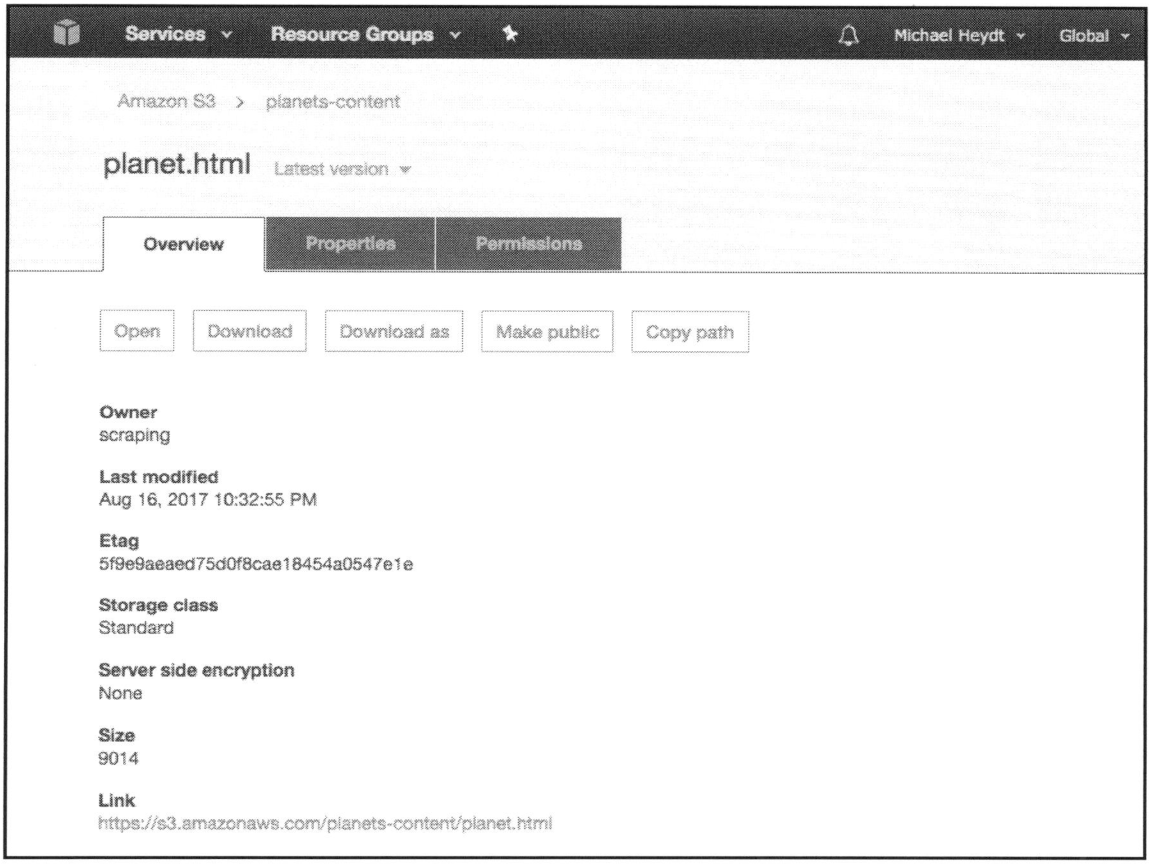

The Properties of the File in S3

How it works

The boto3 library wraps the AWS S3 API in a Pythonic syntax. The `.client()` call authenticates with AWS and gives us an object to use to communicate with S3. Make sure you have your keys in environment variables, as otherwise this will not work.

The bucket name must be globally unique. At the time of writing, this bucket is available, but you will likely need to change the name. The `.create_bucket()` call creates the bucket and sets its ACL. `put_object()` uses the `boto3` upload manager to upload the scraped data into the object in the bucket.

There's more...

There a lot of details to learn for working with S3. You can find API documentation at: `http://docs.aws.amazon.com/AmazonS3/latest/API/Welcome.html`. Boto3 documents can be found at: `https://boto3.readthedocs.io/en/latest/`.

While we only saved a web page, this model can be used to store any type of file based data in S3.

Storing data using MySQL

MySQL is a freely available, open source Relational Database Management System (RDBMS). In this example, we will read the planets data from the website and store it into a MySQL database.

Getting ready

You will need to have access to a MySQL database. You can install one locally installed, in the cloud, within a container. I am using a locally installed MySQL server and have the `root` password set to `mypassword`. You will also need to install the MySQL python library. You can do this with `pip install mysql-connector-python`.

1. The first thing to do is to connect to the database using the `mysql` command at the terminal:

```
# mysql -uroot -pmypassword
mysql: [Warning] Using a password on the command line interface can
be insecure.
Welcome to the MySQL monitor. Commands end with ; or \g.
Your MySQL connection id is 4
Server version: 5.7.19 MySQL Community Server (GPL)

Copyright (c) 2000, 2017, Oracle and/or its affiliates. All rights
reserved.
```

```
Oracle is a registered trademark of Oracle Corporation and/or its
affiliates. Other names may be trademarks of their respective
owners.

Type 'help;' or '\h' for help. Type '\c' to clear the current input
statement.

mysql>
```

2. Now we can create a database that will be used to store our scraped information:

```
mysql> create database scraping;
Query OK, 1 row affected (0.00 sec)
```

3. Now use the new database:

```
mysql> use scraping;
Database changed
```

4. And create a Planets table in the database to store our data:

```
mysql> CREATE TABLE `scraping`.`planets` (
 `id` INT NOT NULL AUTO_INCREMENT,
 `name` VARCHAR(45) NOT NULL,
 `mass` FLOAT NOT NULL,
 `radius` FLOAT NOT NULL,
 `description` VARCHAR(5000) NULL,
 PRIMARY KEY (`id`));
Query OK, 0 rows affected (0.02 sec)
```

Now we are ready to scrape data and put it into the MySQL database.

How to do it

1. The following code (found in `03/store_in_mysql.py`) will read the planets data and write it to MySQL:

```
import mysql.connector
import get_planet_data
from mysql.connector import errorcode
from get_planet_data import get_planet_data

try:
    # open the database connection
    cnx = mysql.connector.connect(user='root',
```

```
password='mypassword',
                                            host="127.0.0.1",
database="scraping")

    insert_sql = ("INSERT INTO Planets (Name, Mass, Radius,
Description) " +
                  "VALUES (%(Name)s, %(Mass)s, %(Radius)s,
%(Description)s)")

    # get the planet data
    planet_data = get_planet_data()

    # loop through all planets executing INSERT for each with the
cursor
    cursor = cnx.cursor()
    for planet in planet_data:
        print("Storing data for %s" % (planet["Name"]))
        cursor.execute(insert_sql, planet)

    # commit the new records
    cnx.commit()

    # close the cursor and connection
    cursor.close()
    cnx.close()

except mysql.connector.Error as err:
    if err.errno == errorcode.ER_ACCESS_DENIED_ERROR:
        print("Something is wrong with your user name or password")
    elif err.errno == errorcode.ER_BAD_DB_ERROR:
        print("Database does not exist")
    else:
        print(err)
else:
    cnx.close()
```

2. This results in the following output:

```
Storing data for Mercury
Storing data for Venus
Storing data for Earth
Storing data for Mars
Storing data for Jupiter
Storing data for Saturn
Storing data for Uranus
Storing data for Neptune
Storing data for Pluto
```

3. Using MySQL Workbench we can see the the records were written to the database (you could use the mysql command line also):

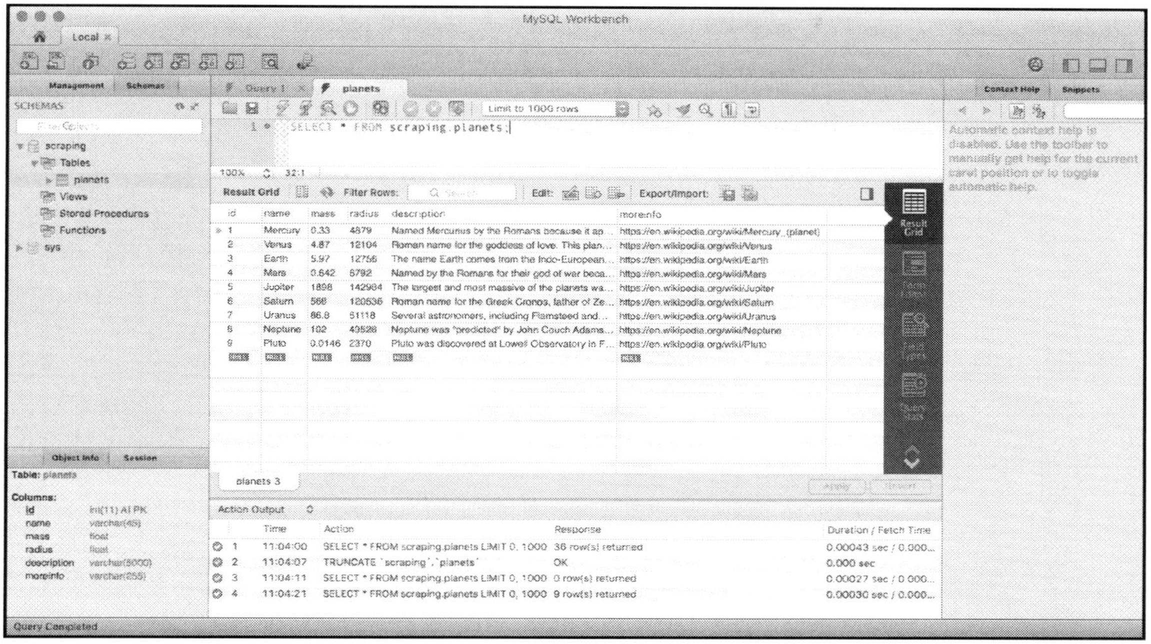

Records displayed using MySQL Workbench

4. The following code can be used to retrieve the data (`03/read_from_mysql.py`):

```
import mysql.connector
from mysql.connector import errorcode

try:
  cnx = mysql.connector.connect(user='root', password='mypassword',
                  host="127.0.0.1", database="scraping")
  cursor = cnx.cursor(dictionary=False)

  cursor.execute("SELECT * FROM scraping.Planets")
  for row in cursor:
    print(row)

  # close the cursor and connection
  cursor.close()
  cnx.close()
```

```
except mysql.connector.Error as err:
  if err.errno == errorcode.ER_ACCESS_DENIED_ERROR:
    print("Something is wrong with your user name or password")
  elif err.errno == errorcode.ER_BAD_DB_ERROR:
    print("Database does not exist")
  else:
    print(err)
finally:
  cnx.close()
```

5. This results in the following output:

```
(1, 'Mercury', 0.33, 4879.0, 'Named Mercurius by the Romans because
it appears to move so swiftly.',
'https://en.wikipedia.org/wiki/Mercury_(planet)')
(2, 'Venus', 4.87, 12104.0, 'Roman name for the goddess of love.
This planet was considered to be the brightest and most beautiful
planet or star in the heavens. Other civilizations have named it
for their god or goddess of love/war.',
'https://en.wikipedia.org/wiki/Venus')
(3, 'Earth', 5.97, 12756.0, "The name Earth comes from the Indo-
European base 'er,'which produced the Germanic noun 'ertho,' and
ultimately German 'erde,' Dutch 'aarde,' Scandinavian 'jord,' and
English 'earth.' Related forms include Greek 'eraze,' meaning 'on
the ground,' and Welsh 'erw,' meaning 'a piece of land.'",
'https://en.wikipedia.org/wiki/Earth')
(4, 'Mars', 0.642, 6792.0, 'Named by the Romans for their god of
war because of its red, bloodlike color. Other civilizations also
named this planet from this attribute; for example, the Egyptians
named it "Her Desher," meaning "the red one."',
'https://en.wikipedia.org/wiki/Mars')
(5, 'Jupiter', 1898.0, 142984.0, 'The largest and most massive of
the planets was named Zeus by the Greeks and Jupiter by the Romans;
he was the most important deity in both pantheons.',
'https://en.wikipedia.org/wiki/Jupiter')
(6, 'Saturn', 568.0, 120536.0, 'Roman name for the Greek Cronos,
father of Zeus/Jupiter. Other civilizations have given different
names to Saturn, which is the farthest planet from Earth that can
be observed by the naked human eye. Most of its satellites were
named for Titans who, according to Greek mythology, were brothers
and sisters of Saturn.', 'https://en.wikipedia.org/wiki/Saturn')
(7, 'Uranus', 86.8, 51118.0, 'Several astronomers, including
Flamsteed and Le Monnier, had observed Uranus earlier but had
recorded it as a fixed star. Herschel tried unsuccessfully to name
his discovery "Georgian Sidus" after George III; the planet was
named by Johann Bode in 1781 after the ancient Greek deity of the
sky Uranus, the father of Kronos (Saturn) and grandfather of Zeus
```

```
(Jupiter).', 'https://en.wikipedia.org/wiki/Uranus')
(8, 'Neptune', 102.0, 49528.0, 'Neptune was "predicted" by John
Couch Adams and Urbain Le Verrier who, independently, were able to
account for the irregularities in the motion of Uranus by correctly
predicting the orbital elements of a trans- Uranian body. Using the
predicted parameters of Le Verrier (Adams never published his
predictions), Johann Galle observed the planet in 1846. Galle
wanted to name the planet for Le Verrier, but that was not
acceptable to the international astronomical community. Instead,
this planet is named for the Roman god of the sea.',
'https://en.wikipedia.org/wiki/Neptune')
(9, 'Pluto', 0.0146, 2370.0, 'Pluto was discovered at Lowell
Observatory in Flagstaff, AZ during a systematic search for a
trans-Neptune planet predicted by Percival Lowell and William H.
Pickering. Named after the Roman god of the underworld who was able
to render himself invisible.',
'https://en.wikipedia.org/wiki/Pluto')
```

How it works

Accessing a MySQL database using the `mysql.connector` involves the use of two classes from the library: `connect` and `cursor`. The `connect` class opens and manages a connection with the database server. From that connection object, we can create a cursor object. This cursor is used for reading and writing data using SQL statements.

In the first example, we used the cursor to insert nine records into the database. Those records are not written to the database until the `commit()` method of the connection is called. This executes the writes of all the rows to the database.

Reading data uses a similar model except that we execute an SQL query (`SELECT`) using the cursor and iterate across the rows that were retrieved. Since we are reading and not writing, there is no need to call `commit()` on the connection.

There's more...

You can learn more about MySQL and install it from: `https://dev.mysql.com/doc/refman/5.7/en/installing.html`. Information on MySQL Workbench is available at: `https://dev.mysql.com/doc/workbench/en/`.

Storing data using PostgreSQL

In this recipe we store our planet data in PostgreSQL. PostgreSQL is an open source relational database management system (RDBMS). It is developed by a worldwide team of volunteers, is not controlled by any corporation or other private entity, and the source code is available free of charge. It has a lot of unique features such as hierarchical data models.

Getting ready

First make sure you have access to a PostgreSQL data instance. Again, you can install one locally, run one in a container, or get an instance in the cloud.

As with MySQL, we need to first create a database. The process is almost identical to that of MySQL but with slightly different commands and parameters.

1. From the terminal execute the psql command at the terminal. This takes you into the psql command processor:

```
# psql -U postgres
psql (9.6.4)
Type "help" for help.
postgres=#
```

2. Now create the scraping database:

```
postgres=# create database scraping;
CREATE DATABASE
postgres=#
```

3. Then switch to the new database:

```
postgres=# \connect scraping
You are now connected to database "scraping" as user "postgres".
scraping=#
```

4. Now we can create the Planets table. We first need to create a sequence table:

```
scraping=# CREATE SEQUENCE public."Planets_id_seq"
scraping-#  INCREMENT 1
scraping-#  START 1
scraping-#  MINVALUE 1
scraping-#  MAXVALUE 9223372036854775807
scraping-#  CACHE 1;
CREATE SEQUENCE
```

```
scraping=# ALTER SEQUENCE public."Planets_id_seq"
scraping-#  OWNER TO postgres;
ALTER SEQUENCE
scraping=#
```

5. And now we can create the table:

```
scraping=# CREATE TABLE public."Planets"
scraping-# (
scraping(# id integer NOT NULL DEFAULT
nextval('"Planets_id_seq"'::regclass),
scraping(# name text COLLATE pg_catalog."default" NOT NULL,
scraping(# mass double precision NOT NULL,
scraping(# radius double precision NOT NULL,
scraping(# description text COLLATE pg_catalog."default" NOT NULL,
scraping(# moreinfo text COLLATE pg_catalog."default" NOT NULL,
scraping(# CONSTRAINT "Planets_pkey" PRIMARY KEY (name)
scraping(# )
scraping-# WITH (
scraping(# OIDS = FALSE
scraping(# )
</span>scraping-# TABLESPACE pg_default;
CREATE TABLE
scraping=#
scraping=# ALTER TABLE public."Planets"
scraping-# OWNER to postgres;
ALTER TABLE
scraping=# \q
```

To access PostgreSQL from Python we will use the `psycopg2` library, so make sure it is installed in your Python environment using `pip install psycopg2`.

We are now ready to write Python to store the planets data in PostgreSQL.

How to do it

We proceed with the recipe as follows:

1. The following code will read the planets data and write it to the database (code in `03/save_in_postgres.py`):

```
import psycopg2
from get_planet_data import get_planet_data

try:
```

```
  # connect to PostgreSQL
  conn = psycopg2.connect("dbname='scraping' host='localhost'
user='postgres' password='mypassword'")

  # the SQL INSERT statement we will use
  insert_sql = ('INSERT INTO public."Planets"(name, mass, radius,
description, moreinfo) ' +
          'VALUES (%(Name)s, %(Mass)s, %(Radius)s, %(Description)s,
%(MoreInfo)s);')

  # open a cursor to access data
  cur = conn.cursor()

  # get the planets data and loop through each
  planet_data = get_planet_data()
  for planet in planet_data:
    # write each record
    cur.execute(insert_sql, planet)

  # commit the new records to the database
  conn.commit()
  cur.close()
  conn.close()

  print("Successfully wrote data to the database")

except Exception as ex:
  print(ex)
```

2. If successful you will see the following:

```
Successfully wrote data to the database
```

3. Using GUI tools such as pgAdmin you can examine the data within the database:

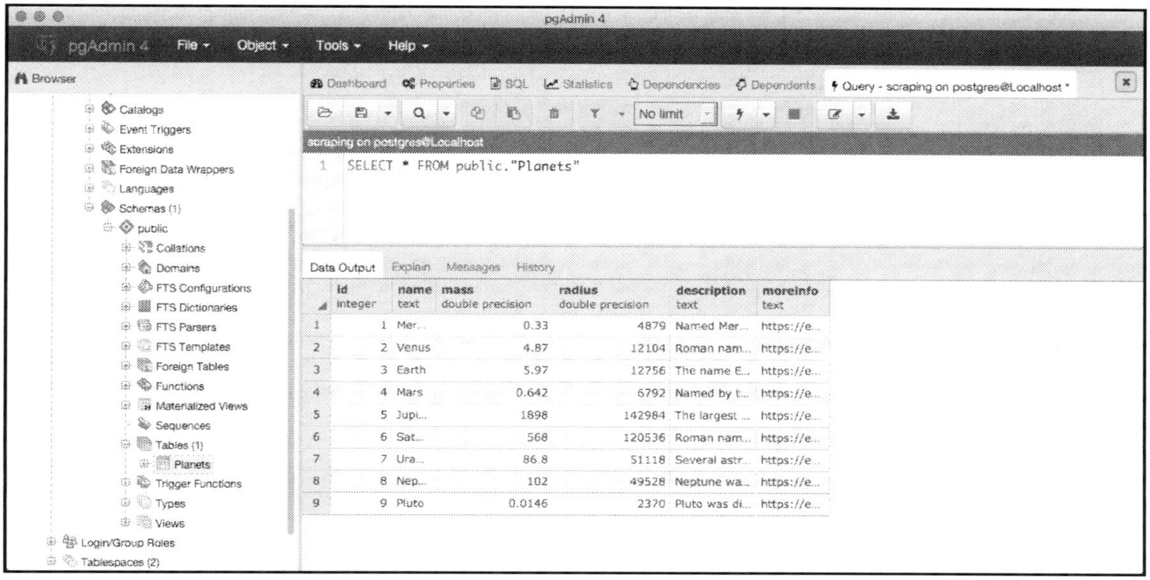

Records Displayed in pgAdmin

4. The data can be queried with the following Python code (found in `03/read_from_postgresql.py`):

```
import psycopg2

try:
  conn = psycopg2.connect("dbname='scraping' host='localhost'
user='postgres' password='mypassword'")

  cur = conn.cursor()
  cur.execute('SELECT * from public."Planets"')
  rows = cur.fetchall()
  print(rows)

  cur.close()
  conn.close()

except Exception as ex:
  print(ex)
```

5. And results in the following output (truncated a little bit:

```
[(1, 'Mercury', 0.33, 4879.0, 'Named Mercurius by the Romans
because it appears to move so swiftly.',
'https://en.wikipedia.org/wiki/Mercury_(planet)'), (2, 'Venus',
4.87, 12104.0, 'Roman name for the goddess of love. This planet was
considered to be the brightest and most beautiful planet or star in
the heavens. Other civilizations have named it for their god or
goddess of love/war.', 'https://en.wikipedia.org/wiki/Venus'), (3,
'Earth', 5.97, 12756.0, "The name Earth comes from the Indo-
European base 'er,'which produced the Germanic noun 'ertho,' and
ultimately German 'erde,' Dutch 'aarde,' Scandinavian 'jord,' and
English 'earth.' Related forms include Greek 'eraze,' meaning 'on
the ground,' and Welsh 'erw,' meaning 'a piece of land.'",
'https://en.wikipedia.org/wiki/Earth'), (4, 'Mars', 0.642, 6792.0,
'Named by the Romans for their god of war because of its red,
bloodlike color. Other civilizations also named this planet from
this attribute; for example, the Egyptians named it
```

How it works

Accessing a PostgreSQL database using the `psycopg2` library as we did involves the use of two classes from the library: `connect` and `cursor`. The `connect` class opens and manages a connection with the database server. From that connection object, we can create a `cursor` object. This cursor is used for reading and writing data using SQL statements.

In the first example, we used the cursor to insert nine records into the database. Those records are not written to the database until the `commit()` method of the connection is called. This executes the writes of all the rows to the database.

Reading data uses a similar model, except that we execute an SQL query (`SELECT`) using the cursor and iterate across the rows that were retrieved. Since we are reading and not writing, there is no need to call `commit()` on the connection.

There's more...

Information on PostgreSQL is available at `https://www.postgresql.org/`. pgAdmin can be obtained at: `https://www.pgadmin.org/` Reference materials for `psycopg` are at: `http://initd.org/psycopg/docs/usage.html`

Storing data in Elasticsearch

Elasticsearch is a search engine based on Lucene. It provides a distributed, multitenant-capable, full-text search engine with an HTTP web interface and schema-free JSON documents. It is a non-relational database (often stated as NoSQL), focusing on the storage of documents instead of records. These documents can be many formats, one of which is useful to us: JSON. This makes using Elasticsearch very simple as we do not need to convert our data to/from JSON. We will use Elasticsearch much more later in the book

For now, let's go and store our planets data in Elasticsearch.

Getting ready

We will access a locally installed Elasticsearch server. To do this from Python, we will use the `Elasticsearch-py` library. It is most likely that you will need to install this using pip: `pip install elasticsearch`.

Unlike PostgreSQL and MySQL, we do not need to create tables in Elasticsearch ahead of time. Elasticsearch does not care about structured data schemas (although it does have indexes), so we don't have to go through this procedure.

How to do it

Writing data to Elasticsearch is really simple. The following Python code performs this task with our planets data (`03/write_to_elasticsearch.py`):

```
from elasticsearch import Elasticsearch
from get_planet_data import get_planet_data

# create an elastic search object
es = Elasticsearch()

# get the data
planet_data = get_planet_data()

for planet in planet_data:
  # insert each planet into elasticsearch server
  res = es.index(index='planets', doc_type='planets_info', body=planet)
  print (res)
```

Executing this results in the following output:

```
{'_index': 'planets', '_type': 'planets_info', '_id':
'AV4qIF3_T0Z2t9T850q6', '_version': 1, 'result': 'created', '_shards':
{'total': 2, 'successful': 1, 'failed': 0}, 'created': True}{'_index':
'planets', '_type': 'planets_info', '_id': 'AV4qIF5QT0Z2t9T850q7',
'_version': 1, 'result': 'created', '_shards': {'total': 2, 'successful':
1, 'failed': 0}, 'created': True}
{'_index': 'planets', '_type': 'planets_info', '_id':
'AV4qIF5XT0Z2t9T850q8', '_version': 1, 'result': 'created', '_shards':
{'total': 2, 'successful': 1, 'failed': 0}, 'created': True}
{'_index': 'planets', '_type': 'planets_info', '_id':
'AV4qIF5fT0Z2t9T850q9', '_version': 1, 'result': 'created', '_shards':
{'total': 2, 'successful': 1, 'failed': 0}, 'created': True}
{'_index': 'planets', '_type': 'planets_info', '_id': 'AV4qIF5mT0Z2t9T850q-
', '_version': 1, 'result': 'created', '_shards': {'total': 2,
'successful': 1, 'failed': 0}, 'created': True}
{'_index': 'planets', '_type': 'planets_info', '_id':
'AV4qIF5rT0Z2t9T850q_', '_version': 1, 'result': 'created', '_shards':
{'total': 2, 'successful': 1, 'failed': 0}, 'created': True}
{'_index': 'planets', '_type': 'planets_info', '_id':
'AV4qIF50T0Z2t9T850rA', '_version': 1, 'result': 'created', '_shards':
{'total': 2, 'successful': 1, 'failed': 0}, 'created': True}
{'_index': 'planets', '_type': 'planets_info', '_id':
'AV4qIF56T0Z2t9T850rB', '_version': 1, 'result': 'created', '_shards':
{'total': 2, 'successful': 1, 'failed': 0}, 'created': True}
{'_index': 'planets', '_type': 'planets_info', '_id':
'AV4qIF6AT0Z2t9T850rC', '_version': 1, 'result': 'created', '_shards':
{'total': 2, 'successful': 1, 'failed': 0}, 'created': True}
```

The output shows the result of each insertion, giving us information such as the `_id` assigned to the document by elasticsearch.

If you have logstash and kibana installed too, you can see the data inside of Kibana:

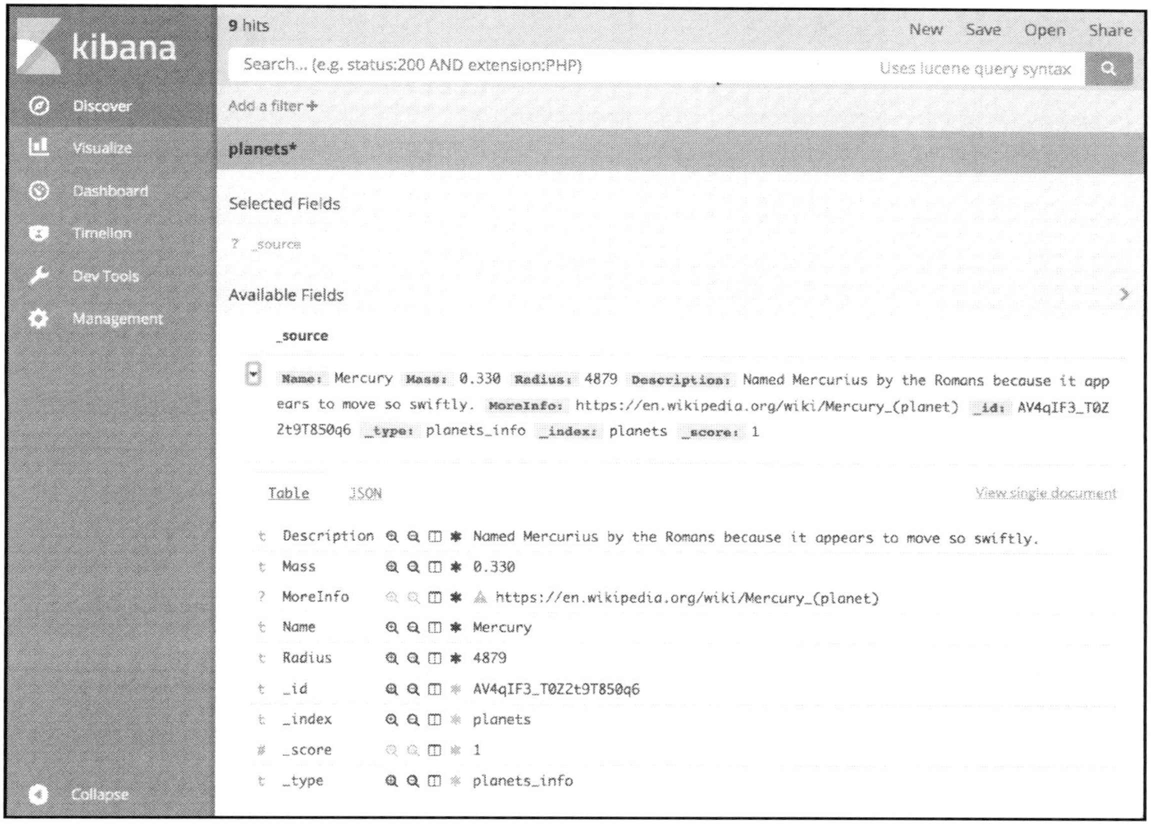

Kibana Showing and Index

And we can query the data with the following Python code. This code retrieves all of the documents in the 'planets' index and prints the name, mass, and radius of each planet (`03/read_from_elasticsearch.py`):

```
from elasticsearch import Elasticsearch

# create an elastic search object
es = Elasticsearch()

res = es.search(index="planets", body={"query": {"match_all": {}}})
```

```
print("Got %d Hits:" % res['hits']['total'])
for hit in res['hits']['hits']:
 print("%(Name)s %(Mass)s: %(Radius)s" % hit["_source"])Got 9 Hits:
```

This results in the following output:

```
Mercury 0.330: 4879
Mars 0.642: 6792
Venus 4.87: 12104
Saturn 568: 120536
Pluto 0.0146: 2370
Earth 5.97: 12756
Uranus 86.8: 51118
Jupiter 1898: 142984
Neptune 102: 49528
```

How it works

Elasticsearch is both a NoSQL database and a search engine. You give documents to Elasticsearch and it parses the data in the documents and creates search indexes for that data automatically.

During the insertion process, we used the `elasticsearch` libraries' `.index()` method and specified an index, named "planets", a document type, `planets_info`, and the finally the body of the document, which is our planet Python object. The `elasticsearch` library that object to JSON and sends it off to Elasticsearch for storage and indexing.

The index parameter is used to inform Elasticsearch how to create an index, which it will use for indexing and which we can use to specify a set of documents to search for when we query. When we performed the query, we specified the same index "planets" and executed a query to match all of the documents.

There's more...

You can find out much more about elasticsearch at: `https://www.elastic.co/products/elasticsearch`. Information on the python API can be found at: `http://pyelasticsearch.readthedocs.io/en/latest/api/`

We will also come back to Elasticsearch in later chapters of the book.

How to build robust ETL pipelines with AWS SQS

Scraping a large quantity of sites and data can be a complicated and slow process. But it is one that can take great advantage of parallel processing, either locally with multiple processor threads, or distributing scraping requests to report scrapers using a message queue system. There may also be the need for multiple steps in a process similar to an Extract, Transform, and Load pipeline (ETL). These pipelines can also be easily built using a message queuing architecture in conjunction with the scraping.

Using a message queuing architecture gives our pipeline two advantages:

- Robustness
- Scalability

The processing becomes robust, as if processing of an individual message fails, then the message can be re-queued for processing again. So if the scraper fails, we can restart it and not lose the request for scraping the page, or the message queue system will deliver the request to another scraper.

It provides scalability, as multiple scrapers on the same, or different, systems can listen on the queue. Multiple messages can then be processed at the same time on different cores or, more importantly, different systems. In a cloud-based scraper, you can scale up the number of scraper instances on demand to handle greater load.

Common message queueing systems that can be used include: Kafka, RabbitMQ, and Amazon SQS. Our example will utilize Amazon SQS, although both Kafka and RabbitMQ are quite excellent to use (we will see RabbitMQ in use later in the book). We use SQS to stay with a model of using AWS cloud-based services as we did earlier in the chapter with S3.

Getting ready

As an example, we will build a vary simple ETL process that will read the main planets page and store the planets data in MySQL. It will also pass a single message for each *more info* link in the page to a queue, where 0 or more processes can receive those requests and perform further processing on those links.

To access SQS from Python, we will revisit using the `boto3` library.

How to do it - posting messages to an AWS queue

The `03/create_messages.py` file contains code to read the planets data and to post the URL in the MoreInfo property to an SQS queue:

```
from urllib.request import urlopen
from bs4 import BeautifulSoup

import boto3
import botocore

# declare our keys (normally, don't hard code this)
access_key="AKIAIXFTCYO7FEL55TCQ"
access_secret_key="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"

# create sqs client
sqs = boto3.client('sqs', "us-west-2",
                   aws_access_key_id = access_key,
                   aws_secret_access_key = access_secret_key)

# create / open the SQS queue
queue = sqs.create_queue(QueueName="PlanetMoreInfo")
print (queue)

# read and parse the planets HTML
html = urlopen("http://127.0.0.1:8080/pages/planets.html")
bsobj = BeautifulSoup(html, "lxml")

planets = []
planet_rows = bsobj.html.body.div.table.findAll("tr", {"class": "planet"})

for i in planet_rows:
  tds = i.findAll("td")
  # get the URL
  more_info_url = tds[5].findAll("a")[0]["href"].strip()
  # send the URL to the queue
  sqs.send_message(QueueUrl=queue["QueueUrl"],
           MessageBody=more_info_url)
  print("Sent %s to %s" % (more_info_url, queue["QueueUrl"]))
```

Run the code in a terminal and you will see output similar to the following:

```
{'QueueUrl':
'https://us-west-2.queue.amazonaws.com/414704166289/PlanetMoreInfo',
'ResponseMetadata': {'RequestId': '2aad7964-292a-5bf6-b838-2b7a5007af22',
'HTTPStatusCode': 200, 'HTTPHeaders': {'server': 'Server', 'date': 'Mon, 28
Aug 2017 20:02:53 GMT', 'content-type': 'text/xml', 'content-length':
'336', 'connection': 'keep-alive', 'x-amzn-requestid': '2aad7964-292a-5bf6-
b838-2b7a5007af22'}, 'RetryAttempts': 0}}
Sent https://en.wikipedia.org/wiki/Mercury_(planet) to
https://us-west-2.queue.amazonaws.com/414704166289/PlanetMoreInfo
Sent https://en.wikipedia.org/wiki/Venus to
https://us-west-2.queue.amazonaws.com/414704166289/PlanetMoreInfo
Sent https://en.wikipedia.org/wiki/Earth to
https://us-west-2.queue.amazonaws.com/414704166289/PlanetMoreInfo
Sent https://en.wikipedia.org/wiki/Mars to
https://us-west-2.queue.amazonaws.com/414704166289/PlanetMoreInfo
Sent https://en.wikipedia.org/wiki/Jupiter to
https://us-west-2.queue.amazonaws.com/414704166289/PlanetMoreInfo
Sent https://en.wikipedia.org/wiki/Saturn to
https://us-west-2.queue.amazonaws.com/414704166289/PlanetMoreInfo
Sent https://en.wikipedia.org/wiki/Uranus to
https://us-west-2.queue.amazonaws.com/414704166289/PlanetMoreInfo
Sent https://en.wikipedia.org/wiki/Neptune to
https://us-west-2.queue.amazonaws.com/414704166289/PlanetMoreInfo
Sent https://en.wikipedia.org/wiki/Pluto to
https://us-west-2.queue.amazonaws.com/414704166289/PlanetMoreInfo
```

Now go into the AWS SQS console. You should see the queue has been created and that it holds 9 messages:

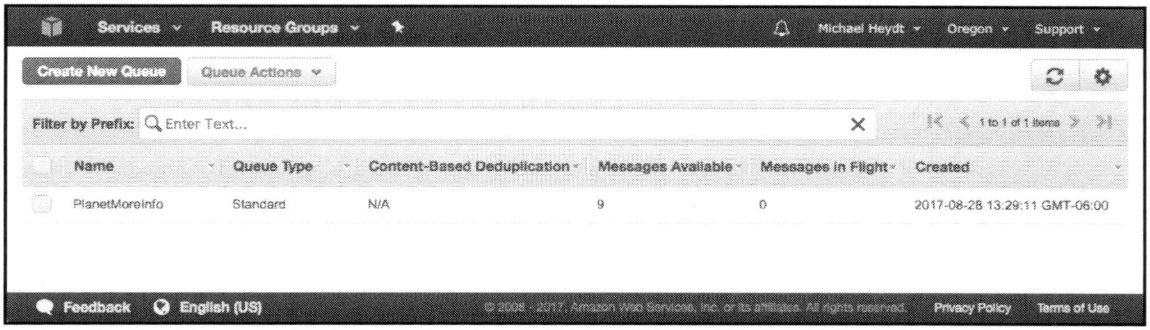

The Queue in SQS

How it works

The code connects to the given account and the us-west-2 region of AWS. A queue is then created if one does not exist. Then, for each planet in the source content, the program sends a message which consists of the *more info* URL for the planet.

At this point, there is no one listening to the queue, so the messages will sit there until eventually read or they expire. The default life for each message is 4 days.

How to do it - reading and processing messages

To process the messages, run the `03/process_messages.py` program:

```
import boto3
import botocore
import requests
from bs4 import BeautifulSoup

print("Starting")

# declare our keys (normally, don't hard code this)
access_key = "AKIAIXFTCYO7FEL55TCQ"
access_secret_key = "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"

# create sqs client
sqs = boto3.client('sqs', "us-west-2",
          aws_access_key_id = access_key,
          aws_secret_access_key = access_secret_key)

print("Created client")

# create / open the SQS queue
queue = sqs.create_queue(QueueName="PlanetMoreInfo")
queue_url = queue["QueueUrl"]
print ("Opened queue: %s" % queue_url)

while True:
  print ("Attempting to receive messages")
  response = sqs.receive_message(QueueUrl=queue_url,
                 MaxNumberOfMessages=1,
                 WaitTimeSeconds=1)
  if not 'Messages' in response:
    print ("No messages")
    continue
```

```
  message = response['Messages'][0]
  receipt_handle = message['ReceiptHandle']
  url = message['Body']

  # parse the page
  html = requests.get(url)
  bsobj = BeautifulSoup(html.text, "lxml")

  # now find the planet name and albedo info
  planet=bsobj.findAll("h1", {"id": "firstHeading"} )[0].text
  albedo_node = bsobj.findAll("a", {"href": "/wiki/Geometric_albedo"})[0]
  root_albedo = albedo_node.parent
  albedo = root_albedo.text.strip()

  # delete the message from the queue
  sqs.delete_message(
    QueueUrl=queue_url,
    ReceiptHandle=receipt_handle
  )

  # print the planets name and albedo info
  print("%s: %s" % (planet, albedo))
```

Run the script using `python process_messages.py`. You will see output similar to the following:

```
Starting
Created client
Opened queue:
https://us-west-2.queue.amazonaws.com/414704166289/PlanetMoreInfo
Attempting to receive messages
Jupiter: 0.343 (Bond)
0.52 (geom.)[3]
Attempting to receive messages
Mercury (planet): 0.142 (geom.)[10]
Attempting to receive messages
Uranus: 0.300 (Bond)
0.51 (geom.)[5]
Attempting to receive messages
Neptune: 0.290 (bond)
0.41 (geom.)[4]
Attempting to receive messages
Pluto: 0.49 to 0.66 (geometric, varies by 35%)[1][7]
Attempting to receive messages
Venus: 0.689 (geometric)[2]
Attempting to receive messages
Earth: 0.367 geometric[3]
```

```
Attempting to receive messages
Mars: 0.170 (geometric)[8]
0.25 (Bond)[7]
Attempting to receive messages
Saturn: 0.499 (geometric)[4]
Attempting to receive messages
No messages
```

How it works

The program connects to SQS and opens the queue. Opening the queue for reading is also done using `sqs.create_queue`, which will simply return the queue if it already exists.

Then, it enters a loop calling `sqs.receive_message`, specifying the URL of the queue, the number of messages to receive in each read, and the maximum amount of time to wait in seconds if there are no messages available.

If a message is read, the URL in the message is retrieved and scraping techniques are used to read the page at the URL and extract the planet's name and information about its albedo.

Note that we retrieve the receipt handle of the message. This is needed to delete the message from the queue. If we do not delete the message, it will be made available in the queue after a period of time. So if our scraper crashed and didn't perform this acknowledgement, the messages will be made available again by SQS for another scraper to process (or the same one when it is back up).

There's more...

You can find more information about S3 at: `https://aws.amazon.com/s3/`. Specifics on the details of the API are available at: `https://aws.amazon.com/documentation/s3/`.

4
Working with Images, Audio, and other Assets

In this chapter, we will cover:

- Downloading media content on the web
- Parsing a URL with urllib to get the filename
- Determining type of content for a URL
- Determining a file extension from a content type
- Downloading and saving images to the local file system
- Downloading and saving images to S3
- Generating thumbnails for images
- Taking website screenshots with Selenium
- Taking a website screenshot with an external service
- Performing OCR on images with pytessaract
- Creating a Video Thumbnail
- Ripping an MP4 video to an MP3

Introduction

A common practice in scraping is the download, storage, and further processing of media content (non-web pages or data files). This media can include images, audio, and video. To store the content locally (or in a service like S3) and do it correctly, we need to know what the type of media is, and it's not enough to trust the file extension in the URL. We will learn how to download and correctly represent the media type based on information from the web server.

Another common task is the generation of thumbnails of images, videos, or even a page of a website. We will examine several techniques of how to generate thumbnails and make website page screenshots. Many times these are used on a new website as thumbnail links to the scraped media that is now stored locally.

Finally, it is often the need to be able to transcode media, such as converting non-MP4 videos to MP4, or changing the bit-rate or resolution of a video. Another scenario is to extract only the audio from a video file. We won't look at video transcoding, but we will rip MP3 audio out of an MP4 file using `ffmpeg`. It's a simple step from there to also transcode video with `ffmpeg`.

Downloading media content from the web

Downloading media content from the web is a simple process: use Requests or another library and download it just like you would HTML content.

Getting ready

There is a class named `URLUtility` in the `urls.py mdoule` in the `util` folder of the solution. This class handles several of the scenarios in this chapter with downloading and parsing URLs. We will be using this class in this recipe and a few others. Make sure the `modules` folder is in your Python path. Also, the example for this recipe is in the `04/01_download_image.py` file.

How to do it

Here is how we proceed with the recipe:

1. The `URLUtility` class can download content from a URL. The code in the recipe's file is the following:

```
import const
from util.urls import URLUtility

util = URLUtility(const.ApodEclipseImage())
print(len(util.data))
```

2. When running this you will see the following output:

```
Reading URL: https://apod.nasa.gov/apod/image/1709/BT5643s.jpg
Read 171014 bytes
171014
```

The example reads `171014` bytes of data.

How it works

The URL is defined as a constant `const.ApodEclipseImage()` in the `const` module:

```
def ApodEclipseImage():
    return "https://apod.nasa.gov/apod/image/1709/BT5643s.jpg"
```

The constructor of the `URLUtility` class has the following implementation:

```
def __init__(self, url, readNow=True):
    """ Construct the object, parse the URL, and download now if
specified"""
    self._url = url
    self._response = None
    self._parsed = urlparse(url)
    if readNow:
        self.read()
```

The constructor stores the URL, parses it, and downloads the file with the `read()` method. The following is the code of the `read()` method:

```
def read(self):
    self._response = urllib.request.urlopen(self._url)
    self._data = self._response.read()
```

This function uses `urlopen` to get a response object, and then reads the stream and stores it as a property of the object. That data can then be retrieved using the data property:

```
@property
def data(self):
    self.ensure_response()
    return self._data
```

The code then simply reports on the length of that data, with the value of `171014`.

There's more...

This class will be used for other tasks such as determining content types, filename, and extensions for those files. We will examine parsing of URLs for filenames next.

Parsing a URL with urllib to get the filename

When downloading content from a URL, we often want to save it in a file. Often it is good enough to save the file in a file with a name found in the URL. But the URL consists of a number of fragments, so how can we find the actual filename from the URL, especially where there are often many parameters after the file name?

Getting ready

We will again be using the `URLUtility` class for this task. The code file for the recipe is `04/02_parse_url.py`.

How to do it

Execute the recipe's file with your python interpreter. It will run the following code:

```
util = URLUtility(const.ApodEclipseImage())
print(util.filename_without_ext)
```

This results in the following output:

```
Reading URL: https://apod.nasa.gov/apod/image/1709/BT5643s.jpg
Read 171014 bytes
The filename is: BT5643s
```

How it works

In the constructor for `URLUtility`, there is a call to `urlib.parse.urlparse`. The following demonstrates using the function interactively:

```
>>> parsed = urlparse(const.ApodEclipseImage())
>>> parsed
ParseResult(scheme='https', netloc='apod.nasa.gov',
path='/apod/image/1709/BT5643s.jpg', params='', query='', fragment='')
```

The `ParseResult` object contains the various components of the URL. The path element contains the path and the filename. The call to the `.filename_without_ext` property returns just the filename without the extension:

```
@property
def filename_without_ext(self):
    filename = os.path.splitext(os.path.basename(self._parsed.path))[0]
    return filename
```

The call to `os.path.basename` returns only the filename portion of the path (including the extension). `os.path.splittext()` then separates the filename and the extension, and the function returns the first element of that tuple/list (the filename).

There's more...

It may seem odd that this does not also return the extension as part of the filename. This is because we cannot assume that the content that we received actually matches the implied type from the extension. It is more accurate to determine this using headers returned by the web server. That's our next recipe.

Determining the type of content for a URL

When performing a GET requests for content from a web server, the web server will return a number of headers, one of which identities the type of the content from the perspective of the web server. In this recipe we learn to use that to determine what the web server considers the type of the content.

Getting ready

We again use the URLUtility class. The code for the recipe is in 04/03_determine_content_type_from_response.py.

How to do it

We proceed as follows:

1. Execute the script for the recipe. It contains the following code:

```
util = URLUtility(const.ApodEclipseImage())
print("The content type is: " + util.contenttype)
```

2. With the following result:

```
Reading URL: https://apod.nasa.gov/apod/image/1709/BT5643s.jpg
Read 171014 bytes
The content type is: image/jpeg
```

How it works

The .contentype property is implemented as follows:

```
@property
def contenttype(self):
    self.ensure_response()
    return self._response.headers['content-type']
```

The `.headers` property of the `_response` object is a dictionary-like class of headers. The `content-type` key will retrieve the `content-type` specified by the server. This call to the `ensure_response()` method simply ensures that the `.read()` function has been executed.

There's more...

The headers in a response contain a wealth of information. If we look more closely at the `headers` property of the response, we can see the following headers are returned:

```
>>> response = urllib.request.urlopen(const.ApodEclipseImage())
>>> for header in response.headers: print(header)
Date
Server
Last-Modified
ETag
Accept-Ranges
Content-Length
Connection
Content-Type
Strict-Transport-Security
```

And we can see the values for each of these headers.

```
>>> for header in response.headers: print(header + " ==> " +
response.headers[header])
Date ==> Tue, 26 Sep 2017 19:31:41 GMT
Server ==> WebServer/1.0
Last-Modified ==> Thu, 31 Aug 2017 20:26:32 GMT
ETag ==> "547bb44-29c06-5581275ce2b86"
Accept-Ranges ==> bytes
Content-Length ==> 171014
Connection ==> close
Content-Type ==> image/jpeg
Strict-Transport-Security ==> max-age=31536000; includeSubDomains
```

Many of these we will not examine in this book, but for the unfamiliar it is good to know that they exist.

Determining the file extension from a content type

It is good practice to use the `content-type` header to determine the type of content, and to determine the extension to use for storing the content as a file.

Getting ready

We again use the `URLUtility` object that we created. The recipe's script is `04/04_determine_file_extension_from_contenttype.py):`.

How to do it

Proceed by running the recipe's script.

An extension for the media type can be found using the `.extension` property:

```
util = URLUtility(const.ApodEclipseImage())
print("Filename from content-type: " + util.extension_from_contenttype)
print("Filename from url: " + util.extension_from_url)
```

This results in the following output:

```
Reading URL: https://apod.nasa.gov/apod/image/1709/BT5643s.jpg
Read 171014 bytes
Filename from content-type: .jpg
Filename from url: .jpg
```

This reports both the extension determined from the file type, and also from the URL. These can be different, but in this case they are the same.

How it works

The following is the implementation of the `.extension_from_contenttype` property:

```
@property
def extension_from_contenttype(self):
    self.ensure_response()

    map = const.ContentTypeToExtensions()
```

```
    if self.contenttype in map:
        return map[self.contenttype]
    return None
```

The first line ensures that we have read the response from the URL. The function then uses a python dictionary, defined in the `const` module, which contains a dictionary of content-types to extension:

```
def ContentTypeToExtensions():
    return {
        "image/jpeg": ".jpg",
        "image/jpg": ".jpg",
        "image/png": ".png"
    }
```

If the content type is in the dictionary, then the corresponding value will be returned. Otherwise, `None` is returned.

Note the corresponding property, `.extension_from_url`:

```
@property
def extension_from_url(self):
    ext = os.path.splitext(os.path.basename(self._parsed.path))[1]
    return ext
```

This uses the same technique as the `.filename` property to parse the URL, but instead returns the `[1]` element, which represents the extension instead of the base filename.

There's more...

As stated, it's best to use the `content-type` header to determine an extension for storing the file locally. There are other techniques than what is provided here, but this is the easiest.

Downloading and saving images to the local file system

Sometimes when scraping we just download and parse data, such as HTML, to extract some data, and then throw out what we read. Other times, we want to keep the downloaded content by storing it as a file.

How to do it

The code example for this recipe is in the `04/05_save_image_as_file.py` file. The portion of the file of importance is:

```
# download the image
item = URLUtility(const.ApodEclipseImage())

# create a file writer to write the data
FileBlobWriter(expanduser("~")).write(item.filename, item.data)
```

Run the script with your Python interpreter and you will get the following output:

```
Reading URL: https://apod.nasa.gov/apod/image/1709/BT5643s.jpg
Read 171014 bytes
Attempting to write 171014 bytes to BT5643s.jpg:
The write was successful
```

How it works

The sample simply writes the data to a file using standard Python file access functions. It does it in an object oriented manner by using a standard interface for writing data and with a file based implementation in the `FileBlobWriter` class:

```
""" Implements the IBlobWriter interface to write the blob to a file """

from interface import implements
from core.i_blob_writer import IBlobWriter

class FileBlobWriter(implements(IBlobWriter)):
    def __init__(self, location):
        self._location = location

    def write(self, filename, contents):
        full_filename = self._location + "/" + filename
        print ("Attempting to write {0} bytes to
{1}:".format(len(contents), filename))

        with open(full_filename, 'wb') as outfile:
            outfile.write(contents)

        print("The write was successful")
```

The class is passed a string representing the directory where the file should be placed. The data is actually written during a later call to the `.write()` method. This method merges the filename and `directory (_location)`, and then opens/creates the file and writes the bytes. The `with` statement ensures that the file is closed.

There's more...

This write could have simply been handled using a function that wraps the code. This object will be reused throughout this chapter. We could use the duck-typing of python, or just a function, but the clarity of interfaces is easier. Speaking of that, the following is the definition of this interface:

```
""" Defines the interface for writing a blob of data to storage """

from interface import Interface

class IBlobWriter(Interface):
   def write(self, filename, contents):
      pass
```

We will also see another implementation of this interface that lets us store files in S3. Through this type of implementation, through interface inheritance, we can easily substitute implementations.

Downloading and saving images to S3

We have seen how to write content into S3 in `Chapter 3`, *Processing Data*. Here we will extend that process into an interface implementation of IBlobWriter to write to S3.

Getting ready

The code example for this recipe is in the `04/06_save_image_in_s3.py` file. Also ensure that you have set your AWS keys as environment variables so that Boto can authenticate the script.

How to do it

We proceed as follows:

1. Run the recipe's script. It will execute the following:

```
# download the image
item = URLUtility(const.ApodEclipseImage())

# store it in S3
S3BlobWriter(bucket_name="scraping-apod").write(item.filename,
item.data)
```

2. Checking in S3, we can see that the bucket was created and the image placed within the bucket:

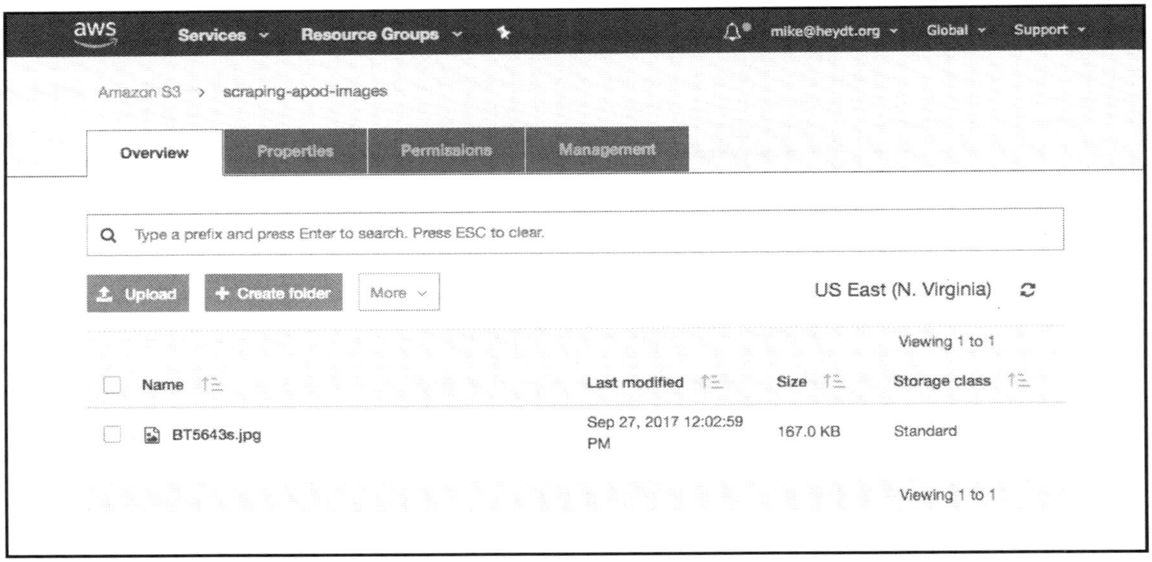

The Image in S3

How it works

The following is the implementation of the `S3BlobWriter`:

```
class S3BlobWriter(implements(IBlobWriter)):
    def __init__(self, bucket_name, boto_client=None):
```

```
        self._bucket_name = bucket_name

        if self._bucket_name is None:
            self.bucket_name = "/"

        # caller can specify a boto client (can reuse and save auth times)
        self._boto_client = boto_client
        # or create a boto client if user did not, use secrets from
environment variables
        if self._boto_client is None:
            self._boto_client = boto3.client('s3')

    def write(self, filename, contents):
        # create bucket, and put the object
        self._boto_client.create_bucket(Bucket=self._bucket_name,
ACL='public-read')
        self._boto_client.put_object(Bucket=self._bucket_name,
                                     Key=filename,
                                     Body=contents,
                                     ACL="public-read")
```

We have seen this code in before in the recipe on writing to S3. This class wraps that up neatly into a reusable interface implementation. When creating an instance, specify the bucket name. Then every call to `.write()` will save in the same bucket.

There's more...

S3 provides a capability on buckets known as enabling a website. Essentially, if you set this option, the content in your bucket will be served via HTTP. We could write many images to this directory and then have them served directly from S3 without implementing a web server!

Generating thumbnails for images

Many times when downloading an image, you do not want to save the full image, but only a thumbnail. Or you may also save both the full-size image and a thumbnail. Thumbnails can be easily created in python using the Pillow library. Pillow is a fork of the Python Image Library, and contains many useful functions for manipulating images. You can find more information on Pillow at `https://python-pillow.org`. In this recipe, we use Pillow to create an image thumbnail.

Getting ready

The script for this recipe is `04/07_create_image_thumbnail.py`. It uses the Pillow library, so make sure you have installed Pillow into your environment with pip or other package management tools:

```
pip install pillow
```

How to do it

Here is how proceed with the recipe:

Run the script for the recipe. It will execute the following code:

```
from os.path import expanduser
import const
from core.file_blob_writer import FileBlobWriter
from core.image_thumbnail_generator import ImageThumbnailGenerator
from util.urls import URLUtility

# download the image and get the bytes
img_data = URLUtility(const.ApodEclipseImage()).data

# we will store this in our home folder
fw = FileBlobWriter(expanduser("~"))

# Create a thumbnail generator and scale the image
tg = ImageThumbnailGenerator(img_data).scale(200, 200)

# write the image to a file
fw.write("eclipse_thumbnail.png", tg.bytes)
```

The result from this will be a file named `eclipse_thumbnail.png` written into your home directory.

The Thumbnail we Created

Pillow keeps the ratio of width and height consistent.

How it works

The `ImageThumbnailGenerator` class wraps calls to Pillow to provide a very simple API for creating a thumbnail for an image:

```
import io
from PIL import Image

class ImageThumbnailGenerator():
    def __init__(self, bytes):
        # Create a pillow image with the data provided
        self._image = Image.open(io.BytesIO(bytes))

    def scale(self, width, height):
        # call the thumbnail method to create the thumbnail
        self._image.thumbnail((width, height))
        return self

    @property
    def bytes(self):
        # returns the bytes of the pillow image

        # save the image to an in memory objects
        bytesio = io.BytesIO()
        self._image.save(bytesio, format="png")
```

```
        # set the position on the stream to 0 and return the underlying
data
        bytesio.seek(0)
        return bytesio.getvalue()
```

The constructor is passed the data for the image and creates a Pillow image object from that data. The thumbnail is created by calling `.thumbnail()` with a tuple representing the desired size of the thumbnail. This resizes the existing image, and Pillow preserves the aspect ratio. It will determine the longer side of the image and scale that to the value in the tuple representing that axis. This image is taller than it is wide, so the thumbnail is made 200 pixels high, and the width is scaled accordingly (in this case, to 160 pixels).

Taking a screenshot of a website

A common scraping task is to create a screenshot of a website. In Python we can create a thumbnail using selenium and webdriver.

Getting ready

The script for this recipe is `04/08_create_website_screenshot.py`. Also, make sure you have selenium in your path and have installed the Python library.

How to do it

Run the script for the recipe. The code in the script is the following:

```
from core.website_screenshot_generator import  WebsiteScreenshotGenerator
from core.file_blob_writer import FileBlobWriter
from os.path import expanduser

# get the screenshot
image_bytes = WebsiteScreenshotGenerator().capture("http://espn.go.com",
500, 500).image_bytes

# save it to a file
FileBlobWriter(expanduser("~")).write("website_screenshot.png",
image_bytes)
```

A `WebsiteScreenshotGenerator` object is created, and then its capture method is called, passing the URL of the website to capture, and a desired width in pixels for the image.

This creates a Pillow image that can be accessed using the `.image` property, and the bytes for the image can be directly accessed using `.image_bytes`. This script gets those bytes and writes them to the `website_screenshot.png` file in you home directory.

You will see the following output from this script:

```
Connected to pydev debugger (build 162.1967.10)
Capturing website screenshot of: http://espn.go.com
Got a screenshot with the following dimensions: (500, 7416)
Cropped the image to: 500 500
Attempting to write 217054 bytes to website_screenshot.png:
The write was successful
```

And our resulting image is the following (the image will vary in its content):

The Screenshot of the Web Page

How it works

The following is the code of the `WebsiteScreenshotGenerator` class:

```
class WebsiteScreenshotGenerator():
    def __init__(self):
        self._screenshot = None

    def capture(self, url, width, height, crop=True):
        print ("Capturing website screenshot of: " + url)
        driver = webdriver.PhantomJS()

        if width and height:
            driver.set_window_size(width, height)

        # go and get the content at the url
        driver.get(url)

        # get the screenshot and make it into a Pillow Image
        self._screenshot =
Image.open(io.BytesIO(driver.get_screenshot_as_png()))
        print("Got a screenshot with the following dimensions:
{0}".format(self._screenshot.size))

        if crop:
            # crop the image
            self._screenshot = self._screenshot.crop((0,0, width, height))
            print("Cropped the image to: {0} {1}".format(width, height))

        return self

    @property
    def image(self):
        return self._screenshot

    @property
    def image_bytes(self):
        bytesio = io.BytesIO()
        self._screenshot.save(bytesio, "PNG")
        bytesio.seek(0)
        return bytesio.getvalue()
```

The call to `driver.get_screenshot_as_png()` does the heavy lifting. It renders the page to a PNG format image and returns the bytes of the image. This data is then converted into a Pillow Image object.

Note in the output that the height of the image returned from webdriver is 7416 pixels, and not 500 as we specified. The PhantomJS renderer will attempt to handle infinitely scrolling web sites, and generally won't constrain the screenshot to the height given to the window.

To actually make the screenshot the specified height, set the crop parameter to `True` (the default). Then this code will use the crop method of the Pillow Image to set the desired height. If you run this code with `crop=False`, then the result would be an image 7416 pixels in height.

Taking a screenshot of a website with an external service

The previous recipe used selenium, webdriver, and PhantomJS to create the screenshot. This obviously requires having those packages installed. If you don't want to install those and still want to make website screenshots, then you can use one of a number of web services that can take screenshots. In this recipe, we will use the service at `www.screenshotapi.io` to create a screenshot.

Getting ready

First, head over to `www.screenshotapi.io` and sign up for a free account:

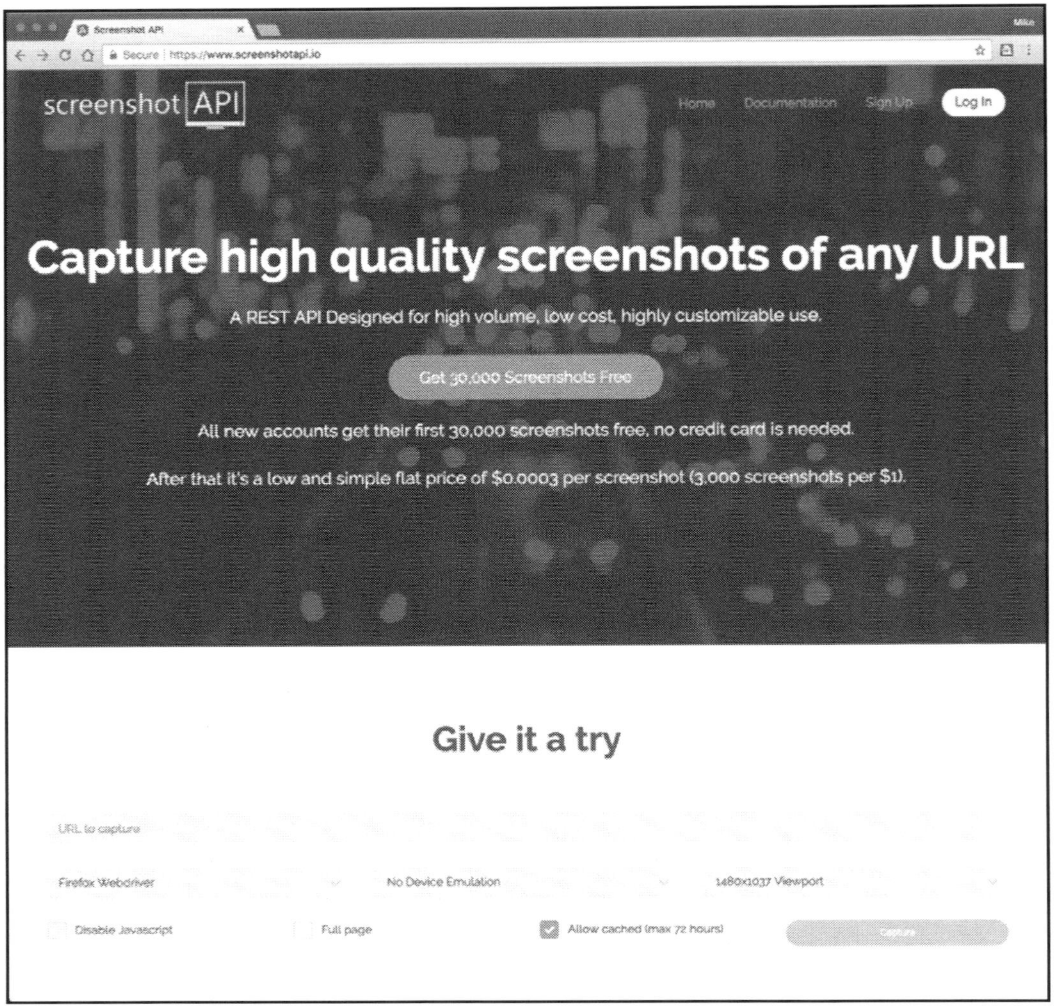

Screenshot of the free account sign up

Once your account is created, proceed to get an API key. This will be needed to authenticate against their service:

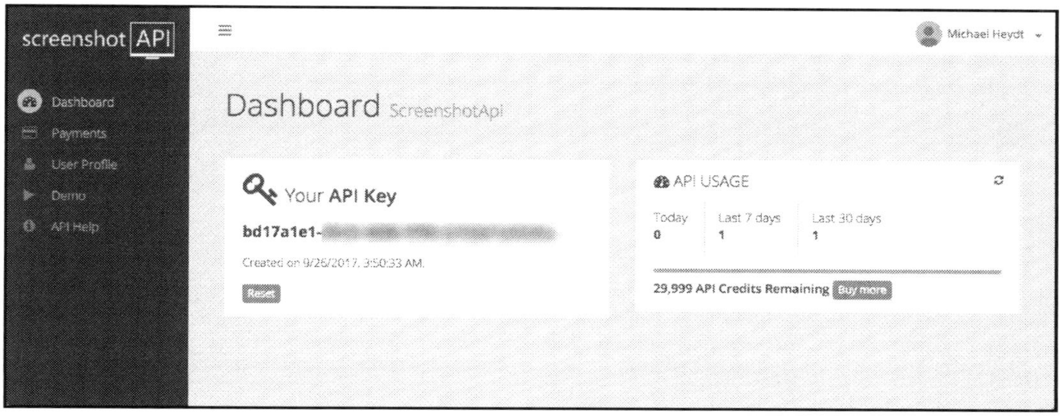

The API Key

How to do it

The script for this example is `04/09_screenshotapi.py`. Give this a run and it will make a screenshot. The code is the following, and is very similar to the previous recipe in structure:

```
from core.website_screenshot_with_screenshotapi import
WebsiteScreenshotGenerator
from core.file_blob_writer import FileBlobWriter
from os.path import expanduser

# get the screenshot
image_bytes = WebsiteScreenshotGenerator("bd17a1e1-db43-4686-9f9b-
b72b67a5535e")\
    .capture("http://espn.go.com", 500, 500).image_bytes

# save it to a file
FileBlobWriter(expanduser("~")).write("website_screenshot.png",
image_bytes)
```

The functional difference to the previous recipe is that we used a different `WebsiteScreenshotGenerator` implementation. This one comes from the `core.website_screenshot_with_screenshotapi` module.

When run, the following will output to the console:

```
Sending request: http://espn.go.com
{"status":"ready","key":"2e9a40b86c95f50ad3f70613798828a8","apiCreditsCost"
:1}
The image key is: 2e9a40b86c95f50ad3f70613798828a8
Trying to retrieve: https://api.screenshotapi.io/retrieve
Downloading image:
https://screenshotapi.s3.amazonaws.com/captures/2e9a40b86c95f50ad3f70613798
828a8.png
Saving screenshot to:
downloaded_screenshot.png2e9a40b86c95f50ad3f70613798828a8
Cropped the image to: 500 500
Attempting to write 209197 bytes to website_screenshot.png:
The write was successful
```

And gives us the following image:

The Website Screenshot from screenshotapi.io

How it works

The following is the code of this `WebsiteScreenshotGenerator`:

```
class WebsiteScreenshotGenerator:
    def __init__(self, apikey):
        self._screenshot = None
        self._apikey = apikey

    def capture(self, url, width, height, crop=True):
        key = self.beginCapture(url, "{0}x{1}".format(width, height),
"true", "firefox", "true")

        print("The image key is: " + key)

        timeout = 30
        tCounter = 0
        tCountIncr = 3

        while True:
            result = self.tryRetrieve(key)
            if result["success"]:
                print("Saving screenshot to: downloaded_screenshot.png" +
key)

                bytes=result["bytes"]
                self._screenshot = Image.open(io.BytesIO(bytes))

                if crop:
                    # crop the image
                    self._screenshot = self._screenshot.crop((0, 0, width,
height))
                    print("Cropped the image to: {0} {1}".format(width,
height))
                break

            tCounter += tCountIncr
            print("Screenshot not yet ready.. waiting for: " +
str(tCountIncr) + " seconds.")
            time.sleep(tCountIncr)
            if tCounter > timeout:
                print("Timed out while downloading: " + key)
                break
        return self

    def beginCapture(self, url, viewport, fullpage, webdriver, javascript):
        serverUrl = "https://api.screenshotapi.io/capture"
```

```
            print('Sending request: ' + url)
            headers = {'apikey': self._apikey}
            params = {'url': urllib.parse.unquote(url).encode('utf8'),
    'viewport': viewport, 'fullpage': fullpage,
                      'webdriver': webdriver, 'javascript': javascript}
            result = requests.post(serverUrl, data=params, headers=headers)
            print(result.text)
            json_results = json.loads(result.text)
            return json_results['key']


        def tryRetrieve(self, key):
            url = 'https://api.screenshotapi.io/retrieve'
            headers = {'apikey': self._apikey}
            params = {'key': key}
            print('Trying to retrieve: ' + url)
            result = requests.get(url, params=params, headers=headers)

            json_results = json.loads(result.text)
            if json_results["status"] == "ready":
                print('Downloading image: ' + json_results["imageUrl"])
                image_result = requests.get(json_results["imageUrl"])
                return {'success': True, 'bytes': image_result.content}
            else:
                return {'success': False}

        @property
        def image(self):
            return self._screenshot

        @property
        def image_bytes(self):
            bytesio = io.BytesIO()
            self._screenshot.save(bytesio, "PNG")
            bytesio.seek(0)
            return bytesio.getvalue()
```

The `screenshotapi.io` API is a REST API. There are two different endpoints:

- `https://api.screenshotapi.io/capture`
- `https://api.screenshotapi.io/retrieve`

The first endpoint is called and passes the URL and other parameters to their service. Upon successful execution, this API returns a key that can be used on the other endpoint to retrieve the image. The screenshot is performed asyncronously, and we need to continually call the `retrieve` API using the key returned from the capture endpoint. This endpoint will return a status value of `ready` when the screenshot is complete. The code simply loops until this is set, an error occurs, or the code times out.

When the snapshot is available, the API returns a URL to the image in the `retrieve` response. The code then retrieves this image and constructs a Pillow Image object from the received data.

There's more...

The `screenshotapi.io` API has many useful parameters. Several of these allow you to adjust which browser engine to use (Firefox, Chrome, or PhantomJS), device emulation, and whether or not to execute JavaScript in the web page. For more details on these options and the API, go to `http://docs.screenshotapi.io/rest-api/`.

Performing OCR on an image with pytesseract

It is possible to extract text from within images using the pytesseract library. In this recipe, we will use pytesseract to extract text from an image. Tesseract is an open source OCR library sponsored by Google. The source is available here: `https://github.com/tesseract-ocr/tesseract`, and you can also find more information on the library there. 0;pytesseract is a thin python wrapper that provides a pythonic API to the executable.

Getting ready

Make sure you have pytesseract installed:

```
pip install pytesseract
```

You will also need to install tesseract-ocr. On Windows, there is an executable installer, which you can get here: `https://github.com/tesseract-ocr/tesseract/wiki/4.0-with-LSTM#400-alpha-for-windows`. On a Linux system, you can use `apt-get`:

```
sudo apt-get tesseract-ocr
```

The easiest means of installation on a Mac is using brew:

```
brew install tesseract
```

The code for this recipe is in `04/10_perform_ocr.py`.

How to do it

Execute the script for the recipe. The script is very straightforward:

```
import pytesseract as pt
from PIL import Image

img = Image.open("textinimage.png")
text = pt.image_to_string(img)
print(text)
```

The image that will be processed is the following:

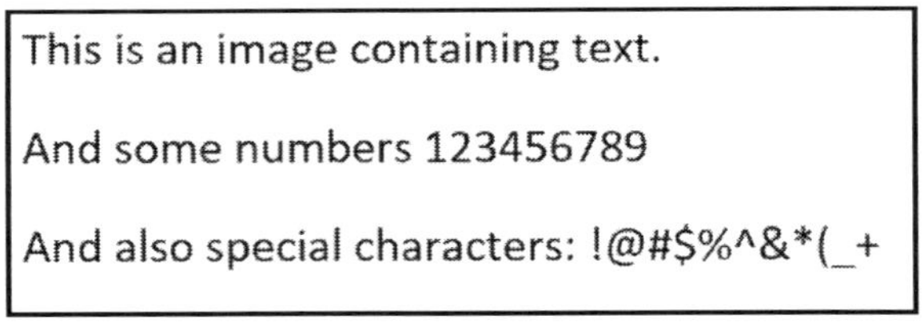
This is an image containing text.
And some numbers 123456789
And also special characters: !@#$%^&*(_+

The Image we will OCR

And the script gives the following output:

```
This is an image containing text.
And some numbers 123456789

And also special characters: !@#$%"&*(_+
```

How it works

The image is first loaded as a Pillow Image object. We can directly pass this object to the pytesseract `image_to_string()` function. That function runs tesseract on the image and returns the text that it found.

There's more...

One of the primary purposes for using OCR in a scraping application is in the solving of text-based captchas. We won't get into captcha solutions as they can be cumbersome and are also documented in other Packt titles.

Creating a Video Thumbnail

You might want to create a thumbnail for a video that you downloaded from a website. These could be used on a page that shows a number of video thumbnails and lets you click on them to watch the specific video.

Getting ready

This sample will use a tool known as ffmpeg. ffmpeg is available at www.ffmpeg.org. Download and install as per the instructions for your operating system.

How to do it

The example script is in `04/11_create_video_thumbnail.py`. It consists of the following code:

```
import subprocess
video_file = 'BigBuckBunny.mp4'
thumbnail_file = 'thumbnail.jpg'
subprocess.call(['ffmpeg', '-i', video_file, '-ss', '00:01:03.000', '-
vframes', '1', thumbnail_file, "-y"])
```

When run you will see output from ffmpeg:

```
 built with Apple LLVM version 8.1.0 (clang-802.0.42)
 configuration: --prefix=/usr/local/Cellar/ffmpeg/3.3.4 --enable-shared --
enable-pthreads --enable-gpl --enable-version3 --enable-hardcoded-tables --
enable-avresample --cc=clang --host-cflags= --host-ldflags= --enable-
libmp3lame --enable-libx264 --enable-libxvid --enable-opencl --enable-
videotoolbox --disable-lzma --enable-vda
 libavutil 55. 58.100 / 55. 58.100
 libavcodec 57. 89.100 / 57. 89.100
 libavformat 57. 71.100 / 57. 71.100
 libavdevice 57. 6.100 / 57. 6.100
 libavfilter 6. 82.100 / 6. 82.100
 libavresample 3. 5. 0 / 3. 5. 0
 libswscale 4. 6.100 / 4. 6.100
 libswresample 2. 7.100 / 2. 7.100
 libpostproc 54. 5.100 / 54. 5.100
Input #0, mov,mp4,m4a,3gp,3g2,mj2, from 'BigBuckBunny.mp4':
 Metadata:
 major_brand : isom
 minor_version : 512
 compatible_brands: mp41
 creation_time : 1970-01-01T00:00:00.000000Z
 title : Big Buck Bunny
 artist : Blender Foundation
 composer : Blender Foundation
 date : 2008
 encoder : Lavf52.14.0
 Duration: 00:09:56.46, start: 0.000000, bitrate: 867 kb/s
 Stream #0:0(und): Video: h264 (Constrained Baseline) (avc1 / 0x31637661),
yuv420p, 320x180 [SAR 1:1 DAR 16:9], 702 kb/s, 24 fps, 24 tbr, 24 tbn, 48
tbc (default)
 Metadata:
 creation_time : 1970-01-01T00:00:00.000000Z
 handler_name : VideoHandler
 Stream #0:1(und): Audio: aac (LC) (mp4a / 0x6134706D), 48000 Hz, stereo,
fltp, 159 kb/s (default)
 Metadata:
 creation_time : 1970-01-01T00:00:00.000000Z
 handler_name : SoundHandler
Stream mapping:
 Stream #0:0 -> #0:0 (h264 (native) -> mjpeg (native))
Press [q] to stop, [?] for help
[swscaler @ 0x7fb50b103000] deprecated pixel format used, make sure you did
set range correctly
Output #0, image2, to 'thumbnail.jpg':
 Metadata:
 major_brand : isom
```

```
minor_version : 512
compatible_brands: mp41
date : 2008
title : Big Buck Bunny
artist : Blender Foundation
composer : Blender Foundation
encoder : Lavf57.71.100
Stream #0:0(und): Video: mjpeg, yuvj420p(pc), 320x180 [SAR 1:1 DAR 16:9],
q=2-31, 200 kb/s, 24 fps, 24 tbn, 24 tbc (default)
Metadata:
creation_time : 1970-01-01T00:00:00.000000Z
handler_name : VideoHandler
encoder : Lavc57.89.100 mjpeg
Side data:
cpb: bitrate max/min/avg: 0/0/200000 buffer size: 0 vbv_delay: -1
frame= 1 fps=0.0 q=4.0 Lsize=N/A time=00:00:00.04 bitrate=N/A speed=0.151x
video:8kB audio:0kB subtitle:0kB other streams:0kB global headers:0kB
muxing overhead: unknown
```

And the output JPG file will be the following JPG image:

The Thumbnail Created from the Video

How it works

The `.ffmpeg` file is actually an executable. The code executes the following ffmpeg command as a sub process:

```
ffmpeg -i BigBuckBunny.mp4 -ss 00:01:03.000 -frames:v 1 thumbnail.jpg -y
```

The input file is `BigBuckBunny.mp4`. The `-ss` option informs where we want to examine the video. `-frames:v` states that we want to extract one frame. Finally we tell `ffmpeg` to write that frame to `thumbnail.jpg` (and `-y` confirms overwriting an existing file).

There's more..

ffmpeg is an incredibly versatile and power tool. A scraper I once created would crawl and find media (actually, commercials played on websites), and store them in a digital archive. The scraper would then send a message through a message queue that would be picked up by a farm of servers whose only job was to run ffmpeg to convert the video into many different formats, bit rates, and also create thumbnails. From that point, more messages would be sent to auditor to use a front end application to check the content for compliance to advertising contract terms. Get to know ffmeg, it is a great tool.

Ripping an MP4 video to an MP3

Now let's examine how to rip the audio from an MP4 video into an MP3 file. The reasons you may want to do this include wanting to take the audio of the video with you (perhaps it's a music video), or you are building a scraper / media collection system that also requires the audio separate from the video.

This task can be accomplished using the `moviepy` library. `moviepy` is a neat library that lets you do all kinds of fun processing on your videos. One of those capabilities is to extract the audio as an MP3.

Getting ready

Make sure that you have moviepy installed in your environment:

```
pip install moviepy
```

We also need to have ffmpeg installed, which we used in the previous recipe, so you should be good to go with this requirement.

How to do it

The code to demonstrate ripping to MP3 is in `04/12_rip_mp3_from_mp4.py`. `moviepy` makes this process incredibly easy.

1. The following rips the MP4 downloaded in the previous recipe:

```
import moviepy.editor as mp
clip = mp.VideoFileClip("BigBuckBunny.mp4")
clip.audio.write_audiofile("movie_audio.mp3")
```

2. When running this, you will see output, such as the following, as the file is ripped. This only took a few seconds:

```
[MoviePy] Writing audio in movie_audio.mp3
100%|██████████| 17820/17820 [00:16<00:00, 1081.67it/s]
[MoviePy] Done.
```

3. When complete, you will have an MP3 file:

```
# ls -l *.mp3
-rw-r--r--@ 1 michaelheydt  staff  12931074 Sep 27 21:44 movie_audio.mp3
```

There's more...

For more info on moviepy, check out the project site at `http://zulko.github.io/moviepy/`.

5
Scraping - Code of Conduct

In this chapter, we will cover:

- Scraping legality and scraping politely
- Respecting robots.txt
- Crawling using the sitemap
- Crawling with delays
- Using identifiable user agents
- Setting the number of concurrent requests per domain
- Using auto throttling
- Caching responses

Introduction

While you can technically scrape any website, it is important to know whether scraping is legal or not. We will discuss scraping legal concerns, explore general rules of thumb, and see best practices to scrape politely and minimize potential damage to the target websites.

Scraping legality and scraping politely

There's no real code in this recipe. It's simply an exposition of some of the concepts related to the legal issues involved in scraping. I'm not a lawyer, so don't take anything I write here as legal advice. I'll just point out a few things you need to be concerned with when using a scraper.

Getting ready

The legality of scraping breaks down into two issues:

- Ownership of content
- Denial of service

Fundamentally, anything posted on the web is open for reading. Every time you load a page, any page, your browser downloads that content from the web server and visually presents it to you. So in a sense, you and your browser are already scraping anything you look at on the web. And by the nature of the web, because someone is posting content publicly on the web, they are inherently asking you to take that information, but often only for specific purposes.

The big issue comes with creating automated tools that directly look for and make copies of *things* on the internet, with a *thing* being either data, images, videos, or music - essentially things that are created by others and represent something that has value to the creator, or owners. These items may create issues when explicitly making a copy of the item for your own personal use, and are much more likely to create issues when making a copy and using that copy for your or others' gain.

Videos, books, music, and images are some of the obvious items of concern over the legality of making copies either for personal or commercial use. In general, if you scrape content such as this from open sites, such as those that do not require authorized access or require payment for access to the content, then you are fine. There are also *fair use* rules that allow the reuse of content in certain situations, such as small amounts of document sharing in a classroom scenario, where knowledge that is published for people to learn is shared and there is no real economic impact.

Scraping of *data* from websites is often a much fuzzier problem. By data I mean information that is provided as a service. A good example, from my experience, is energy prices that are published to a provider's website. These are often provided as a convenience to customers, but not for you to scrape freely and use the data for your own commercial analytics service. That data can often be used without concern if you are just collecting it for a non-public database or you are only using for your own use, then it is likely fine. But if you use that database to drive your own website and share that content under your own name, then you might want to watch out.

The point is, check out the disclaimers / terms of service on the site for what you can do with that information. It should be documented, but if it is not, then that does not mean that you are in the clear to go crazy. Always be careful and use common sense, as you are taking other peoples content for you own purposes.

The other concern, which I lump into a concept known as denial of service, relates to the actual process of collecting information and how often you do it. The process of manually reading content on a site differs significantly to writing automated bots that relentlessly badger web servers for content. Taken to an extreme, this access frequency could be so significant that it denies other legitimate users access to the content, hence denying them service. It can also increase costs for the hosters of the content by increasing their cost for bandwidth, or even electrical costs for running the servers.

A well managed website will identify these types of repeated and frequent access and shut them down using tools such as web application firewalls with rules to block your access based on IP address, headers, and cookies. In other cases, these may be identified and your ISP contacted to get you to stop doing these tasks. Remember, you are never truly anonymous, and smart hosters can figure out who you are, exactly what you accessed, and when you accessed it.

How to do it

So how do you go about being a good scraper? There are several factors to this that we will cover in this chapter:

- You can start with respecting the `robots.txt` file
- Don't crawl every link you find on a site, just those given in a site map
- Throttle your requests, so as do as Han Solo said to Chewbacca: Fly Casual; or, don't look like you are repeatedly taking content by Crawling Casual
- Identify yourself so that you are known to the site

Respecting robots.txt

Many sites want to be crawled. It is inherent in the nature of the beast: Web hosters put content on their sites to be seen by humans. But it is also important that other computers see the content. A great example is search engine optimization (SEO). SEO is a process where you actually design your site to be crawled by spiders such as Google, so you are actually encouraging scraping. But at the same time, a publisher may only want specific parts of their site crawled, and to tell crawlers to keep their spiders off of certain portions of the site, either it is not for sharing, or not important enough to be crawled and wast the web server resources.

The rules of what you are and are not allowed to crawl are usually contained in a file that is on most sites known as `robots.txt`. The `robots.txt` is a human readable but parsable file, which can be used to identify the places you are allowed, and not allowed, to scrape.

The format of the `robots.txt` file is unfortunately not standard and anyone can make their own modifications, but there is very strong consensus on the format. A `robots.txt` file is normally found at the root URL of the site. To demonstrate a`robots.txt` file, the following code contains excerpts of the one provided by Amazon at `http://amazon.com/robots.txt`. I've edited it down to just show the important concepts:

```
User-agent: *
Disallow: /exec/obidos/account-access-login
Disallow: /exec/obidos/change-style
Disallow: /exec/obidos/flex-sign-in
Disallow: /exec/obidos/handle-buy-box
Disallow: /exec/obidos/tg/cm/member/
Disallow: /gp/aw/help/id=sss
Disallow: /gp/cart
Disallow: /gp/flex

...

Allow: /wishlist/universal*
Allow: /wishlist/vendor-button*
Allow: /wishlist/get-button*

...

User-agent: Googlebot
Disallow: /rss/people/*/reviews
Disallow: /gp/pdp/rss/*/reviews
Disallow: /gp/cdp/member-reviews/
Disallow: /gp/aw/cr/

...
Allow: /wishlist/universal*
Allow: /wishlist/vendor-button*
Allow: /wishlist/get-button*
```

It can be seen that there are three main elements in the file:

- A user agent declaration for which the following lines, until the end of file or next user agent statement, are to be applied
- A set of URLs that are allowed to be crawled
- A set of URLs are prohibited from being crawled

The syntax is actually quite simple, and Python libraries exist to help us implement the rules contained within `robots.txt`. We will be using the `reppy` library to facilitate honoring `robots.txt`.

Getting ready

Let's examine how to demonstrate using `robots.txt` with the reppy library. For more information on reppy, see its GitHub page at `https://github.com/seomoz/reppy`.

`reppy` can be installed like this:

```
pip install reppy
```

However, I found that on my Mac I got an error during installation, and it required the following command:

```
CFLAGS=-stdlib=libc++ pip install reppy
```

General information/searching on Google for a `robots.txt` Python parsing library will generally guide you toward using the robotparser library. This library is available for Python 2.x. For Python 3, it has been moved into the `urllib` library. However, I have found that this library reports incorrect values in specific scenarios. I'll point that out in our example.

How to do it

To run the recipe, execute the code in `05/01_sitemap.py`. The script will examine whether several URLs are allowed to be crawled on amazon.com. When running it, you will see the following output:

```
True: http://www.amazon.com/
False: http://www.amazon.com/gp/dmusic/
True: http://www.amazon.com/gp/dmusic/promotions/PrimeMusic/
False: http://www.amazon.com/gp/registry/wishlist/
```

How it works

1. The script begins by importing `reppy.robots`:

```
from reppy.robots import Robots
```

2. The code then uses `Robots` to fetch the `robots.txt` for amazon.com.

```
url = "http://www.amazon.com"
robots = Robots.fetch(url + "/robots.txt")
```

3. Using the content that was fetched, the script checks several URLs for accessibility:

```
paths = [
    '/',
    '/gp/dmusic/',
    '/gp/dmusic/promotions/PrimeMusic/',
    '/gp/registry/wishlist/'
]

for path in paths:
 print("{0}: {1}".format(robots.allowed(path, '*'), url + path))
```

The results of this code is the following:

```
True: http://www.amazon.com/
False: http://www.amazon.com/gp/dmusic/
True: http://www.amazon.com/gp/dmusic/promotions/PrimeMusic/
False: http://www.amazon.com/gp/registry/wishlist/
```

The call to `robots.allowed` is given the URL and the user agent. It returns `True` or `False` based upon whether the URL is allowed to be crawled. In this case, the results where True, False, True and False for the specified URLs. Let's examine how.

The / URL has no entry in `robots.txt`, so it is allowed by default. But in the file under the * user agent group are the following two lines:

```
Disallow: /gp/dmusic/
Allow: /gp/dmusic/promotions/PrimeMusic
```

/gp/dmusic is not allowed, so False is returned. /gp/dmusic/promotions/PrimeMusic is explicitly allowed. If the Allowed: entry was not specified, then the Disallow: /gp/dmusic/ line would also disallow any further paths down from /gp/dmusic/. This essentially says that any URLs starting with /gp/dmusic/ are disallowed, except that you are allowed to crawl /gp/dmusic/promotions/PrimeMusic.

Here is where there is a difference when using the `robotparser` library. `robotparser` reports that `/gp/dmusic/promotions/PrimeMusic` is disallowed. The library does not handle this type of scenario correctly, as it stops scanning `robots.txt` at the first match, and does not continue further into the file to look for any overrides of this kind.

There's more...

First, for detailed information on `robots.txt`, see `https://developers.google.com/search/reference/robots_txt`.

Note that not all sites have a `robots.txt`, and its absence does not imply you have free rights to crawl all the content.

Also, a `robots.txt` file may contain information on where to find the sitemap(s) for the website. We examine these sitemaps in the next recipe.

Scrapy can also read `robots.txt` and find sitemaps for you.

Crawling using the sitemap

A sitemap is a protocol that allows a webmaster to inform search engines about URLs on a website that are available for crawling. A webmaster would want to use this as they actually want their information to be crawled by a search engine. The webmaster wants to make that content available for you to find, at least through search engines. But you can also use this information to your advantage.

A sitemap lists the URLs on a site, and allows a webmasters to specify additional information about each URL:

- When it was last updated
- How often the content changes
- How important the URL is in relation to others

Sitemaps are useful on websites where:

- Some areas of the website are not available through the browsable interface; that is, you cannot reach those pages
- Ajax, Silverlight, or Flash content is used but not normally processed by search engines
- The site is very large and there is a chance for the web crawlers to overlook some of the new or recently updated content
- When websites have a huge number of pages that are isolated or not well linked together
- When a website has few external links

A sitemap file has the following structure:

```
<?xml version="1.0" encoding="utf-8"?>
<urlset xmlns="http://www.sitemaps.org/schemas/sitemap/0.9"
   xmlns:xsi="http://www.w3.org/2001/XMLSchema-instance"
   xsi:schemaLocation="http://www.sitemaps.org/schemas/sitemap/0.9
http://www.sitemaps.org/schemas/sitemap/0.9/sitemap.xsd">
    <url>
        <loc>http://example.com/</loc>
        <lastmod>2006-11-18</lastmod>
        <changefreq>daily</changefreq>
        <priority>0.8</priority>
    </url>
</urlset>
```

Each URL in the site will be represented with a `<url></url>` tag, with all those tags wrapped in an outer `<urlset></urlset>` tag. There will always a `<loc></loc>` tag specifying the URL. The other three tags are optional.

Sitemaps files can be incredibly large, so they are often broken into multiple files and then referenced by a single sitemap index file. This file has the following format:

```
<?xml version="1.0" encoding="UTF-8"?>
<sitemapindex xmlns="http://www.sitemaps.org/schemas/sitemap/0.9">
   <sitemap>
      <loc>http://www.example.com/sitemap1.xml.gz</loc>
      <lastmod>2014-10-01T18:23:17+00:00</lastmod>
   </sitemap>
</sitemapindex>
```

In most cases, the `sitemap.xml` file is found at the root of the domain. As an example, for nasa.gov it is `https://www.nasa.gov/sitemap.xml`. But note that this is not a standard, and different sites may have the map, or maps, at different locations.

A sitemap for a particular website may also be located within the site's `robots.txt` file. As an example, the `robots.txt` file for microsoft.com ends with the following:

```
Sitemap: https://www.microsoft.com/en-us/explore/msft_sitemap_index.xml
Sitemap: https://www.microsoft.com/learning/sitemap.xml
Sitemap: https://www.microsoft.com/en-us/licensing/sitemap.xml
Sitemap: https://www.microsoft.com/en-us/legal/sitemap.xml
Sitemap: https://www.microsoft.com/filedata/sitemaps/RW5xN8
Sitemap: https://www.microsoft.com/store/collections.xml
Sitemap: https://www.microsoft.com/store/productdetailpages.index.xml
```

Therefore, to get microsoft.com's sitemaps, we would first need to read the `robots.txt` file and extract that information.

Let's now look at parsing a sitemap.

Getting ready

Everything you need is in the `05/02_sitemap.py` script, along with the `sitemap.py` file in then same folder. The `sitemap.py` file implements a basic sitemap parser that we will use in the main script. For the purposes of this example, we will get the sitemap data for nasa.gov.

How to do it

First execute the `05/02_sitemap.py` file. Make sure that the associated `sitemap.py` file is in the same directory or your path. When running, after a few seconds you will get output similar to the following:

```
Found 35511 urls
{'lastmod': '2017-10-11T18:23Z', 'loc':
'http://www.nasa.gov/centers/marshall/history/this-week-in-nasa-history-apo
llo-7-launches-oct-11-1968.html', 'tag': 'url'}
{'lastmod': '2017-10-11T18:22Z', 'loc':
'http://www.nasa.gov/feature/researchers-develop-new-tool-to-evaluate-iceph
obic-materials', 'tag': 'url'}
{'lastmod': '2017-10-11T17:38Z', 'loc':
'http://www.nasa.gov/centers/ames/entry-systems-vehicle-development/roster.
html', 'tag': 'url'}
{'lastmod': '2017-10-11T17:38Z', 'loc':
'http://www.nasa.gov/centers/ames/entry-systems-vehicle-development/about.h
tml', 'tag': 'url'}
{'lastmod': '2017-10-11T17:22Z', 'loc':
'http://www.nasa.gov/centers/ames/earthscience/programs/MMS/instruments',
'tag': 'url'}
{'lastmod': '2017-10-11T18:15Z', 'loc':
'http://www.nasa.gov/centers/ames/earthscience/programs/MMS/onepager',
'tag': 'url'}
{'lastmod': '2017-10-11T17:10Z', 'loc':
'http://www.nasa.gov/centers/ames/earthscience/programs/MMS', 'tag': 'url'}
{'lastmod': '2017-10-11T17:53Z', 'loc':
'http://www.nasa.gov/feature/goddard/2017/nasa-s-james-webb-space-telescope
-and-the-big-bang-a-short-qa-with-nobel-laureate-dr-john', 'tag': 'url'}
{'lastmod': '2017-10-11T17:38Z', 'loc':
'http://www.nasa.gov/centers/ames/entry-systems-vehicle-development/index.h
tml', 'tag': 'url'}
{'lastmod': '2017-10-11T15:21Z', 'loc':
'http://www.nasa.gov/feature/mark-s-geyer-acting-deputy-associate-administr
ator-for-technical-human-explorations-and-operations', 'tag': 'url'}
```

The program found 35,511 URLs throughout all of the nasa.gov sitemaps! The code only printed the first 10 as this would have been quite a bit of output. Using this info to initialize a crawl of all of these URLs will definitely take quite a long time!

But this is also the beauty of the sitemap. Many, if not all, of these results have a `lastmod` tag that tells you when the content at the end of that associated URL was last modified. If you are implementing a polite crawler of nasa.gov, you would want to keep these URLs and their timestamp in a database, and then before crawling that URL check to see if the content has actually changed, and don't crawl if it hasn't.

Now let's see how this actually worked.

How it works

The recipe works as follows:

1. The script starts by calling `get_sitemap()`:

```
map = sitemap.get_sitemap("https://www.nasa.gov/sitemap.xml")
```

2. This is given a URL to the sitemap.xml file (or any other file - non-gzipped). The implementation simply gets the content at the URL and returns it:

```
def get_sitemap(url):
    get_url = requests.get(url)

    if get_url.status_code == 200:
        return get_url.text
    else:
        print ('Unable to fetch sitemap: %s.' % url)
```

3. The bulk of the work is done by passing that content to `parse_sitemap()`. In the case of nasa.gov, this sitemap contains the following content, a sitemap index file:

```
<?xml version="1.0" encoding="UTF-8"?>
<?xml-stylesheet type="text/xsl"
href="//www.nasa.gov/sitemap.xsl"?>
<sitemapindex xmlns="http://www.sitemaps.org/schemas/sitemap/0.9">
<sitemap><loc>http://www.nasa.gov/sitemap-1.xml</loc><lastmod>2017-
10-11T19:30Z</lastmod></sitemap>
<sitemap><loc>http://www.nasa.gov/sitemap-2.xml</loc><lastmod>2017-
10-11T19:30Z</lastmod></sitemap>
<sitemap><loc>http://www.nasa.gov/sitemap-3.xml</loc><lastmod>2017-
10-11T19:30Z</lastmod></sitemap>
<sitemap><loc>http://www.nasa.gov/sitemap-4.xml</loc><lastmod>2017-
10-11T19:30Z</lastmod></sitemap>
</sitemapindex>
```

4. `process_sitemap()` starts with a call to `process_sitemap()`:

```
def parse_sitemap(s):
    sitemap = process_sitemap(s)
```

5. This function starts by calling `process_sitemap()`, which returns a list of Python dictionary objects with `loc`, `lastmod`, `changeFreq`, and priority key value pairs:

```
def process_sitemap(s):
    soup = BeautifulSoup(s, "lxml")
    result = []

    for loc in soup.findAll('loc'):
        item = {}
        item['loc'] = loc.text
        item['tag'] = loc.parent.name
        if loc.parent.lastmod is not None:
            item['lastmod'] = loc.parent.lastmod.text
        if loc.parent.changeFreq is not None:
            item['changeFreq'] = loc.parent.changeFreq.text
        if loc.parent.priority is not None:
            item['priority'] = loc.parent.priority.text
        result.append(item)

    return result
```

6. This is performed by parsing the sitemap using `BeautifulSoup` and `lxml`. The `loc` property is always `set`, and `lastmod`, `changeFreq` and priority are set if there is an an associated XML tag. The .tag property itself just notes whether this content was retrieved from a `<sitemap>` tag or a `<url>` tag (`<loc>` tags can be on either).
   `parse_sitemap()` then continues with processing those results one by one:

```
while sitemap:
    candidate = sitemap.pop()

    if is_sub_sitemap(candidate):
        sub_sitemap = get_sitemap(candidate['loc'])
        for i in process_sitemap(sub_sitemap):
            sitemap.append(i)
    else:
        result.append(candidate)
```

7. Each item is examined. If it is from a sitemap index file (the URL ends in .xml and the .tag is the sitemap), then we need to read that .xml file and parse its content, whose results are placed into our list of items to process. In this example, four sitemap files are identified, and each of these are read, processed, parsed, and their URLs added to the result.
   To demonstrate some of this content, the following are the first few lines of sitemap-1.xml:

```
<?xml version="1.0" encoding="UTF-8"?>
<?xml-stylesheet type="text/xsl"
href="//www.nasa.gov/sitemap.xsl"?>
<urlset xmlns="http://www.sitemaps.org/schemas/sitemap/0.9">
<url><loc>http://www.nasa.gov/</loc><changefreq>daily</changefreq><
priority>1.0</priority></url>
<url><loc>http://www.nasa.gov/connect/apps.html</loc><lastmod>2017-
08-14T22:15Z</lastmod><changefreq>yearly</changefreq></url>
<url><loc>http://www.nasa.gov/socialmedia</loc><lastmod>2017-09-29T
21:47Z</lastmod><changefreq>monthly</changefreq></url>
<url><loc>http://www.nasa.gov/multimedia/imagegallery/iotd.html</lo
c><lastmod>2017-08-21T22:00Z</lastmod><changefreq>yearly</changefre
q></url>
<url><loc>http://www.nasa.gov/archive/archive/about/career/index.ht
ml</loc><lastmod>2017-08-04T02:31Z</lastmod><changefreq>yearly</cha
ngefreq></url>
```

Overall, this one sitemap has 11,006 lines, so roughly 11,000 URLs! And in total, as was reported, there are 35,511 URLs across all three sitemaps.

There's more...

Sitemap files may also be zipped, and end in a .gz extension. This is because it likely contains many URLs and the compression will save a lot of space. While the code we used does not process gzip sitemap files, it is easy to add this using functions in the gzip library.

Scrapy also provides a facility for starting crawls using the sitemap. One of these is a specialization of the Spider class, SitemapSpider. This class has the smarts to parse the sitemap for you, and then start following the URLs. To demonstrate, the script `05/03_sitemap_scrapy.py` will start the crawl at the nasa.gov top-level sitemap index:

```
import scrapy
from scrapy.crawler import CrawlerProcess

class Spider(scrapy.spiders.SitemapSpider):
    name = 'spider'
```

```
    sitemap_urls = ['https://www.nasa.gov/sitemap.xml']

    def parse(self, response):
        print("Parsing: ", response)

if __name__ == "__main__":
    process = CrawlerProcess({
        'DOWNLOAD_DELAY': 0,
        'LOG_LEVEL': 'DEBUG'
    })
    process.crawl(Spider)
    process.start()
```

When running this, there will be a ton of output, as the spider is going to start crawling all 30000+ URLs. Early in the output, you will see output such as the following:

```
2017-10-11 20:34:27 [scrapy.core.engine] DEBUG: Crawled (200) <GET
https://www.nasa.gov/sitemap.xml> (referer: None)
2017-10-11 20:34:27 [scrapy.downloadermiddlewares.redirect] DEBUG:
Redirecting (301) to <GET https://www.nasa.gov/sitemap-4.xml> from <GET
http://www.nasa.gov/sitemap-4.xml>
2017-10-11 20:34:27 [scrapy.downloadermiddlewares.redirect] DEBUG:
Redirecting (301) to <GET https://www.nasa.gov/sitemap-2.xml> from <GET
http://www.nasa.gov/sitemap-2.xml>
2017-10-11 20:34:27 [scrapy.downloadermiddlewares.redirect] DEBUG:
Redirecting (301) to <GET https://www.nasa.gov/sitemap-3.xml> from <GET
http://www.nasa.gov/sitemap-3.xml>
2017-10-11 20:34:27 [scrapy.downloadermiddlewares.redirect] DEBUG:
Redirecting (301) to <GET https://www.nasa.gov/sitemap-1.xml> from <GET
http://www.nasa.gov/sitemap-1.xml>
2017-10-11 20:34:27 [scrapy.core.engine] DEBUG: Crawled (200) <GET
https://www.nasa.gov/sitemap-4.xml> (referer: None)
```

Scrapy has found all of the sitemaps and read in their content. Soon afterwards, you will start to see a number of redirections and notifications that certain pages are being parsed:

```
2017-10-11 20:34:30 [scrapy.downloadermiddlewares.redirect] DEBUG:
Redirecting (302) to <GET
https://www.nasa.gov/image-feature/jpl/pia21629/neptune-from-saturn/> from
<GET https://www.nasa.gov/image-feature/jpl/pia21629/neptune-from-saturn>
2017-10-11 20:34:30 [scrapy.downloadermiddlewares.redirect] DEBUG:
Redirecting (302) to <GET
https://www.nasa.gov/centers/ames/earthscience/members/nasaearthexchange/Ra
makrishna_Nemani/> from <GET
https://www.nasa.gov/centers/ames/earthscience/members/nasaearthexchang
```

```
e/Ramakrishna_Nemani>
Parsing: <200
https://www.nasa.gov/exploration/systems/sls/multimedia/sls-hardware-being-
moved-on-kamag-transporter.html>
Parsing: <200 https://www.nasa.gov/exploration/systems/sls/M17-057.html>
```

Crawling with delays

Fast scraping is considered a bad practice. Continuously pounding a website for pages can burn up CPU and bandwidth, and a robust site will identify you doing this and block your IP. And if you are unlucky, you might get a nasty letter for violating terms of service!

The technique of delaying requests in your crawler depends upon how your crawler is implemented. If you are using Scrapy, then you can set a parameter that informs the crawler how long to wait between requests. In a simple crawler just sequentially processing URLs in a list, you can insert a thread.sleep statement.

Things can get more complicated if you have implemented a distributed cluster of crawlers that spread the load of page requests, such as using a message queue with competing consumers. That can have a number of different solutions, which are beyond the scope provided in this context.

Getting ready

We will examine using Scrapy with delays. The sample is in `o5/04_scrape_with_delay.py`.

How to do it

Scrapy by default imposes a delay of 0 seconds between page requests. That is, it does not wait between requests by default.

1. This can be controlled using the `DOWNLOAD_DELAY` setting. To demonstrate, let's run the script from the command line:

```
05 $ scrapy runspider 04_scrape_with_delay.py -s LOG_LEVEL=WARNING
Parsing: <200 https://blog.scrapinghub.com>
Parsing: <200 https://blog.scrapinghub.com/page/2/>
Parsing: <200 https://blog.scrapinghub.com/page/3/>
Parsing: <200 https://blog.scrapinghub.com/page/4/>
```

```
Parsing: &lt;200 https://blog.scrapinghub.com/page/5/>
Parsing: <200 https://blog.scrapinghub.com/page/6/>
Parsing: <200 https://blog.scrapinghub.com/page/7/>
Parsing: <200 https://blog.scrapinghub.com/page/8/>
Parsing: <200 https://blog.scrapinghub.com/page/9/>
Parsing: <200 https://blog.scrapinghub.com/page/10/>
Parsing: <200 https://blog.scrapinghub.com/page/11/>
Total run time: 0:00:07.006148
Michaels-iMac-2:05 michaelheydt$
```

This crawls all of the pages at blog.scrapinghub.com, and reports the total time to perform the crawl. `LOG_LEVEL=WARNING` removes most logging output and just gives out the output from print statements. This used the default wait between pages of 0 and resulted in a crawl roughly seven seconds in length.

2. The wait between pages can be set using the `DOWNLOAD_DELAY` setting. The following delays for five seconds between page requests:

```
05 $ scrapy runspider 04_scrape_with_delay.py -s DOWNLOAD_DELAY=5 -
s LOG_LEVEL=WARNING
Parsing: <200 https://blog.scrapinghub.com>
Parsing: <200 https://blog.scrapinghub.com/page/2/>
Parsing: <200 https://blog.scrapinghub.com/page/3/>
Parsing: <200 https://blog.scrapinghub.com/page/4/>
Parsing: <200 https://blog.scrapinghub.com/page/5/>
Parsing: <200 https://blog.scrapinghub.com/page/6/>
Parsing: <200 https://blog.scrapinghub.com/page/7/>
Parsing: <200 https://blog.scrapinghub.com/page/8/>
Parsing: <200 https://blog.scrapinghub.com/page/9/>
Parsing: <200 https://blog.scrapinghub.com/page/10/>
Parsing: <200 https://blog.scrapinghub.com/page/11/>
Total run time: 0:01:01.099267
```

By default, this does not actually wait 5 seconds. It will wait `DOWNLOAD_DELAY` seconds, but by a random factor between 0.5 and 1.5 times `DOWNLOAD_DELAY`. Why do this? This makes your crawler look "less robotic." You can turn this off by using the `RANDOMIZED_DOWNLOAD_DELAY=False` setting.

How it works

This crawler is implemented as a Scrapy spider. The class definition begins with declaring the spider name and the start URL:

```
class Spider(scrapy.Spider):
    name = 'spider'
    start_urls = ['https://blog.scrapinghub.com']
```

The parse method looks for CSS 'div.prev-post > a', and follows those links.

The scraper also defines a close method, which is called by Scrapy when the crawl is complete:

```
def close(spider, reason):
    start_time = spider.crawler.stats.get_value('start_time')
    finish_time = spider.crawler.stats.get_value('finish_time')
    print("Total run time: ", finish_time-start_time)
```

This accesses the spiders crawler stats object, retrieves the start and finish time for the spider, and reports the difference to the user.

There's more...

The script also defines code for when executing the script directly with Python:

```
if __name__ == "__main__":
    process = CrawlerProcess({
        'DOWNLOAD_DELAY': 5,
        'RANDOMIZED_DOWNLOAD_DELAY': False,
        'LOG_LEVEL': 'DEBUG'
    })
    process.crawl(Spider)
    process.start()
```

This begins by creating a CrawlerProcess object. This object can be passed a dictionary representing the settings and values to configure the crawl with. This defaults to a five-second delay, without randomization, and an output level of DEBUG.

Using identifiable user agents

What happens if you violate the terms of service and get flagged by the website owner? How can you help the site owners in contacting you, so that they can nicely ask you to back off to what they consider a reasonable level of scraping?

What you can do to facilitate this is add info about yourself in the User-Agent header of the requests. We have seen an example of this in `robots.txt` files, such as from amazon.com. In their `robots.txt` is an explicit statement of a user agent for Google: GoogleBot.

During scraping, you can embed your own information within the User-Agent header of the HTTP requests. To be polite, you can enter something such as 'MyCompany-MyCrawler (mybot@mycompany.com)'. The remote server, if tagging you in violation, will definitely be capturing this information, and if provided like this, it gives them a convenient means of contacting your instead of just shutting you down.

How to do it

Setting the user agent differs depending upon what tools you use. Ultimately, it is just ensuring that the User-Agent header is set to a string that you specify. When using a browser, this is normally set by the browser to identity the browser and the operating system. But you can put anything you want into this header. When using requests, it is very straightforward:

```
url = 'https://api.github.com/some/endpoint'
headers = {'user-agent': 'MyCompany-MyCrawler (mybot@mycompany.com)'}
r = requests.get(url, headers=headers)
```

When using Scrapy, it is as simple as configuring a setting:

```
process = CrawlerProcess({
    'USER_AGENT': 'MyCompany-MyCrawler (mybot@mycompany.com)'
})
process.crawl(Spider)
process.start()
```

How it works

Outgoing HTTP requests have a number of different headers. These ensure that the User-Agent header is set to this value for all requests made of the target web server.

There's more...

While it is possible to set any content you want in the User-Agent header, some web servers will inspect the User-Agent header and make decisions on how to respond based upon the content. A common example of this is using the header to identify mobile devices to provide a mobile presentation.

But some sites also only allow access to content to specific User-Agent values. Setting your own value could have the effect of having the web server not respond or return other errors, such as unauthorized. So when you use this technique, make sure to check it will work.

Setting the number of concurrent requests per domain

It is generally inefficient to crawl a site one URL at a time. Therefore, there is normally a number of simultaneous page requests made to the target site at any given time. Normally, the remote web server can quite effectively handle multiple simultaneous requests, and on your end you are just waiting for data to come back in for each, so concurrency generally works well for your scraper.

But this is also a pattern that smart websites can identify and flag as suspicious activity. And there are practical limits on both your crawler's end and the website. The more concurrent requests that are made, the more memory, CPU, network connections, and network bandwidth is required on both sides. These have costs involved, and there are practical limits on these values too.

So it is generally a good practice to set a limit on the number of requests that you will simultaneously make to any web server.

How it works

There are number of techniques that can be used to control concurrency levels, and the process can often be quite complicated with controlling multiple requests and threads of execution. We won't discuss here how this is done at the thread level and only mention the construct built into Scrapy.

Scrapy is inherently concurrent in its requests. By default, Scrapy will dispatch at most eight simultaneous requests to any given domain. You can change this using the `CONCURRENT_REQUESTS_PER_DOMAIN` setting. The following sets the value to 1 concurrent request:

```
process = CrawlerProcess({
    'CONCURRENT_REQUESTS_PER_DOMAIN': 1
})
process.crawl(Spider)
process.start()
```

Using auto throttling

Fairly closely tied to controlling the maximum level of concurrency is the concept of throttling. Websites vary in their ability to handle requests, both across multiple websites and on a single website at different times. During periods of slower response times, it makes sense to lighten up of the number of requests during that time. This can be a tedious process to monitor and adjust by hand.

Fortunately for us, scrapy also provides an ability to do this via an extension named `AutoThrottle`.

How to do it

AutoThrottle can easily be configured using the `AUTOTHROTTLE_TARGET_CONCURRENCY` setting:

```
process = CrawlerProcess({
    'AUTOTHROTTLE_TARGET_CONCURRENCY': 3
})
process.crawl(Spider)
process.start()
```

How it works

scrapy tracks the latency on each request. Using that information, it can adjust the delay between requests to a specific domain so that there are no more than `AUTOTHROTTLE_TARGET_CONCURRENCY` requests simultaneously active for that domain, and that the requests are evenly distributed in any given time span.

There's more...

There are lot of options for controlling throttling. You can get an overview of them at https://doc.scrapy.org/en/latest/topics/autothrottle.html?&_ga=2.54316072.1404351387.1507758575-507079265.1505263737#settings.

Using an HTTP cache for development

The development of a web crawler is a process of exploration, and one that will iterate through various refinements to retrieve the requested information. During the development process, you will often be hitting remote servers, and the same URLs on those servers, over and over. This is not polite. Fortunately, scrapy also comes to the rescue by providing caching middleware that is specifically designed to help in this situation.

How to do it

Scrapy will cache requests using a middleware module named HttpCacheMiddleware. Enabling it is as simple as configuring the `HTTPCACHE_ENABLED` setting to `True`:

```
process = CrawlerProcess({
    'AUTOTHROTTLE_TARGET_CONCURRENCY': 3
})
process.crawl(Spider)
process.start()
```

How it works

The implementation of HTTP caching is simple, yet complex at the same time. The `HttpCacheMiddleware` provided by Scrapy has a plethora of configuration options based upon your needs. Ultimately, it comes down to storing each URL and its content in a store along with an associated duration for cache expiration. If a second request is made for a URL within the expiration interval, then the local copy will be retrieved instead of making a remote request. If the time has expired, then the contents are fetched from the web server, stored in the cache, and a new expiration time set.

There's more...

There are many options for configuration scrapy caching, including means of storing content (file system, DBM, or LevelDB), cache policies, and how Http Cache-Control directives from the server are handled. To explore these options, check out the following URL: `https://doc.scrapy.org/en/latest/topics/downloader-middleware.html?_ga=2.50242598.1404351387.1507758575-507079265.1505263737#dummy-policy-default`.

6
Scraping Challenges and Solutions

In this chapter, we will cover:

- Retrying failed page downloads
- Supporting page redirects
- Waiting for content to be available in Selenium
- Limiting crawling to a single domain
- Processing infinitely scrolling pages
- Controlling the depth of a crawl
- Controlling the length of a crawl
- Handling paginated websites
- Handling forms and form-based authorization
- Handling basic authorization
- Preventing bans by scraping via proxies
- Randomizing user agents
- Caching responses

Introduction

Developing a reliable scraper is never easy, there are so many *what ifs* that we need to take into account. What if the website goes down? What if the response returns unexpected data? What if your IP is throttled or blocked? What if authentication is required? While we can never predict and cover all *what ifs*, we will discuss some common traps, challenges, and workarounds.

Note that several of the recipes require access to a website that I have provided as a Docker container. They require more logic than the simple, static site we used in earlier chapters. Therefore, you will need to pull and run a Docker container using the following Docker commands:

```
docker pull mheydt/pywebscrapecookbook
docker run -p 5001:5001 pywebscrapecookbook
```

Retrying failed page downloads

Failed page requests can be easily handled by Scrapy using retry middleware. When installed, Scrapy will attempt retries when receiving the following HTTP error codes:

```
[500, 502, 503, 504, 408]
```

The process can be further configured using the following parameters:

- `RETRY_ENABLED` (True/False - default is True)
- `RETRY_TIMES` (# of times to retry on any errors - default is 2)
- `RETRY_HTTP_CODES` (a list of HTTP error codes which should be retried - default is [500, 502, 503, 504, 408])

How to do it

The `06/01_scrapy_retry.py` script demonstrates how to configure Scrapy for retries. The script file contains the following configuration for Scrapy:

```
process = CrawlerProcess({
    'LOG_LEVEL': 'DEBUG',
    'DOWNLOADER_MIDDLEWARES':
        {
            "scrapy.downloadermiddlewares.retry.RetryMiddleware": 500
```

```
        },
        'RETRY_ENABLED': True,
        'RETRY_TIMES': 3
})
process.crawl(Spider)
process.start()
```

How it works

Scrapy will pick up the configuration for retries as specified when the spider is run. When encountering errors, Scrapy will retry up to three times before giving up.

Supporting page redirects

Page redirects in Scrapy are handled using redirect middleware, which is enabled by default. The process can be further configured using the following parameters:

- `REDIRECT_ENABLED`: (True/False - default is True)
- `REDIRECT_MAX_TIMES`: (The maximum number of redirections to follow for any single request - default is 20)

How to do it

The script in `06/02_scrapy_redirects.py` demonstrates how to configure Scrapy to handle redirects. This configures a maximum of two redirects for any page. Running the script reads the NASA sitemap and crawls that content. This contains a large number of redirects, many of which are redirects from HTTP to HTTPS versions of URLs. There will be a lot of output, but here are a few lines demonstrating the output:

```
Parsing: <200 https://www.nasa.gov/content/earth-expeditions-above/>
['http://www.nasa.gov/content/earth-expeditions-above',
'https://www.nasa.gov/content/earth-expeditions-above']
```

This particular URL was processed after one redirection, from an HTTP to an HTTPS version of the URL. The list defines all of the URLs that were involved in the redirection.

You will also be able to see where redirection exceeded the specified level (2) in the output pages. The following is one example:

```
2017-10-22 17:55:00 [scrapy.downloadermiddlewares.redirect] DEBUG:
Discarding <GET http://www.nasa.gov/topics/journeytomars/news/index.html>:
max redirections reached
```

How it works

The spider is defined as the following:

```
class Spider(scrapy.spiders.SitemapSpider):
    name = 'spider'
    sitemap_urls = ['https://www.nasa.gov/sitemap.xml']

    def parse(self, response):
        print("Parsing: ", response)
        print (response.request.meta.get('redirect_urls'))
```

This is identical to our previous NASA sitemap based crawler, with the addition of one line printing the `redirect_urls`. In any call to `parse`, this metadata will contain all redirects that occurred to get to this page.

The crawling process is configured with the following code:

```
process = CrawlerProcess({
    'LOG_LEVEL': 'DEBUG',
    'DOWNLOADER_MIDDLEWARES':
        {
            "scrapy.downloadermiddlewares.redirect.RedirectMiddleware": 500
        },
    'REDIRECT_ENABLED': True,
    'REDIRECT_MAX_TIMES': 2
})
```

Redirect is enabled by default, but this sets the maximum number of redirects to 2 instead of the default of 20.

Waiting for content to be available in Selenium

A common problem with dynamic web pages is that even after the whole page has loaded, and hence the `get()` method in Selenium has returned, there still may be content that we need to access later as there are outstanding Ajax requests from the page that are still pending completion. An example of this is needing to click a button, but the button not being enabled until all data has been loaded asyncronously to the page after loading.

Take the following page as an example: `http://the-internet.herokuapp.com/dynamic_loading/2`. This page finishes loading very quickly and presents us with a **Start** button:

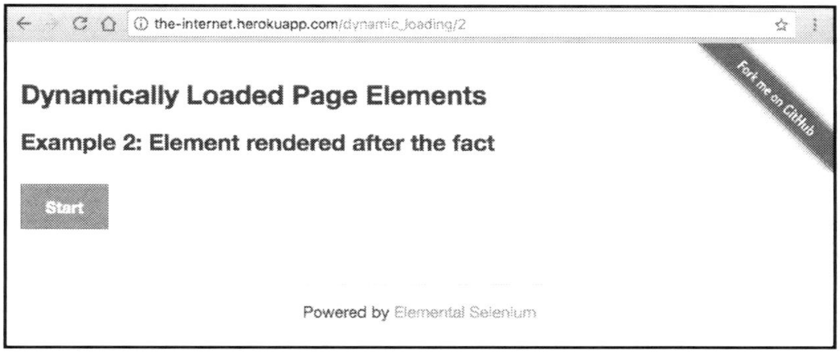

The Start button presented on screen

When pressing the button, we are presented with a progress bar for five seconds:

The status bar while waiting

And when this is completed, we are presented with **Hello World!**

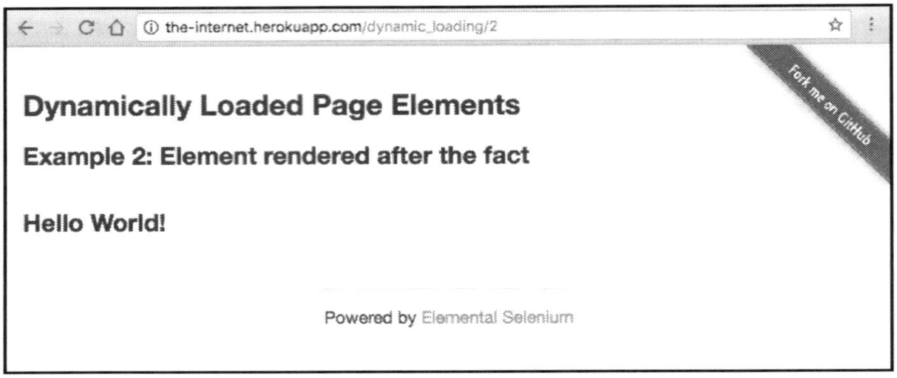

After the page is completely rendered

Now suppose we want to scrape this page to get the content that is exposed only after the button is pressed and after the wait? How do we do this?

How to do it

We can do this using Selenium. We will use two features of Selenium. The first is the ability to click on page elements. The second is the ability to wait until an element with a specific ID is available on the page.

1. First, we get the button and click it. The button's HTML is the following:

```
<div id='start'>
   <button>Start</button>
</div>
```

2. When the button is pressed and the load completes, the following HTML is added to the document:

```
<div id='finish'>
   <h4>Hello World!"</h4>
</div>
```

3. We will use the Selenium driver to find the Start button, click it, and then wait until a `div` with an ID of `'finish'` is available. Then we get that element and return the text in the enclosed `<h4>` tag.

You can try this by running `06/03_press_and_wait.py`. It's output will be the following:

```
clicked
Hello World!
```

Now let's see how it worked.

How it works

Let us break down the explanation:

1. We start by importing the required items from Selenium:

   ```
   from selenium import webdriver
   from selenium.webdriver.support import ui
   ```

2. Now we load the driver and the page:

   ```
   driver = webdriver.PhantomJS()
   driver.get("http://the-internet.herokuapp.com/dynamic_loading/2")
   ```

3. With the page loaded, we can retrieve the button:

   ```
   button =
   driver.find_element_by_xpath("//*/div[@id='start']/button")
   ```

4. And then we can click the button:

   ```
   button.click()
   print("clicked")
   ```

5. Next we create a `WebDriverWait` object:

```
wait = ui.WebDriverWait(driver, 10)
```

6. With this object, we can request Selenium's UI wait for certain events. This also sets a maximum wait of 10 seconds. Now using this, we can wait until we meet a criterion; that an element is identifiable using the following XPath:

```
wait.until(lambda driver:
driver.find_element_by_xpath("//*/div[@id='finish']"))
```

7. When this completes, we can retrieve the h4 element and get its enclosing text:

```
finish_element=driver.find_element_by_xpath("//*/div[@id='finish']/
h4")
print(finish_element.text)
```

Limiting crawling to a single domain

We can inform Scrapy to limit the crawl to only pages within a specified set of domains. This is an important task, as links can point to anywhere on the web, and we often want to control where crawls end up going. Scrapy makes this very easy to do. All that needs to be done is setting the `allowed_domains` field of your scraper class.

How to do it

The code for this example is `06/04_allowed_domains.py`. You can run the script with your Python interpreter. It will execute and generate a ton of output, but if you keep an eye on it, you will see that it only processes pages on nasa.gov.

How it works

The code is the same as previous NASA site crawlers except that we include `allowed_domains=['nasa.gov']`:

```
class Spider(scrapy.spiders.SitemapSpider):
    name = 'spider'
    sitemap_urls = ['https://www.nasa.gov/sitemap.xml']
    allowed_domains=['nasa.gov']

    def parse(self, response):
        print("Parsing: ", response)
```

The NASA site is fairly consistent with staying within its root domain, but there are occasional links to other sites such as content on boeing.com. This code will prevent moving to those external sites.

Processing infinitely scrolling pages

Many websites have replaced "previous/next" pagination buttons with an infinite scrolling mechanism. These websites use this technique to load more data when the user has reached the bottom of the page. Because of this, strategies for crawling by following the "next page" link fall apart.

While this would seem to be a case for using browser automation to simulate the scrolling, it's actually quite easy to figure out the web pages' Ajax requests and use those for crawling instead of the actual page. Let's look at `spidyquotes.herokuapp.com/scroll` as an example.

Getting ready

Open `http://spidyquotes.herokuapp.com/scroll` in your browser. This page will load additional content when you scroll to the bottom of the page:

Screenshot of the quotes to scrape

Once the page is open, go into your developer tools and select the network panel. Then, scroll to the bottom of the page. You will see new content in the network panel:

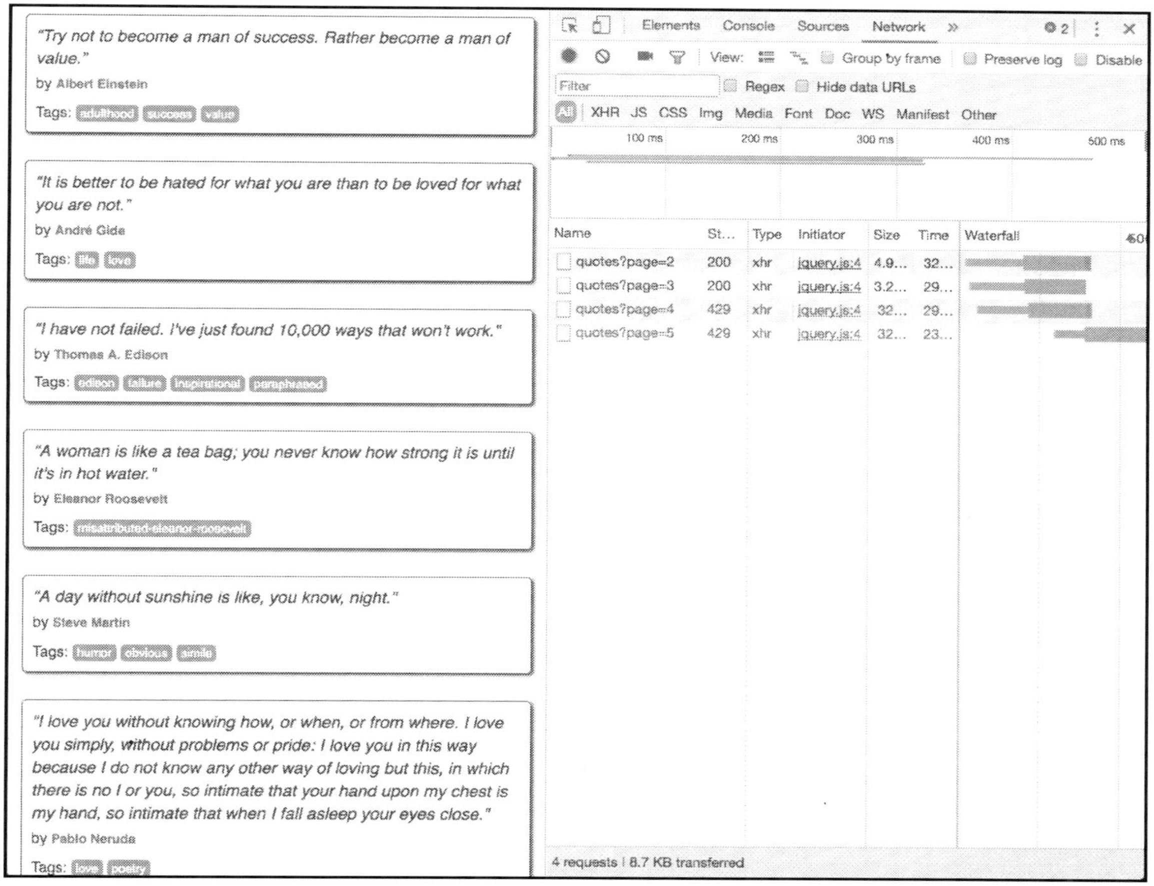

Screenshot of the developer tools options

When we click on one of the links, we can see the following JSON:

```
{
"has_next": true,
"page": 2,
"quotes": [{
"author": {
"goodreads_link": "/author/show/82952.Marilyn_Monroe",
"name": "Marilyn Monroe",
"slug": "Marilyn-Monroe"
```

```
},
"tags": ["friends", "heartbreak", "inspirational", "life", "love",
"sisters"],
"text": "\u201cThis life is what you make it...."
}, {
"author": {
"goodreads_link": "/author/show/1077326.J_K_Rowling",
"name": "J.K. Rowling",
"slug": "J-K-Rowling"
},
"tags": ["courage", "friends"],
"text": "\u201cIt takes a great deal of bravery to stand up to our enemies,
but just as much to stand up to our friends.\u201d"
},
```

This is great because all we need to do is continually generate requests to `/api/quotes?page=x`, increasing `x` until the `has_next` tag exists in the reply document. If there are no more pages, then this tag will not be in the document.

How to do it

The `06/05_scrapy_continuous.py` file contains a Scrapy agent, which crawls this set of pages. Run it with your Python interpreter and you will see output similar to the following (the following is multiple excerpts from the output):

```
<200 http://spidyquotes.herokuapp.com/api/quotes?page=2>
2017-10-29 16:17:37 [scrapy.core.scraper] DEBUG: Scraped from <200
http://spidyquotes.herokuapp.com/api/quotes?page=2>
{'text': "“This life is what you make it. No matter what, you're going to
mess up sometimes, it's a universal truth. But the good part is you get to
decide how you're going to mess it up. Girls will be your friends - they'll
act like it anyway. But just remember, some come, some go. The ones that
stay with you through everything - they're your true best friends. Don't
let go of them. Also remember, sisters make the best friends in the world.
As for lovers, well, they'll come and go too. And baby, I hate to say it,
most of them - actually pretty much all of them are going to break your
heart, but you can't give up because if you give up, you'll never find your
soulmate. You'll never find that half who makes you whole and that goes for
everything. Just because you fail once, doesn't mean you're gonna fail at
everything. Keep trying, hold on, and always, always, always believe in
yourself, because if you don't, then who will, sweetie? So keep your head
high, keep your chin up, and most importantly, keep smiling, because life's
a beautiful thing and there's so much to smile about.”", 'author': 'Marilyn
Monroe', 'tags': ['friends', 'heartbreak', 'inspirational', 'life', 'love',
'sisters']}
```

```
2017-10-29 16:17:37 [scrapy.core.scraper] DEBUG: Scraped from <200
http://spidyquotes.herokuapp.com/api/quotes?page=2>
{'text': '"It takes a great deal of bravery to stand up to our enemies, but
just as much to stand up to our friends."', 'author': 'J.K. Rowling',
'tags': ['courage', 'friends']}
2017-10-29 16:17:37 [scrapy.core.scraper] DEBUG: Scraped from <200
http://spidyquotes.herokuapp.com/api/quotes?page=2>
{'text': ""If you can't explain it to a six year old, you don't understand
it yourself."", 'author': 'Albert Einstein', 'tags': ['simplicity',
'understand']}
```

When this gets to page 10 it will stop as it will see that there is no next page flag set in the content.

How it works

Let's walk through the spider to see how this works. The spider starts with the following definition of the start URL:

```
class Spider(scrapy.Spider):
    name = 'spidyquotes'
    quotes_base_url = 'http://spidyquotes.herokuapp.com/api/quotes'
    start_urls = [quotes_base_url]
    download_delay = 1.5
```

The parse method then prints the response and also parses the JSON into the data variable:

```
    def parse(self, response):
        print(response)
        data = json.loads(response.body)
```

Then it loops through all the items in the quotes element of the JSON objects. For each item, it yields a new Scrapy item back to the Scrapy engine:

```
        for item in data.get('quotes', []):
            yield {
                'text': item.get('text'),
                'author': item.get('author', {}).get('name'),
                'tags': item.get('tags'),
            }
```

It then checks to see if the data JSON variable has a `'has_next'` property, and if so it gets the next page and yields a new request back to Scrapy to parse the next page:

```
if data['has_next']:
    next_page = data['page'] + 1
    yield scrapy.Request(self.quotes_base_url + "?page=%s" % next_page)
```

There's more...

It is also possible to process infinite, scrolling pages using Selenium. The following code is in `06/06_scrape_continuous_twitter.py`:

```
from selenium import webdriver
import time

driver = webdriver.PhantomJS()

print("Starting")
driver.get("https://twitter.com")
scroll_pause_time = 1.5

# Get scroll height
last_height = driver.execute_script("return document.body.scrollHeight")
while True:
    print(last_height)
    # Scroll down to bottom
    driver.execute_script("window.scrollTo(0,
document.body.scrollHeight);")

    # Wait to load page
    time.sleep(scroll_pause_time)

    # Calculate new scroll height and compare with last scroll height
    new_height = driver.execute_script("return document.body.scrollHeight")
    print(new_height, last_height)

    if new_height == last_height:
        break
    last_height = new_height
```

The output would be similar to the following:

```
Starting
4882
8139 4882
8139
11630 8139
11630
15055 11630
15055
15055 15055
Process finished with exit code 0
```

This code starts by loading the page from Twitter. The call to .get() will return when the page is fully loaded. The scrollHeight is then retrieved, and the program scrolls to that height and waits for a moment for the new content to load. The scrollHeight of the browser is retrieved again, and if different than last_height, it will loop and continue processing. If the same as last_height, no new content has loaded and you can then continue on and retrieve the HTML for the completed page.

Controlling the depth of a crawl

The depth of a crawl can be controlled using Scrapy DepthMiddleware middleware. The depth middleware limits the number of follows that Scrapy will take from any given link. This option can be useful for controlling how deep you go into a particular crawl. This is also used to keep a crawl from going on too long, and useful if you know that the content you are crawling for is located within a certain number of degrees of separation from the pages at the start of your crawl.

How to do it

The depth control middleware is installed in the middleware pipeline by default. An example of depth limiting is contained in the 06/06_limit_depth.py script. This script crawls the static site provided with the source code on port 8080, and allows you to configure the depth limit. This site consists of three levels: 0, 1, and 2, and has three pages at each level. The files are named CrawlDepth<level><pagenumber>.html. Page 1 on each level links to the other two pages on the same level, as well as to the first page on the next level. Links to higher levels end at level 2. This structure is great for examining how depth processing is handled in Scrapy.

How it works

The limiting of depth can be performed by setting the `DEPTH_LIMIT` parameter:

```
process = CrawlerProcess({
    'LOG_LEVEL': 'CRITICAL',
    'DEPTH_LIMIT': 2,
    'DEPT_STATS': True
})
```

A depth limit of 1 means we will only crawl one level, which means it will process the URLs specified in `start_urls`, and then any URLs found within those pages. With `DEPTH_LIMIT` we get the following output:

```
Parsing: <200 http://localhost:8080/CrawlDepth0-1.html>
Requesting crawl of: http://localhost:8080/CrawlDepth0-2.html
Requesting crawl of: http://localhost:8080/Depth1/CrawlDepth1-1.html
Parsing: <200 http://localhost:8080/Depth1/CrawlDepth1-1.html>
Requesting crawl of: http://localhost:8080/Depth1/CrawlDepth1-2.html
Requesting crawl of: http://localhost:8080/Depth1/depth1/CrawlDepth1-2.html
Requesting crawl of: http://localhost:8080/Depth1/depth2/CrawlDepth2-1.html
Parsing: <200 http://localhost:8080/CrawlDepth0-2.html>
Requesting crawl of: http://localhost:8080/CrawlDepth0-3.html
<scrapy.statscollectors.MemoryStatsCollector object at 0x109f754e0>
Crawled: ['http://localhost:8080/CrawlDepth0-1.html',
'http://localhost:8080/Depth1/CrawlDepth1-1.html',
'http://localhost:8080/CrawlDepth0-2.html']
Requested: ['http://localhost:8080/CrawlDepth0-2.html',
'http://localhost:8080/Depth1/CrawlDepth1-1.html',
'http://localhost:8080/Depth1/CrawlDepth1-2.html',
'http://localhost:8080/Depth1/depth1/CrawlDepth1-2.html',
'http://localhost:8080/Depth1/depth2/CrawlDepth2-1.html',
'http://localhost:8080/CrawlDepth0-3.html']
```

The crawl starts with `CrawlDepth0-1.html`. That page has two lines, one to `CrawlDepth0-2.html` and one to `CrawlDepth1-1.html`. They are then requested to be parsed. Considering that the start page is at depth 0, those pages are at depth 1, the limit of our depth. Therefore, we will see those two pages being parsed. However, note that all the links from those two pages, although requesting to be parsed, are then ignored by Scrapy as they are at depth 2, which exceeds the specified limit.

Now change the depth limit to 2:

```
process = CrawlerProcess({
    'LOG_LEVEL': 'CRITICAL',
    'DEPTH_LIMIT': 2,
    'DEPT_STATS': True
})
```

The output then becomes as follows:

```
Parsing: <200 http://localhost:8080/CrawlDepth0-1.html>
Requesting crawl of: http://localhost:8080/CrawlDepth0-2.html
Requesting crawl of: http://localhost:8080/Depth1/CrawlDepth1-1.html
Parsing: <200 http://localhost:8080/Depth1/CrawlDepth1-1.html>
Requesting crawl of: http://localhost:8080/Depth1/CrawlDepth1-2.html
Requesting crawl of: http://localhost:8080/Depth1/depth1/CrawlDepth1-2.html
Requesting crawl of: http://localhost:8080/Depth1/depth2/CrawlDepth2-1.html
Parsing: <200 http://localhost:8080/CrawlDepth0-2.html>
Requesting crawl of: http://localhost:8080/CrawlDepth0-3.html
Parsing: <200 http://localhost:8080/Depth1/depth2/CrawlDepth2-1.html>
Parsing: <200 http://localhost:8080/CrawlDepth0-3.html>
Parsing: <200 http://localhost:8080/Depth1/CrawlDepth1-2.html>
Requesting crawl of: http://localhost:8080/Depth1/CrawlDepth1-3.html
<scrapy.statscollectors.MemoryStatsCollector object at 0x10d3d44e0>
Crawled: ['http://localhost:8080/CrawlDepth0-1.html',
'http://localhost:8080/Depth1/CrawlDepth1-1.html',
'http://localhost:8080/CrawlDepth0-2.html',
'http://localhost:8080/Depth1/depth2/CrawlDepth2-1.html',
'http://localhost:8080/CrawlDepth0-3.html',
'http://localhost:8080/Depth1/CrawlDepth1-2.html']
Requested: ['http://localhost:8080/CrawlDepth0-2.html',
'http://localhost:8080/Depth1/CrawlDepth1-1.html',
'http://localhost:8080/Depth1/CrawlDepth1-2.html',
'http://localhost:8080/Depth1/depth1/CrawlDepth1-2.html',
'http://localhost:8080/Depth1/depth2/CrawlDepth2-1.html',
'http://localhost:8080/CrawlDepth0-3.html',
'http://localhost:8080/Depth1/CrawlDepth1-3.html']
```

Note that the three pages previously ignored with `DEPTH_LIMIT` set to 1 are now parsed. And now, links found at that depth, such as for the page `CrawlDepth1-3.html`, are now ignored as their depth exceeds 2.

Controlling the length of a crawl

The length of a crawl, in terms of number of pages that can be parsed, can be controlled with the `CLOSESPIDER_PAGECOUNT` setting.

How to do it

We will be using the script in `06/07_limit_length.py`. The script and scraper are the same as the NASA sitemap crawler with the addition of the following configuration to limit the number of pages parsed to 5:

```
if __name__ == "__main__":
    process = CrawlerProcess({
        'LOG_LEVEL': 'INFO',
        'CLOSESPIDER_PAGECOUNT': 5
    })
    process.crawl(Spider)
    process.start()
```

When this is run, the following output will be generated (interspersed in the logging output):

```
<200
https://www.nasa.gov/exploration/systems/sls/multimedia/sls-hardware-being-
moved-on-kamag-transporter.html>
<200 https://www.nasa.gov/exploration/systems/sls/M17-057.html>
<200
https://www.nasa.gov/press-release/nasa-awards-contract-for-center-protecti
ve-services-for-glenn-research-center/>
<200 https://www.nasa.gov/centers/marshall/news/news/icymi1708025/>
<200
https://www.nasa.gov/content/oracles-completed-suit-case-flight-series-to-a
scension-island/>
<200
https://www.nasa.gov/feature/goddard/2017/asteroid-sample-return-mission-su
ccessfully-adjusts-course/>
<200 https://www.nasa.gov/image-feature/jpl/pia21754/juling-crater/>
```

How it works

Note that we set the page limit to 5, but the example actually parsed 7 pages. The value for `CLOSESPIDER_PAGECOUNT` should be considered a value that Scrapy will do as a minimum, but which may be exceeded by a small amount.

Handling paginated websites

Pagination breaks large sets of content into a number of pages. Normally, these pages have a previous/next page link for the user to click. These links can generally be found with XPath or other means and then followed to get to the next page (or previous). Let's examine how to traverse across pages with Scrapy. We'll look at a hypothetical example of crawling the results of an automated internet search. The techniques directly apply to many commercial sites with search capabilities, and are easily modified for those situations.

Getting ready

We will demonstrate handling pagination with an example that crawls a set of pages from the website in the provided container. This website models five pages with previous and next links on each page, along with some embedded data within each page that we will extract.

The first page of the set can be seen at `http://localhost:5001/pagination/page1.html`. The following image shows this page open, and we are inspecting the **Next** button:

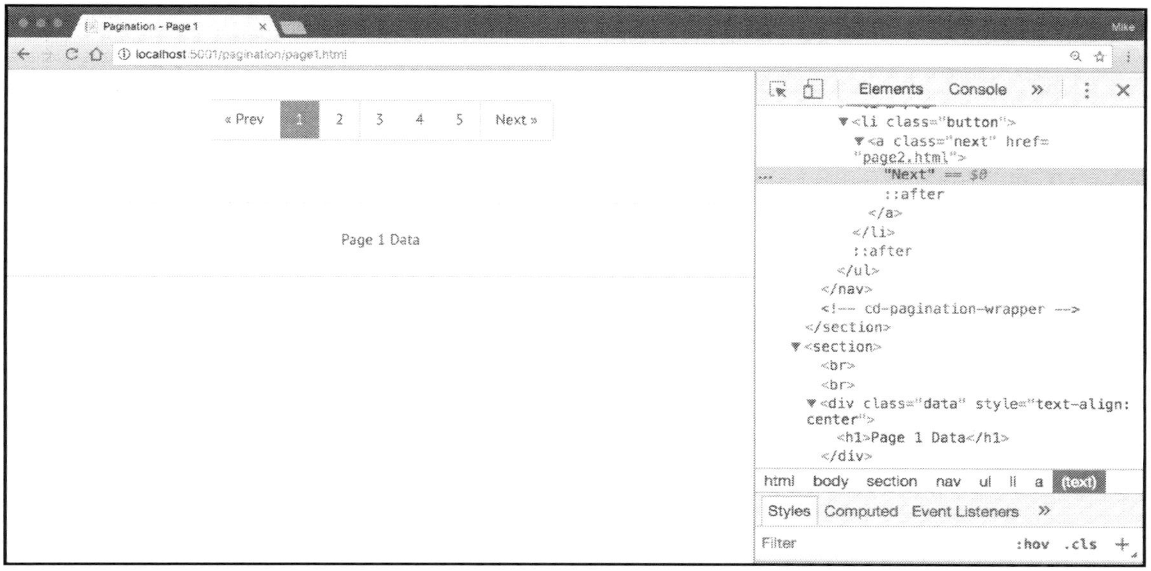

Inspecting the Next button

There are two parts of the page that are of interest. The first is the link for the Next button. It's a fairly common practice that this link has a class that identifies the link as being for the next page. We can use that info to find this link. In this case, we can find it using the following XPath:

```
//*/a[@class='next']
```

The second item of interest is actually retrieving the data we want from the page. On these pages, this is identified by a `<div>` tag with a `class="data"` attribute. These pages only have one data item, but in this example of crawling the pages resulting in a search, we will pull multiple items.

Now let's go and actually run a scraper for these pages.

How to do it

There is a script named `06/08_scrapy_pagination.py`. Run this script with Python and there will be a lot of output from Scrapy, most of which will be the standard Scrapy debugging output. However, within that output you will see that we extracted the data items on all five pages:

```
Page 1 Data
Page 2 Data
Page 3 Data
Page 4 Data
Page 5 Data
```

How it works

The code begins with the definition of `CrawlSpider` and the start URL:

```
class PaginatedSearchResultsSpider(CrawlSpider):
    name = "paginationscraper"
    start_urls = [
"http://localhost:5001/pagination/page1.html"
    ]
```

Then the rules field is defined, which informs Scrapy how to parse each page to look for links. This code uses the XPath discussed earlier to find the Next link in the page. Scrapy will use this rule on every page to find the next page to process, and will queue that request for processing after the current page. For each page that is found, the callback parameter informs Scrapy which method to call for processing, in this case `parse_result_page`:

```
rules = (
# Extract links for next pages
    Rule(LinkExtractor(allow=(),
restrict_xpaths=("//*/a[@class='next']")),
callback='parse_result_page', follow=True),
)
```

A single list variable named `all_items` is declared to hold all the items we find:

```
all_items = []
```

Then the `parse_start_url` method is defined. Scrapy will call this to parse the initial URL in the crawl. The function simply defers that processing to `parse_result_page`:

```
def parse_start_url(self, response):
    return self.parse_result_page(response)
```

The `parse_result_page` method then uses XPath to find the text inside of the `<h1>` tag within the `<div class="data">` tag. It then appends that text to the `all_items` list:

```
def parse_result_page(self, response):
    data_items = response.xpath("//*/div[@class='data']/h1/text()")
for data_item in data_items:
    self.all_items.append(data_item.root)
```

Upon the crawl being completed, the `closed()` method is called and writes out the content of the `all_items` field:

```
def closed(self, reason):
    for i in self.all_items:
        print(i)
```

The crawler is run using Python as a script using the following:

```
if __name__ == "__main__":
    process = CrawlerProcess({
        'LOG_LEVEL': 'DEBUG',
        'CLOSESPIDER_PAGECOUNT': 10
    })
    process.crawl(ImdbSearchResultsSpider)
    process.start()
```

Note the use of the `CLOSESPIDER_PAGECOUNT` property being set to `10`. This exceeds the number of pages on this site, but in many (or most) cases there will likely be thousands of pages in a search result. It's a good practice to stop after an appropriate number of pages. This is good behavior a crawler, as the relevance of items to your search drops dramatically after a few pages, so crawling beyond the first few pages has greatly diminishing returns and it's generally best to stop after a few pages.

There's more...

As mentioned at the start of the recipe, this is easy to modify for various automatic searches on various content sites. This practice can push the limits of acceptable use, so it has been generalized here. But for more actual examples, visit my blog at: `www.smac.io`.

Handling forms and forms-based authorization

We are often required to log into a site before we can crawl its content. This is usually done through a form where we enter a user name and password, press *Enter*, and then granted access to previously hidden content. This type of form authentication is often called cookie authorization, as when we authorize, the server creates a cookie that it can use to verify that you have signed in. Scrapy respects these cookies, so all we need to do is somehow automate the form during our crawl.

Getting ready

We will crawl a page in the containers web site at the following URL: `http://localhost:5001/home/secured`. On this page, and links from that page, there is content we would like to scrape. However, this page is blocked by a login. When opening the page in a browser, we are presented with the following login form, where we can enter `darkhelmet` as the user name and `vespa` as the password:

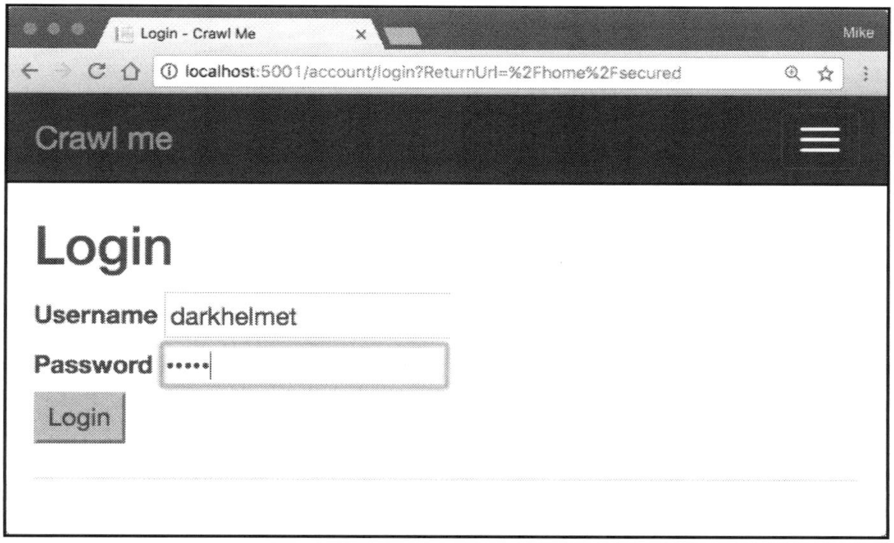

Username and password credentials are entered

Upon pressing *Enter* we are authenticated and taken to our originally desired page.

There's not a great deal of content there, but the message is enough to verify that we have logged in, and our scraper knows that too.

How to do it

We proceed with the recipe as follows:

1. If you examine the HTML for the sign-in page, you will have noticed the following form code:

```
<form action="/Account/Login" method="post"><div>
 <label for="Username">Username</label>
 <input type="text" id="Username" name="Username" value="" />
 <span class="field-validation-valid" data-valmsg-for="Username"
data-valmsg-replace="true"></span></div>
<div>
 <label for="Password">Password</label>
 <input type="password" id="Password" name="Password" />
 <span class="field-validation-valid" data-valmsg-for="Password"
data-valmsg-replace="true"></span>
 </div>
```

```
 <input type="hidden" name="returnUrl" />
<input name="submit" type="submit" value="Login"/>
 <input name="__RequestVerificationToken" type="hidden"
value="CfDJ8CqzjGWzUMJKkKCmxuBIgZf3UkeXZnVKBwRV_Wu4qUkprH8b_2jno5-1
SGSNjFqlFgLie84xI2ZBkhHDzwgUXpz6bbBwER0v_-
fP5iTITiZi2VfyXzLD_beXUp5cgjCS5AtkIayWThJSI36InzBqj2A" /></form>
```

2. To get the form processors in Scrapy to work, we will need the IDs of the username and password fields in this form. They are `Username` and `Password` respectively. Now we can create a spider using this information. This spider is in the script file, `06/09_forms_auth.py`. The spider definition starts with the following:

```
class Spider(scrapy.Spider):
    name = 'spider'
    start_urls = ['http://localhost:5001/home/secured']
    login_user = 'darkhelmet'
    login_pass = 'vespa'
```

3. We define two fields in the class, `login_user` and `login_pass`, to hold the username we want to use. The crawl will also start at the specified URL.
4. The `parse` method is then changed to examine if the page contains a login form. This is done by using XPath to see if there is an input form of type password and with an `id` of `Password`:

```
def parse(self, response):
    print("Parsing: ", response)

    count_of_password_fields =
int(float(response.xpath("count(//*/input[@type='password' and
@id='Password'])").extract()[0]))
    if count_of_password_fields > 0:
        print("Got a password page")
```

5. If that field is found, we then return a `FormRequest` to Scrapy, generated using its `from_response` method:

```
return scrapy.FormRequest.from_response(
    response,
    formdata={'Username': self.login_user, 'Password':
self.login_pass},
    callback=self.after_login)
```

6. This function is passed the response, and then a dictionary specifying the IDs of fields that need data inserted along with those values. A callback is then defined to be executed after this FormRequest is executed by Scrapy, and to which is passed the content of the resulting form:

```
def after_login(self, response):
    if "This page is secured" in str(response.body):
        print("You have logged in ok!")
```

7. This callback simply looks for the words `This page is secured`, which are only returned if the login is successful. When running this successfully, we will see the following output from our scraper's print statements:

```
Parsing: <200
http://localhost:5001/account/login?ReturnUrl=%2Fhome%2Fsecured>
Got a password page
You have logged in ok!
```

How it works

When you create a `FormRequest`, your are instructing Scrapy to construct a form POST request on behalf of your process, using the data in the specified dictionary as the form parameters in the POST request. It constructs this request and sends it to the server. Upon receipt of the answer in that POST, it calls the specified callback function.

There's more...

This technique is also useful in form entries of many other kinds, not just login forms. This can be used to automate, then execute, any type of HTML form request, such as making orders, or those used for executing search operations.

Handling basic authorization

Some websites use a form of authorization known as *basic authorization*. This was popular before other means of authorization, such as cookie auth or OAuth. It is also common on corporate intranets and some web APIs. In basic authorization, a header is added to the HTTP request. This header, `Authorization`, is passed the Basic string and then a base64 encoding of the values `<username>:<password>`. So in the case of darkhelmet, this header would look as follows:

```
Authorization: Basic ZGFya2hlbG1ldDp2ZXNwYQ==, with
ZGFya2hlbG1ldDp2ZXNwYQ== being darkhelmet:vespa base 64 encoded.
```

Note that this is no more secure than sending it in plain-text, (although when performed over HTTPS it is secure.) However, for the most part, is has been subsumed for more robust authorization forms, and even cookie authorization allows for more complex features such as claims:

How to do it

Supporting basic auth in Scrapy is straightforward. To get this to work for a spider and a given site the spider is crawling, simply define the `http_user`, `http_pass`, and `name` fields in your scraper. The following demonstrates:

```
class SomeIntranetSiteSpider(CrawlSpider):
    http_user = 'someuser'
    http_pass = 'somepass'
    name = 'intranet.example.com'
    # .. rest of the spider code omitted ...
```

How it works

When the spider crawls any pages on the given site specified by the name, it will use the values of `http_user` and `http_pass` to construct the appropriate header.

There's more...

Note, this task is performed by the `HttpAuthMiddleware` module of Scrapy. More info on basic authorization is also available at: `https://developer.mozilla.org/en-US/docs/Web/HTTP/Authentication`.

Preventing bans by scraping via proxies

Sometimes you may get blocked by a site that your are scraping because you are identified as a scraper, and sometimes this happens because the webmaster sees the scrape requests coming from a uniform IP, at which point they simply block access to that IP.

To help prevent this problem, it is possible to use proxy randomization middleware within Scrapy. There exists a library, `scrapy-proxies`, which implements a proxy randomization feature.

Getting ready

You can get `scrapy-proxies` from GitHub at `https://github.com/aivarsk/scrapy-proxies` or by installing it using `pip install scrapy_proxies`.

How to do it

Use of `scrapy-proxies` is done by configuration. It starts by configuring `DOWNLOADER_MIDDLEWARES`, and making sure they have `RetryMiddleware`, `RandomProxy`, and `HttpProxyMiddleware` installed. The following would be a typical configuration:

```
# Retry many times since proxies often fail
RETRY_TIMES = 10
# Retry on most error codes since proxies fail for different reasons
RETRY_HTTP_CODES = [500, 503, 504, 400, 403, 404, 408]

DOWNLOADER_MIDDLEWARES = {
 'scrapy.downloadermiddlewares.retry.RetryMiddleware': 90,
 'scrapy_proxies.RandomProxy': 100,
 'scrapy.downloadermiddlewares.httpproxy.HttpProxyMiddleware': 110,
}
```

The the `PROXY_LIST` setting is configured to point to a file containing a list of proxies:

```
PROXY_LIST = '/path/to/proxy/list.txt'
```

Then, we need to let Scrapy know the `PROXY_MODE`:

```
# Proxy mode
# 0 = Every requests have different proxy
# 1 = Take only one proxy from the list and assign it to every requests
# 2 = Put a custom proxy to use in the settings
PROXY_MODE = 0
```

If `PROXY_MODE` is `2`, then you must specify a `CUSTOM_PROXY`:

```
CUSTOM_PROXY = "http://host1:port"
```

How it works

This configuration essentially tells Scrapy that if a request for a page fails with any of the `RETRY_HTTP_CODES`, and for up to `RETRY_TIMES` per URL, then use a proxy from within the file specified by `PROXY_LIST`, and by using the pattern defined by `PROXY_MODE`. With this, you can have Scrapy fail back to any number of proxy servers to retry the request from a different IP address and/or port.

Randomizing user agents

Which user agent you use can have an effect on the success of your scraper. Some websites will flat out refuse to serve content to specific user agents. This can be because the user agent is identified as a scraper that is banned, or the user agent is for an unsupported browser (namely Internet Explorer 6).

Another reason for control over the scraper is that content may be rendered differently by the web server depending on the specified user agent. This is currently common for mobile sites, but it can also be used for desktops, to do things such as delivering simpler content for older browsers.

Therefore, it can be useful to set the user agent to other values than the defaults. Scrapy defaults to a user agent named `scrapybot`. This can be configured by using the `BOT_NAME` parameter. If you use Scrapy projects, Scrapy will set the agent to the name of your project.

For more complicated schemes, there are two popular extensions that can be used: `scrapy-fake-agent` and `scrapy-random-useragent`.

How to do it

We proceed with the recipe as follows:

1. `scrapy-fake-useragent` is available on GitHub at `https://github.com/alecxe/scrapy-fake-useragent`, and `scrapy-random-useragent` is available at `https://github.com/cnu/scrapy-random-useragent`. You can include them using `pip install scrapy-fake-agent` and/or `pip install scrapy-random-useragent`.
2. `scrapy-random-useragent` will select a random user agent for each of your requests from a file. It is configured in two settings:

```
DOWNLOADER_MIDDLEWARES = {
'scrapy.contrib.downloadermiddleware.useragent.UserAgentMiddleware'
: None,
    'random_useragent.RandomUserAgentMiddleware': 400
}
```

3. This disables the existing `UserAgentMiddleware`, and replaces it with the implementation provided in `RandomUserAgentMiddleware`. Then, you configure a reference to a file containing a list of user agent names:

```
USER_AGENT_LIST = "/path/to/useragents.txt"
```

4. Once configured, each request will use a random user agent from the file.
5. `scrapy-fake-useragent` uses a different model. It retrieves user agents from an online database tracking the most common user agents in use. Configuring Scrapy for its use is done with the following settings:

```
DOWNLOADER_MIDDLEWARES = {
    'scrapy.downloadermiddlewares.useragent.UserAgentMiddleware':
None,
    'scrapy_fake_useragent.middleware.RandomUserAgentMiddleware':
400,
}
```

6. It also has the ability to set the type of user agent used, to values such as mobile or desktop, to force selection of user agents in those two categories. This is performed using the `RANDOM_UA_TYPE` setting, which defaults to random.

7. If using `scrapy-fake-useragent` with any proxy middleware, then you may want to randomize per proxy. This can be done by setting `RANDOM_UA_PER_PROXY` to True. Also, you will want to set the priority of `RandomUserAgentMiddleware` to be greater than `scrapy-proxies`, so that the proxy is set before being handled.

Caching responses

Scrapy comes with the ability to cache HTTP requests. This can greatly reduce crawling times if pages have already been visited. By enabling the cache, Scrapy will store every request and response.

How to do it

There is a working example in the `06/10_file_cache.py` script. In Scrapy, caching middleware is disabled by default. To enable this cache, set `HTTPCACHE_ENABLED` to `True` and `HTTPCACHE_DIR` to a directory on the file system (using a relative path will create the directory in the project's data folder). To demonstrate, this script runs a crawl of the NASA site, and caches the content. It is configured using the following:

```
if __name__ == "__main__":
    process = CrawlerProcess({
        'LOG_LEVEL': 'CRITICAL',
        'CLOSESPIDER_PAGECOUNT': 50,
        'HTTPCACHE_ENABLED': True,
        'HTTPCACHE_DIR': "."
    })
    process.crawl(Spider)
    process.start()
```

We ask Scrapy to cache using files and to create a sub-directory in the current folder. We also instruct it to limit the crawl to roughly 500 pages. When running this, the crawl will take roughly a minute (depending on your internet speed), and there will be roughly 500 lines of output.

After the first execution, you can see that there is now a `.scrapy` folder in your directory that contains the cache data. The structure will look like the following:

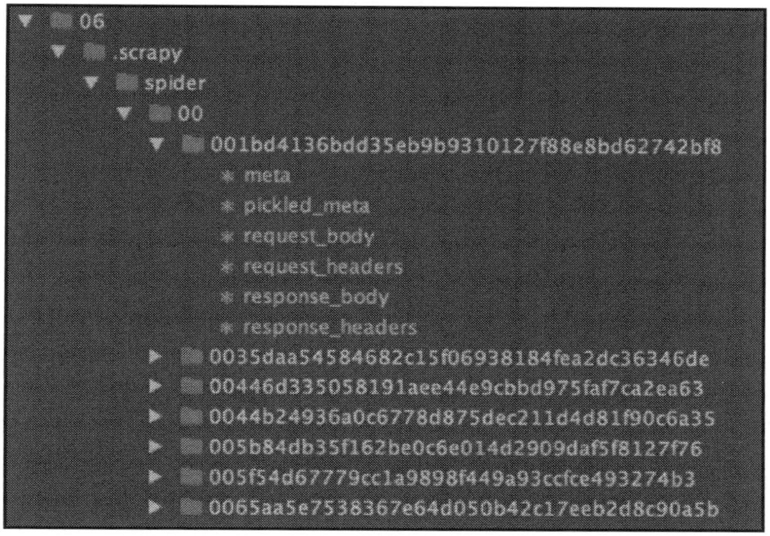

Running the script again will only take a few seconds, and will produce the same output/reporting of pages parsed, except that this time the content will come from the cache instead of HTTP requests.

There's more...

There are many configurations and options for caching in Scrapy. By default, the cache expiration, specified by `HTTPCACHE_EXPIRATION_SECS`, is set to 0. 0 means the cache items never expire, so once written, Scrapy will never request that item via HTTP again. Realistically, you will want to set this to some value that does expire.

File storage for the cache is only one of the options for caching. Items can also be cached in DMB and LevelDB by setting the `HTTPCACHE_STORAGE` setting to `scrapy.extensions.httpcache.DbmCacheStorage` or `scrapy.extensions.httpcache.LeveldbCacheStorage`, respectively. You could also write your own code, to store page content in another type of database or cloud storage if you feel so inclined.

Finally, we come to cache policy. Scrapy comes with two policies built in: Dummy (the default), and RFC2616. This can be set by changing the `HTTPCACHE_POLICY` setting to `scrapy.extensions.httpcache.DummyPolicy` or `scrapy.extensions.httpcache.RFC2616Policy`.

The RFC2616 policy enables HTTP cache-control awareness with operations including the following:

- Do not attempt to store responses/requests with no-store cache-control directive set
- Do not serve responses from cache if no-cache cache-control directive is set even for fresh responses
- Compute freshness lifetime from max-age cache-control directive
- Compute freshness lifetime from Expires response header
- Compute freshness lifetime from Last-Modified response header (heuristic used by Firefox)
- Compute current age from Age response header
- Compute current age from Date header
- Revalidate stale responses based on Last-Modified response header
- Revalidate stale responses based on ETag response header
- Set Date header for any received response missing it
- Support max-stale cache-control directive in requests

7
Text Wrangling and Analysis

In this chapter, we will cover:

- Installing NLTK
- Performing sentence splitting
- Performing tokenization
- Performing stemming
- Performing lemmatization
- Identifying and removing stop words
- Calculating the frequency distribution of words
- Identifying and removing rare words
- Identifying and removing short words
- Removing punctuation marks
- Piecing together n-grams
- Scraping a job listing from StackOverflow
- Reading and cleaning the description in the job listCreating a word cloud from a StackOverflow job listing

Introduction

Mining the data is often the most interesting part of the job, and text is one of the most common data sources. We will be using the NLTK toolkit to introduce common natural language processing concepts and statistical models. Not only do we want to find quantitative data, such as numbers within data that we have scraped, we also want to be able to analyze various characteristics of textual information. This analysis of textual information is often lumped into a category known as natural language processing (NLP). There exists a library for Python, NLTK, that provides rich capabilities. We will investigate several of it's capabilities.

Installing NLTK

In this recipe we learn to install NTLK, the natural language toolkit for Python.

How to do it

We proceed with the recipe as follows:

1. The core of NLTK can be installed using pip:

```
pip install nltk
```

2. Some processes, such as those we will use, require an additional download of various data sets that they use to perform various analyses. They can be downloaded by executing the following:

```
import nltk
nltk.download()
showing info
https://raw.githubusercontent.com/nltk/nltk_data/gh-pages/index.xml
```

3. On a Mac, this actually pops up the following window:

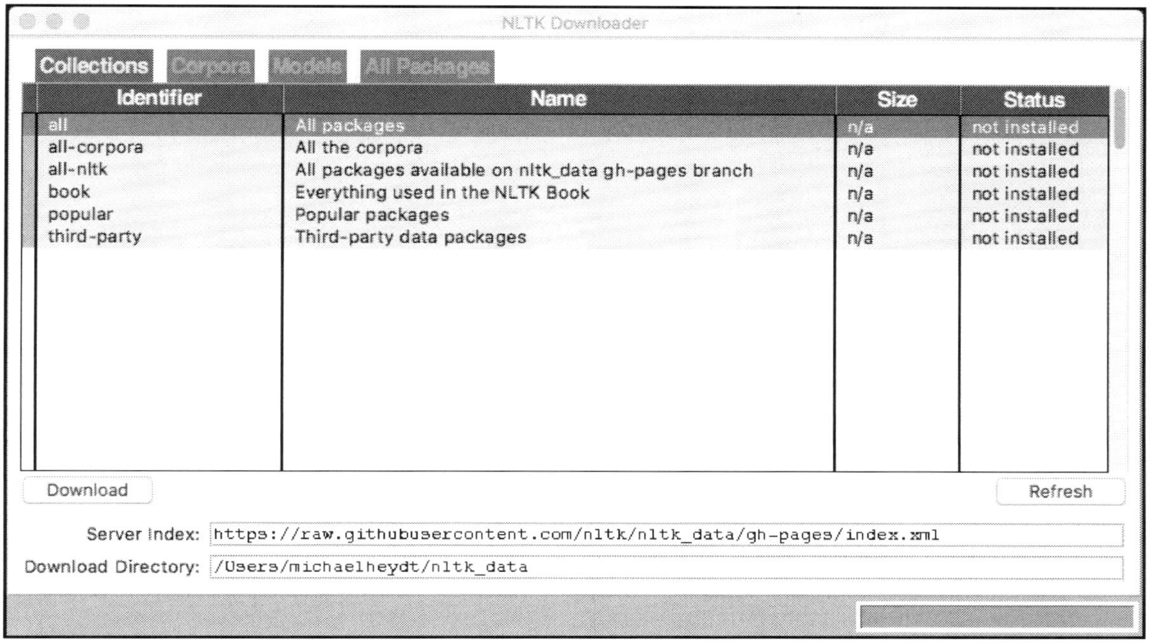

The NTLK GUI

Select install **all** and press the **Download** button. The tools will begin to download a number of data sets. This can take a while, so grab a coffee or beer and check back every now and then. When completed, you are ready to progress to the next recipe.

Performing sentence splitting

Many NLP processes require splitting a large amount of text into sentences. This may seem to be a simple task, but for computers it can be problematic. A simple sentence splitter can look just for periods (.), or use other algorithms such as predictive classifiers. We will examine two means of sentence splitting with NLTK.

How to do it

We will use a sentence stored in thee `07/sentence1.txt` file. It has the following content, which was pulled from a random job listing on StackOverflow:

> *We are seeking developers with demonstrable experience in: ASP.NET, C#, SQL Server, and AngularJS. We are a fast-paced, highly iterative team that has to adapt quickly as our factory grows. We need people who are comfortable tackling new problems, innovating solutions, and interacting with every facet of the company on a daily basis. Creative, motivated, able to take responsibility and support the applications you create. Help us get rockets out the door faster!*

The first example of sentence splitting is in the `07/01_sentence_splitting1.py` file. This uses the built-in sentence splitter in NLTK, which uses an internal boundary detection algorithm:

1. First we import the sentence tokenizer from NLTK:

```
from nltk.tokenize import sent_tokenize
```

2. Then load the file:

```
with open('sentence1.txt', 'r') as myfile:
    data=myfile.read().replace('\n', '')
```

3. Then the sentence is split using `sent_tokenize`, and the sentences are reported:

```
sentences = sent_tokenize(data)

for s in sentences:
    print(s)
```

This results in the following output:

```
We are seeking developers with demonstrable experience in: ASP.NET, C#, SQL
Server, and AngularJS.
We are a fast-paced, highly iterative team that has to adapt quickly as our
factory grows.
We need people who are comfortable tackling new problems, innovating
solutions, and interacting with every facet of the company on a daily
basis.
Creative, motivated, able to take responsibility and support the
applications you create.
Help us get rockets out the door faster!
```

4. If you want to create your own tokenizer and train it yourself, then you can use the `PunktSentenceTokenizer` class. `sent_tokenize` is actually a derived class of this class that implements sentence splitting in English by default. But there are 17 different language models you can pick from:

```
Michaels-iMac-2:~ michaelheydt$ ls ~/nltk_data/tokenizers/punkt
PY3   finnish.pickle  portuguese.pickle
README          french.pickle   slovene.pickle
czech.pickle    german.pickle   spanish.pickle
danish.pickle   greek.pickle    swedish.pickle
dutch.pickle    italian.pickle  turkish.pickle
english.pickle  norwegian.pickle
estonian.pickle polish.pickle
```

5. You can select the desired language by using the language parameter. As an example, the following would split based on using German:

```
sentences = sent_tokenize(data, language="german")
```

There's more...

To learn more about this algorithm, you can read the source paper available at `http://citeseerx.ist.psu.edu/viewdoc/download?doi=10.1.1.85.5017rep=rep1type=pdf`.

Performing tokenization

Tokenization is the process of converting text into tokens. These tokens can be paragraphs, sentences, and common individual words, and are commonly based at the word level. NLTK comes with a number of tokenizers that will be demonstrated in this recipe.

How to do it

The code for this example is in the `07/02_tokenize.py` file. This extends the sentence splitter to demonstrate five different tokenization techniques. The first sentence in the file will be the only one tokenized so that we keep the amount of output to a reasonable amount:

1. The first step is to simply use the built-in Python string `.split()` method. This results in the following:

```
print(first_sentence.split())
['We', 'are', 'seeking', 'developers', 'with', 'demonstrable',
'experience', 'in:', 'ASP.NET,', 'C#,', 'SQL', 'Server,', 'and',
'AngularJS.']
```

The sentence is split on space boundaries. Note that punctuation such as ":" and "," are included in the resulting tokens.

2. The following demonstrates using the tokenizers built into NLTK. First, we need to import them:

```
from nltk.tokenize import word_tokenize, regexp_tokenize,
wordpunct_tokenize, blankline_tokenize
```

The following demonstrates using the `word_tokenizer`:

```
print(word_tokenize(first_sentence))
['We', 'are', 'seeking', 'developers', 'with', 'demonstrable',
'experience', 'in', ':', 'ASP.NET', ',', 'C', '#', ',', 'SQL',
'Server', ',', 'and', 'AngularJS', '.']
```

The result now has also split the punctuation into their own tokens.

The following uses the regex tokenizer, which allows you to apply any regex expression as a tokenizer. It uses a `'\w+'` regex and has the following result:

```
print(regexp_tokenize(first_sentence, pattern='\w+'))
['We', 'are', 'seeking', 'developers', 'with', 'demonstrable',
'experience', 'in', 'ASP', 'NET', 'C', 'SQL', 'Server', 'and', 'AngularJS']
```

The `wordpunct_tokenizer` has the following results:

```
print(wordpunct_tokenize(first_sentence))
['We', 'are', 'seeking', 'developers', 'with', 'demonstrable',
'experience', 'in', ':', 'ASP', '.', 'NET', ',', 'C', '#,', 'SQL',
'Server', ',', 'and', 'AngularJS', '.']
```

And `blankline_tokenize` produces the following:

```
print(blankline_tokenize(first_sentence))
['We are seeking developers with demonstrable experience in: ASP.NET, C#,
SQL Server, and AngularJS.']
```

As can be seen, this is not quite a simple problem as might be thought. Depending upon the type of text being tokenized, you can come out with quite different results.

Performing stemming

Stemming is the process of cutting down a token to its *stem*. Technically, it is the process or reducing inflected (and sometimes derived) words to their word stem - the base root form of the word. As an example, the words *fishing*, *fished*, and *fisher* stem from the root word *fish*. This helps to reduce the set of words being processed into a smaller base set that is more easily processed.

The most common algorithm for stemming was created by Martin Porter, and NLTK provides an implementation of this algorithm in the PorterStemmer. NLTK also provides an implementation of a Snowball stemmer, which was also created by Porter, and designed to handle languages other than English. There is one more implementation provided by NLTK referred to as a Lancaster stemmer. The Lancaster stemmer is considered the most aggressive stemmer of the three.

How to do it

NLTK provides an implementation of the Porter stemming algorithm in its PorterStemmer class. An instance of this can easily be created by the following code:

```
>>> from nltk.stem import PorterStemmer
>>> pst = PorterStemmer()
>>> pst.stem('fishing')
'fish'
```

The script in the `07/03_stemming.py` file applies the Porter and Lancaster stemmers to the first sentence of our input file. The primary section of the code performing the stemming is the following:

```
pst = PorterStemmer()
lst = LancasterStemmer()

print("Stemming results:")

for token in regexp_tokenize(sentences[0], pattern='\w+'):
    print(token, pst.stem(token), lst.stem(token))
```

And this results in the following output:

```
Stemming results:
We We we
are are ar
seeking seek seek
developers develop develop
with with with
demonstrable demonstr demonst
experience experi expery
in in in
ASP asp asp
NET net net
C C c
SQL sql sql
Server server serv
and and and
AngularJS angularj angulars
```

Looking at the results, it can be seen that the Lancaster stemmer is indeed more aggressive than the Porter stemmer, as several of the words have been cut down further with the latter stemmer.

Performing lemmatization

Lemmatization is a more methodical process of converting words to their base. Where stemming generally just chops off the ends of words, lemmatization takes into account the morphological analysis of words, evaluating the context and part of speech to determine the inflected form, and makes a decision between different rules to determine the root.

How to do it

Lemmatization can be utilized in NTLK using the `WordNetLemmatizer`. This class uses the WordNet service, an online semantic database to make its decisions. The code in the `07/04_lemmatization.py` file extends the previous stemming example to also calculate the lemmatization of each word. The code of importance is the following:

```
from nltk.stem import PorterStemmer
from nltk.stem.lancaster import LancasterStemmer
from nltk.stem import WordNetLemmatizer

pst = PorterStemmer()
lst = LancasterStemmer()
wnl = WordNetLemmatizer()

print("Stemming / lemmatization results")
for token in regexp_tokenize(sentences[0], pattern='\w+'):
    print(token, pst.stem(token), lst.stem(token), wnl.lemmatize(token))
```

And it results in the following output:

```
Stemming / lemmatization results
We We we We
are are ar are
seeking seek seek seeking
developers develop develop developer
with with with with
demonstrable demonstr demonst demonstrable
experience experi expery experience
in in in in
ASP asp asp ASP
NET net net NET
C C c C
SQL sql sql SQL
Server server serv Server
and and and and
AngularJS angularj angulars AngularJS
```

There is a small amount of variance in the results using the lemmatization process. The point of this is that, depending upon your data, one of these may be more suitable for your needs than the other, so give all of them a try if needed.

Determining and removing stop words

Stop words are common words that, in a natural language processing situation, do not provide much contextual meaning. These words are often the most common words in a language. These tend to, at least in English, be articles and pronouns, such as *I, me, the, is, which, who, at,* among others. Processing of meaning in documents can often be facilitated by removal of these words before processing, and hence many tools support this ability. NLTK is one of these, and comes with support for stop word removal for roughly 22 languages.

How to do it

Proceed with the recipe as follows (code is available in `07/06_freq_dist.py`):

1. The following demonstrates stop word removal using NLTK. First, start with importing stop words:

```
>>> from nltk.corpus import stopwords
```

2. Then select the stop words for your desired language. The following selects English:

```
>>> stoplist = stopwords.words('english')
```

3. The English stop list has 153 words:

```
>>> len(stoplist)
153
```

4. That's not too many that we can't show them all here:

```
>>> stoplist
 ['i', 'me', 'my', 'myself', 'we', 'our', 'ours', 'ourselves',
'you', 'your', 'yours', 'yourself', 'yourselves', 'he', 'him',
'his', 'himself', 'she', 'her', 'hers', 'herself', 'it', 'its',
'itself', 'they', 'them', 'their', 'theirs', 'themselves', 'what',
'which', 'who', 'whom', 'this', 'that', 'these', 'those', 'am',
'is', 'are', 'was', 'were', 'be', 'been', 'being', 'have', 'has',
'had', 'having', 'do', 'does', 'did', 'doing', 'a', 'an', 'the',
'and', 'but', 'if', 'or', 'because', 'as', 'until', 'while', 'of',
'at', 'by', 'for', 'with', 'about', 'against', 'between', 'into',
'through', 'during', 'before', 'after', 'above', 'below', 'to',
'from', 'up', 'down', 'in', 'out', 'on', 'off', 'over', 'under',
'again', 'further', 'then', 'once', 'here', 'there', 'when',
```

```
'where', 'why', 'how', 'all', 'any', 'both', 'each', 'few', 'more',
'most', 'other', 'some', 'such', 'no', 'nor', 'not', 'only', 'own',
'same', 'so', 'than', 'too', 'very', 's', 't', 'can', 'will',
'just', 'don', 'should', 'now', 'd', 'll', 'm', 'o', 're', 've',
'y', 'ain', 'aren', 'couldn', 'didn', 'doesn', 'hadn', 'hasn',
'haven', 'isn', 'ma', 'mightn', 'mustn', 'needn', 'shan',
'shouldn', 'wasn', 'weren', 'won', 'wouldn']
```

5. The removal of stop words from a list of words can be performed easily with a simple python statement. This is demonstrated in the `07/05_stopwords.py` file. The script starts with the required imports and readies the sentence we want to process:

```
from nltk.tokenize import sent_tokenize
from nltk.tokenize import regexp_tokenize
from nltk.corpus import stopwords

with open('sentence1.txt', 'r') as myfile:
    data = myfile.read().replace('\n', '')

sentences = sent_tokenize(data)
first_sentence = sentences[0]

print("Original sentence:")
print(first_sentence)
```

6. This yields the following output, which we are familiar with:

```
Original sentence:
We are seeking developers with demonstrable experience in: ASP.NET,
C#, SQL Server, and AngularJS.
```

7. Next we tokenize that sentence:

```
tokenized = regexp_tokenize(first_sentence, '\w+')
print("Tokenized:", tokenized)
```

8. With the following output:

```
Tokenized: ['We', 'are', 'seeking', 'developers', 'with',
'demonstrable', 'experience', 'in', 'ASP', 'NET', 'C', 'SQL',
'Server', 'and', 'AngularJS']
```

9. Then we can remove tokens that are in the stop list with the following statements:

```
stoplist = stopwords.words('english')
cleaned = [word for word in tokenized if word not in stoplist]
print("Cleaned:", cleaned)
```

Using the following output:

```
Cleaned: ['We', 'seeking', 'developers', 'demonstrable', 'experience',
'ASP', 'NET', 'C', 'SQL', 'Server', 'AngularJS']
```

There's more...

Stop word removal has its purposes. It is helpful, as we will see in a later recipe where we create a word cloud (stop words don't give much information in a word cloud), but can also be detrimental. Many other NLP processes that deduce meaning based upon sentence structure can be greatly hampered by their removal.

Calculating the frequency distributions of words

A frequency distribution counts the number of occurrences of distinct data values. These are of value as we can use them to determine which words or phrases within a document are most common, and from that infer those that have greater or lesser value.

Frequency distributions can be calculated using several different techniques. We will examine them using the facilities built into NLTK.

How to do it

NLTK provides a class, `ntlk.probabilities.FreqDist`, that allow us to very easily calculate the frequency distribution of values in a list. Let's examine using this class (code is in `07/freq_dist.py`):

1. To create a frequency distribution using NLTK, start by importing the feature from NTLK (and also tokenizers and stop words):

```
from nltk.probabilities import FreqDist
from nltk.tokenize import regexp_tokenize
from nltk.corpus import stopwords
```

2. Then we can use the `FreqDist` function to create a frequency distribution given a list of words. We will examine this by reading in the contents of `wotw.txt` (The War of the Worlds - courtesy of Gutenberg), tokenizing, and removing stop words:

```
with open('wotw.txt', 'r') as file:
    data = file.read()
tokens = [word.lower() for word in regexp_tokenize(data, '\w+')]
stoplist = stopwords.words('english')
without_stops = [word for word in tokens if word not in stoplist]
```

3. We can then calculate the frequency distribution of the remaining words:

```
freq_dist = FreqDist(without_stops)
```

4. `freq_dist` is a dictionary of words to the counts of those words. The following prints all of them (only a few lines of output shown as there are thousands of unique words):

```
print('Number of words: %s' % len(freq_dist))
for key in freq_dist.keys():
    print(key, freq_dist[key])
Number of words: 6613
shall 8
dwell 1
worlds 2
inhabited 1
lords 1
world 26
things 64
```

5. We can use the frequency distribution to identify the most common words. The following reports the 10 most common words:

```
print(freq_dist.most_common(10))
[('one', 201), ('upon', 172), ('said', 166), ('martians', 164),
('people', 159), ('came', 151), ('towards', 129), ('saw', 129),
('man', 126), ('time', 122)]
```

I was hoping that martians was in the top 5. It's number 4.

There's more...

We can also use this to identify the least common words, by slicing the result of `.most_common()` with a negative value. As an example, the following finds the 10 least common words:

```
print(freq_dist.most_common()[-10:])
[('bitten', 1), ('gibber', 1), ('fiercer', 1), ('paler', 1), ('uglier', 1),
('distortions', 1), ('haunting', 1), ('mockery', 1), ('beds', 1), ('seers',
1)]
```

There are quite a few words with only one occurrence, so this only gets a subset of those values. The number of words with only one occurrence can be determined by the following (truncated due to there being 3,224 words):

```
dist_1 = [item[0] for item in freq_dist.items() if item[1] == 1]
print(len(dist_1), dist_1)

3224 ['dwell', 'inhabited', 'lords', 'kepler', 'quoted', 'eve', 'mortal',
'scrutinised', 'studied', 'scrutinise', 'multiply', 'complacency', 'globe',
'infusoria', ...
```

Identifying and removing rare words

We can remove words with low occurences by leveraging the ability to find words with low frequency counts, that fall outside of a certain deviation of the norm, or just from a list of words considered to be rare within the given domain. But the technique we will use works the same for either.

How to do it

Rare words can be removed by building a list of those rare words and then removing them from the set of tokens being processed. The list of rare words can be determined by using the frequency distribution provided by NTLK. Then you decide what threshold should be used as a rare word threshold:

1. The script in the `07/07_rare_words.py` file extends that of the frequency distribution recipe to identify words with two or fewer occurrences and then removes those words from the tokens:

```
with open('wotw.txt', 'r') as file:
    data = file.read()

tokens = [word.lower() for word in regexp_tokenize(data, '\w+')]
stoplist = stopwords.words('english')
without_stops = [word for word in tokens if word not in stoplist]

freq_dist = FreqDist(without_stops)

print('Number of words: %s' % len(freq_dist))

# all words with one occurrence
dist = [item[0] for item in freq_dist.items() if item[1] <= 2]
print(len(dist))
not_rare = [word for word in without_stops if word not in dist]

freq_dist2 = FreqDist(not_rare)
print(len(freq_dist2))
```

The output results in:

```
Number of words: 6613
4361
2252
```

Through these two steps, removing stop words and then words with 2 or fewer occurrences, we have moved the total number of words from 6,613 to 2,252, which is roughly one third.

Identifying and removing rare words

Removal of short words can also be useful in removing noise words from the content. The following examines removing words of a certain length or shorter. It also demonstrates the opposite by selecting the words not considered short (having a length of more than the specified short word length).

How to do it

We can leverage the frequency distribution from NLTK to efficiently calculate the short words. We could just scan all of the words in the source, but it is simply more efficient to scan the lengths of all of the keys in the resulting distribution as it will be a significantly smaller set of data:

1. The script in the `07/08_short_words.py` file exemplifies this process. It starts by loading the content of `wotw.txt` and then calculating the word frequency distribution (after short word removal). Then it identifies the words of thee characters or less:

```
short_word_len = 3
short_words = [word for word in freq_dist.keys() if len(word) <=
short_word_len]
print('Distinct # of words of len <= %s: %s' % (short_word_len,
len(short_words)))
```

This results in:

```
Distinct # of words of len <= 3: 184
```

2. The words not considered short can be found by changing the logic operator in the list comprehension:

```
unshort_words = [word for word in freq_dist.keys() if len(word) >
short_word_len]
print('Distinct # of word > len %s: %s' % (short_word_len,
len(unshort_words)))
```

And results in:

```
Distinct # of word > len 3: 6429
```

Removing punctuation marks

Depending upon the tokenizer used, and the input to those tokenizers, it may be desired to remove punctuation from the resulting list of tokens. The `regexp_tokenize` function with `'\w+'` as the expression removes punctuation well, but `word_tokenize` does not do it very well and will return many punctuation marks as their own tokens.

How to do it

Removing punctuation marks from our tokens is done similarly to the removal of other words within our tokens by using a list comprehension and only selecting those items that are not punctuation marks. The script `07/09_remove_punctuation.py` file demonstrates this. Let's walk through the process:

1. We'll start with the following, which will `word_tokenize` a string from a job listing:

```
>>> content = "Strong programming experience in C#, ASP.NET/MVC,
JavaScript/jQuery and SQL Server"
>>> tokenized = word_tokenize(content)
>>> stop_list = stopwords.words('english')
>>> cleaned = [word for word in tokenized if word not in stop_list]
>>> print(cleaned)
['Strong', 'programming', 'experience', 'C', '#', ',',
'ASP.NET/MVC', ',', 'JavaScript/jQuery', 'SQL', 'Server']
```

2. Now we can remove the punctuation with the following:

```
>>> punctuation_marks = [':', ',', '.', "``", "''", '(', ')', '-',
'!', '#']
>>> tokens_cleaned = [word for word in cleaned if word not in
punctuation_marks]
>>> print(tokens_cleaned)
['Strong', 'programming', 'experience', 'C', 'ASP.NET/MVC',
'JavaScript/jQuery', 'SQL', 'Server']
```

3. This process can be encapsulated in a function. The following is in the `07/punctuation.py` file, and will remove punctuation:

```
def remove_punctuation(tokens):
    punctuation = [':', ',', '.', "``", "''", '(', ')', '-', '!',
'#']
    return [token for token in tokens if token not in punctuation]
```

There's more...

Removal of punctuation and symbols can be a difficult problem. While they don't add value to many searches, punctuation can also be required to be kept as part of a token. Take the case of searching a job site and trying to find C# programming positions, such as in the example in this recipe. The tokenization of C# gets split into two tokens:

```
>>> word_tokenize("C#")
['C', '#']
```

We actually have two problems here. By having C and # separated, we lost knowledge of C# being in the source content. And then if we removed the # from the tokens, then we lose that information as we also cannot reconstruct C# from adjacent tokens.

Piecing together n-grams

Much has been written about NLTK being used to identify n-grams within text. An n-gram is a set of words, *n* words in length, that are common within a document/corpus (occurring 2 or more times). A 2-gram is any two words commonly repeated, a 3-gram is a three word phrase, and so on. We will not look into determining the n-grams in a document. We will focus on reconstructing known n-grams from our token streams, as we will consider those n-grams to be more important to a search result than the 2 or 3 independent words found in any order.

In the domain of parsing job listings, important 2-grams can be things such as **Computer Science**, **SQL Server**, **Data Science**, and **Big Data**. Additionally, we could consider C# a 2-gram of `'C'` and `'#'`, and hence why we might not want to use the regex parser or `'#'` as punctuation when processing a job listing.

We need to have a strategy to recognize these known combinations from out token stream. Let's look at how to do this.

How to do it

First, this example does not intend to make an exhaustive examination or one that is optimally performant. Just one that is simple to understand and can be easily applied and extended to our example of parsing job listings:

1. We will examine this process using the following sentences from a `StackOverflow` job listing for SpaceX:

   We are seeking developers with demonstrable experience in: ASP.NET, C#, SQL Server, and AngularJS. We are a fast-paced, highly iterative team that has to adapt quickly as our factory grows.

2. There are a number of high value 2-grams in these two sentences (and I think job listings are a great place to look for 2-grams). Just looking at it, I can pick out the following as being important:

- ASP.NET
- C#
- SQL Server
- fast-paced
- highly iterative
- adapt quickly
- demonstrable experience

3. Now, while these may not be 2-grams in the technical definition, when we parse them, they will all be separated into independent tokens. This can be shown in the `07/10-ngrams.py` file, and in the following example:

```
from nltk.tokenize import word_tokenize
from nltk.corpus import stopwords

with open('job-snippet.txt', 'r') as file:
    data = file.read()

tokens = [word.lower() for word in word_tokenize(data)]
stoplist = stopwords.words('english')
without_stops = [word for word in tokens if word not in stoplist]
print(without_stops)
```

This produces the following output:

```
['seeking', 'developers', 'demonstrable', 'experience', ':', 'asp.net',
',', 'c', '#', ',', 'sql', 'server', ',', 'angularjs', '.', 'fast-paced',
',', 'highly', 'iterative', 'team', 'adapt', 'quickly', 'factory', 'grows',
'.']
```

We want to remove punctuation from this set, but we would like to do it after constructing some 2-grams, specifically so that we can piece "C#" back into a single token.

4. The script in the `07/10-reconstruct-2grams.py` file demonstrates a function to facilitate this. First, we need to describe the 2-grams that we want to reconstruct. In this file, they are defined as the following:

```
grams = {
    "c": [{"#": ""}],
    "sql": [{"server": " "}],
    "fast": [{"paced": "-"}],
    "highly": [{"iterative": " "}],
    "adapt": [{"quickly": " "}],
    "demonstrable": [{"experience", " "}]
}
```

`grams` is a dictionary, where the keys specify the `"Left"` side of the 2-gram. Each key has a list of dictionaries, where each dictionary key can be the right side of the 2-gram, and the value is a string that will be placed between the left and right.

5. With this definition, we are able to see `"C"` and `"#"` in our tokens be reconstructed to "C#". `"SQL"` and `"Server"` will be `"SQL Server"`. `"fast"` and `"paced"` will result in `"faced-paced"`.
So we just need a function to make this all work. This function is defined in the `07/buildgrams.py` file:

```
def build_2grams(tokens, patterns):
    results = []
    left_token = None
    for i, t in enumerate(tokens):
        if left_token is None:
            left_token = t
            continue

        right_token = t

        if left_token.lower() in patterns:
            right = patterns[left_token.lower()]
            if right_token.lower() in right:
```

```
                results.append(left_token +
right[right_token.lower()] + right_token)
                left_token = None
            else:
                results.append(left_token)
        else:
            results.append(left_token)
            left_token = right_token

    if left_token is not None:
        results.append(left_token)
    return results
```

6. This function, given a set of tokens and a dictionary in the format described earlier, will return a revised set of tokens with any matching 2-grams put into a single token. The following demonstrates some simple cases of its use:

```
grams = {
    'c': {'#': ''}
}
print(build_2grams(['C'], grams))
print(build_2grams(['#'], grams))
print(build_2grams(['C', '#'], grams))
print(build_2grams(['c', '#'], grams))
```

This results in the following output:

```
['C']
['#']
['C#']
['c#']
```

7. Now let's apply it to our input. The complete script for this is in the `07/10-reconstruct-2grams.py` file (and adds a few 2-grams):

```
grams = {
    "c": {"#": ""},
    "sql": {"server": " "},
    "fast": {"paced": "-"},
    "highly": {"iterative": " "},
    "adapt": {"quickly": " "},
    "demonstrable": {"experience": " "},
    "full": {"stack": " "},
    "enterprise": {"software": " "},
    "bachelor": {"s": "'"},
    "computer": {"science": " "},
    "data": {"science":  " "},
```

```
        "current": {"trends": " "},
        "real": {"world": " "},
        "paid": {"relocation": " "},
        "web": {"server": " "},
        "relational": {"database": " "},
        "no": {"sql": " "}
    }

with open('job-snippet.txt', 'r') as file:
    data = file.read()

tokens = word_tokenize(data)
stoplist = stopwords.words('english')
without_stops = [word for word in tokens if word not in stoplist]
result = remove_punctuation(build_2grams(without_stops, grams))
print(result)
```

The results are the following:

```
['We', 'seeking', 'developers', 'demonstrable experience', 'ASP.NET', 'C#',
'SQL Server', 'AngularJS', 'We', 'fast-paced', 'highly iterative', 'team',
'adapt quickly', 'factory', 'grows']
```

Perfect!

There's more...

We are providing a dictionary to the `build_2grams()` function that defines rules for identifying 2-grams. In this example, we predefined these 2-grams. It is possible to use NLTK to find 2-grams (and n-grams in general), but with this small sample of one job positing, it's likely that none will be found.

Scraping a job listing from StackOverflow

Now let's pull a bit of this together to scrape information from a StackOverflow job listing. We are going to look at just one listing at this time so that we can learn the structure of these pages and pull information from them. In later chapters, we will look at aggregating results from multiple listings. Let's now just learn how to do this.

Getting ready

StackOverflow actually makes it quite easy to scrape data from their pages. We are going to use content from a posting at `https://stackoverflow.com/jobs/122517/spacex-enterprise-software-engineer-full-stack-spacex?so=p&sec=True&pg=1&offset=22&cl=Amazon%3b+`. This likely will not be available at the time you read it, so I've included the HTML of this page in the `07/spacex-job-listing.html` file, which we will use for the examples in this chapter.

StackOverflow job listings pages are very structured. It's probably because they're created by programmers and for programmers. The page (at the time of writing) looks like the following:

A StackOverflow job listing

All of this information is codified within the HTML of the page. You can see for yourself by analyzing the page content. But what StackOverflow does that is so great is that it puts much of its page data in an embedded JSON object. This is placed within a `<script type="application/ld+json">` HTML tag, so it's really easy to find. The following shows a truncated section of this tag (the description is truncated, but all the tags are shown):

```
<script type="application/ld+json">
{
  "@context": "http://schema.org",
  "@type": "JobPosting",
  "title": "SpaceX Enterprise Software Engineer, Full Stack",
  "skills": [
    "c#",
    "sql",
    "javascript",
    "asp.net",
    "angularjs"
  ],
  "description": "<h2>About this job</h2>\r\n<p><span>Location
<span>Industry: <strong>Aerospace, Information Technology, Web
<br/><h2>Job description</h2> <p><strong>Full Stack Enterprise&
financial systems, the restaurant, and even the public home pag
are seeking developers with demonstrable experience in: ASP.NET
the company on a daily basis. Creative, motivated, able to take
mathematics, or similar technical discipline.</li>\r\n<li>3+ ye
Understanding of SQL. Ability to write performant SQL. Ability
Demonstrated ability creating rich web interfaces using a moder
site, and rich client side application from scratch.</li>\r\n<l
development as it changes rapidly. Strong knowledge of computer
  "datePosted": "2017-11-01",
  "validThrough": "2018-09-30",
  "employmentType": "FULL_TIME",
  "experienceRequirements": "Mid-Level, Senior",
  "industry": [
    "Aerospace",
    "Information Technology",
    "Web Development"
  ],
  "jobBenefits": [
    "Stock Awards and 401k plan",
    "Full medical, dental, and vision insurance",
    "Free gym membership",
    "In-house restaurant, coffee bar, and frozen yogurt",
    "Flexible work hours",
    "Relocation expenses covered",
    "Onsite Dental",
    "Onsite Medical Clinic"
  ],
  "hiringOrganization": {
    "@type": "Organization",
    "name": "SpaceX",
    "sameAs": "http://www.spacex.com",
    "logo": "https://i.stack.imgur.com/ZrgLD.png",
    "description": "<p>SpaceX was founded under the belief that
Mars.</p>"
  },
  "jobLocation": [
    {
      "@type": "Place",
      "address": {
        "@type": "PostalAddress",
        "addressCountry": "US",
        "addressRegion": "CA",
        "addressLocality": "Hawthorne",
        "streetAddress": "Rocket Road",
        "postalCode": "90250"
      }
    }
  ]
}
</script>
```

The JSON embedded in a job listing

This makes it very easy to get the content, as we can simply retrieve the page, find this tag, and then convert this JSON into a Python object with the `json` library. In addition to the actual job description, is also included much of the "**metadata**" of the job posting, such as skills, industries, benefits, and location information. We don't need to search the HTML for the information - just find this tag and load the JSON. Note that if we want to find items, such as **Job Responsibilities,** we still need to parse the description. Also note that the description contains full HTML, so when parsing that, we would need to still deal with HTML tags.

How to do it

Let's go and get the job description from this page. We will simply retrieve the contents in this recipe. We will clean it up in the next recipe.

The full code for this example is in the `07/12_scrape_job_stackoverflow.py` file. Let's walk through it:

1. First we read the file:

```
with open("spacex-job-listing.txt", "r") as file:
    content = file.read()
```

2. Then we load the content into a `BeautifulSoup` object, and retrieve the `<script type="application/ld+json">` tag:

```
bs = BeautifulSoup(content, "lxml")
script_tag = bs.find("script", {"type": "application/ld+json"})
```

3. Now that we have that tag, we can load its contents into a Python dictionary using the `json` library:

```
job_listing_contents = json.loads(script_tag.contents[0])
print(job_listing_contents)
```

The output of this looks like the following (this is truncated for brevity):


```
{'@context': 'http://schema.org', '@type': 'JobPosting', 'title': 'SpaceX
Enterprise Software Engineer, Full Stack', 'skills': ['c#', 'sql',
'javascript', 'asp.net', 'angularjs'], 'description': '<h2>About this
job</h2>\r\n<p><span>Location options: <strong>Paid
relocation</strong></span><br/><span>Job type:
<strong>Permanent</strong></span><br/><span>Experience level: <strong>Mid-
Level, Senior</strong></span><br/><span>Role: <strong>Full Stack
Developer</strong></span><br/><span>Industry: <strong>Aerospace,
Information Technology, Web Development</strong></span><br/><span>Company
size: <strong>1k-5k people</strong></span><br/><span>Company type:
<strong>Private</strong></span><br/></p><br/><br/><h2>Technologies</h2>
<p>c#, sql, javascript, asp.net, angularjs</p> <br/><br/><h2>Job
description</h2> <p><strong>Full Stack Enterprise Software
Engineer</strong></p>\r\n<p>The EIS (Enterprise Information Systems) team
writes the software that builds rockets and powers SpaceX. We are
responsible for
```


4. This is great because we can now do some simple tasks with this without involving HTML parsing. As an example, we can retrieve the skills required for the job with just the following code:

```
# print the skills
for skill in job_listing_contents["skills"]:
    print(skill)
```

It produces the following output:

```
c#
sql
javascript
asp.net
angularjs
```

There's more...

The description is still stored in HTML within the description property of this JSON object. We will examine the parsing of that data in the next recipe.

Reading and cleaning the description in the job listing

The description of the job listing is still in HTML. We will want to extract the valuable content out of this data, so we will need to parse this HTML and perform tokenization, stop word removal, common word removal, do some tech 2-gram processing, and in general all of those different processes. Let's look at doing these.

Getting ready

I have collapsed the code for determining tech-based 2-grams into the `07/tech2grams.py` file. We will use the `tech_2grams` function within the file.

How to do it...

The code for this example is in the `07/13_clean_jd.py` file. It continues on where the `07/12_scrape_job_stackoverflow.py` file ends:

1. We start by creating a `BeautifulSoup` object from the description key of the description we loaded. We will also print this to see what it looks like:

```
desc_bs = BeautifulSoup(job_listing_contents["description"],
"lxml")
print(desc_bs)

<p><span>Location options: <strong>Paid
relocation</strong></span><br/><span>Job type:
<strong>Permanent</strong></span><br/><span>Experience level:
<strong>Mid-Level, Senior</strong></span><br/><span>Role:
<strong>Full Stack Developer</strong></span><br/><span>Industry:
<strong>Aerospace, Information Technology, Web
Development</strong></span><br/><span>Company size: <strong>1k-5k
people</strong></span><br/><span>Company type:
<strong>Private</strong></span><br/></p><br/><br/><h2>Technologies<
/h2> <p>c#, sql, javascript, asp.net, angularjs</p>
<br/><br/><h2>Job description</h2> <p><strong>Full Stack Enterprise
Software Engineer</strong></p>
<p>The EIS (Enterprise Information Systems) team writes the
software that builds rockets and powers SpaceX. We are responsible
for all of the software on the factory floor, the warehouses, the
financial systems, the restaurant, and even the public home page.
```

```
Elon has called us the "nervous system" of SpaceX because we
connect all of the other teams at SpaceX to ensure that the entire
rocket building process runs smoothly.</p>
<p><strong>Responsibilities:</strong></p>
<ul>
<li>We are seeking developers with demonstrable experience in:
ASP.NET, C#, SQL Server, and AngularJS. We are a fast-paced, highly
iterative team that has to adapt quickly as our factory grows. We
need people who are comfortable tackling new problems, innovating
solutions, and interacting with every facet of the company on a
daily basis. Creative, motivated, able to take responsibility and
support the applications you create. Help us get rockets out the
door faster!</li>
</ul>
<p><strong>Basic Qualifications:</strong></p>
<ul>
<li>Bachelor's degree in computer science, engineering, physics,
mathematics, or similar technical discipline.</li>
<li>3+ years of experience developing across a full-stack:  Web
server, relational database, and client-side
(HTML/Javascript/CSS).</li>
</ul>
<p><strong>Preferred Skills and Experience:</strong></p>
<ul>
<li>Database - Understanding of SQL. Ability to write performant
SQL. Ability to diagnose queries, and work with DBAs.</li>
<li>Server - Knowledge of how web servers operate on a low-level.
Web protocols. Designing APIs. How to scale web sites. Increase
performance and diagnose problems.</li>
<li>UI - Demonstrated ability creating rich web interfaces using a
modern client side framework. Good judgment in UX/UI design.
Understands the finer points of HTML, CSS, and Javascript - know
which tools to use when and why.</li>
<li>System architecture - Knowledge of how to structure a database,
web site, and rich client side application from scratch.</li>
<li>Quality - Demonstrated usage of different testing patterns,
continuous integration processes, build deployment systems.
Continuous monitoring.</li>
<li>Current - Up to date with current trends, patterns, goings on
in the world of web development as it changes rapidly. Strong
knowledge of computer science fundamentals and applying them in the
real-world.</li>
</ul> <br/><br/></body></html>
```

2. We want to go through this and remove all of the HTML and only be left with the text of the description. That will be what we then tokenize. Fortunately, throwing out all the HTML tags is easy with `BeautifulSoup`:

```
just_text = desc_bs.find_all(text=True)
print(just_text)

['About this job', '\n', 'Location options: ', 'Paid relocation',
'Job type: ', 'Permanent', 'Experience level: ', 'Mid-Level,
Senior', 'Role: ', 'Full Stack Developer', 'Industry: ',
'Aerospace, Information Technology, Web Development', 'Company
size: ', '1k-5k people', 'Company type: ', 'Private',
'Technologies', ' ', 'c#, sql, javascript, asp.net, angularjs', '
', 'Job description', ' ', 'Full Stack Enterprise\xa0Software
Engineer', '\n', 'The EIS (Enterprise Information Systems) team
writes the software that builds rockets and powers SpaceX. We are
responsible for all of the software on the factory floor, the
warehouses, the financial systems, the restaurant, and even the
public home page. Elon has called us the "nervous system" of SpaceX
because we connect all of the other teams at SpaceX to ensure that
the entire rocket building process runs smoothly.', '\n',
'Responsibilities:', '\n', '\n', 'We are seeking developers with
demonstrable experience in: ASP.NET, C#, SQL Server, and AngularJS.
We are a fast-paced, highly iterative team that has to adapt
quickly as our factory grows. We need people who are comfortable
tackling new problems, innovating solutions, and interacting with
every facet of the company on a daily basis. Creative, motivated,
able to take responsibility and support the applications you
create. Help us get rockets out the door faster!', '\n', '\n',
'Basic Qualifications:', '\n', '\n', "Bachelor's degree in computer
science, engineering, physics, mathematics, or similar technical
discipline.", '\n', '3+ years of experience developing across a
full-stack:\xa0 Web server, relational database, and client-side
(HTML/Javascript/CSS).', '\n', '\n', 'Preferred Skills and
Experience:', '\n', '\n', 'Database - Understanding of SQL. Ability
to write performant SQL. Ability to diagnose queries, and work with
DBAs.', '\n', 'Server - Knowledge of how web servers operate on a
low-level. Web protocols. Designing APIs. How to scale web sites.
Increase performance and diagnose problems.', '\n', 'UI -
Demonstrated ability creating rich web interfaces using a modern
client side framework. Good judgment in UX/UI design.\xa0
Understands the finer points of HTML, CSS, and Javascript - know
which tools to use when and why.', '\n', 'System architecture -
Knowledge of how to structure a database, web site, and rich client
side application from scratch.', '\n', 'Quality - Demonstrated
usage of different testing patterns, continuous integration
processes, build deployment systems. Continuous monitoring.', '\n',
```

```
'Current - Up to date with current trends, patterns, goings on in
the world of web development as it changes rapidly. Strong
knowledge of computer science fundamentals and applying them in the
real-world.', '\n', ' ']
```

Just super! We now have this, and it is already broken down into what can be considered sentences!

3. Let's join these all together, word tokenize them, get rid of stop words, and also apply common tech job 2-grams:

```
joined = ' '.join(just_text)
tokens = word_tokenize(joined)

stop_list = stopwords.words('english')
with_no_stops = [word for word in tokens if word not in stop_list]
cleaned = remove_punctuation(two_grammed)
print(cleaned)
```

And this has the following output:

```
['job', 'Location', 'options', 'Paid relocation', 'Job', 'type',
'Permanent', 'Experience', 'level', 'Mid-Level', 'Senior', 'Role', 'Full-
Stack', 'Developer', 'Industry', 'Aerospace', 'Information Technology',
'Web Development', 'Company', 'size', '1k-5k', 'people', 'Company', 'type',
'Private', 'Technologies', 'c#', 'sql', 'javascript', 'asp.net',
'angularjs', 'Job', 'description', 'Full-Stack', 'Enterprise Software',
'Engineer', 'EIS', 'Enterprise', 'Information', 'Systems', 'team',
'writes', 'software', 'builds', 'rockets', 'powers', 'SpaceX',
'responsible', 'software', 'factory', 'floor', 'warehouses', 'financial',
'systems', 'restaurant', 'even', 'public', 'home', 'page', 'Elon',
'called', 'us', 'nervous', 'system', 'SpaceX', 'connect', 'teams',
'SpaceX', 'ensure', 'entire', 'rocket', 'building', 'process', 'runs',
'smoothly', 'Responsibilities', 'seeking', 'developers', 'demonstrable
experience', 'ASP.NET', 'C#', 'SQL Server', 'AngularJS', 'fast-paced',
'highly iterative', 'team', 'adapt quickly', 'factory', 'grows', 'need',
'people', 'comfortable', 'tackling', 'new', 'problems', 'innovating',
'solutions', 'interacting', 'every', 'facet', 'company', 'daily', 'basis',
'Creative', 'motivated', 'able', 'take', 'responsibility', 'support',
'applications', 'create', 'Help', 'us', 'get', 'rockets', 'door', 'faster',
'Basic', 'Qualifications', 'Bachelor', "'s", 'degree', 'computer science',
'engineering', 'physics', 'mathematics', 'similar', 'technical',
'discipline', '3+', 'years', 'experience', 'developing', 'across', 'full-
stack', 'Web server', 'relational database', 'client-side',
'HTML/Javascript/CSS', 'Preferred', 'Skills', 'Experience', 'Database',
'Understanding', 'SQL', 'Ability', 'write', 'performant', 'SQL', 'Ability',
'diagnose', 'queries', 'work', 'DBAs', 'Server', 'Knowledge', 'web',
```

```
'servers', 'operate', 'low-level', 'Web', 'protocols', 'Designing', 'APIs',
'scale', 'web', 'sites', 'Increase', 'performance', 'diagnose', 'problems',
'UI', 'Demonstrated', 'ability', 'creating', 'rich', 'web', 'interfaces',
'using', 'modern', 'client-side', 'framework', 'Good', 'judgment', 'UX/UI',
'design', 'Understands', 'finer', 'points', 'HTML', 'CSS', 'Javascript',
'know', 'tools', 'use', 'System', 'architecture', 'Knowledge', 'structure',
'database', 'web', 'site', 'rich', 'client-side', 'application', 'scratch',
'Quality', 'Demonstrated', 'usage', 'different', 'testing', 'patterns',
'continuous integration', 'processes', 'build', 'deployment', 'systems',
'Continuous monitoring', 'Current', 'date', 'current trends', 'patterns',
'goings', 'world', 'web development', 'changes', 'rapidly', 'Strong',
'knowledge', 'computer science', 'fundamentals', 'applying', 'real-world']
```

I think that's a very nice and refined set of keywords pulled out of that job listing.

8

Searching, Mining and Visualizing Data

In this chapter, we will cover:

- Geocoding an IP address
- Collecting IP addresses of Wikipedia edits
- Visualizing contributor location frequency on Wikipedia
- Creating a word cloud from a StackOverflow job listing
- Crawling links on Wikipedia
- Visualizing page relationships on Wikipedia
- Calculating degrees of separation between Wikipedia pages

Introduction

In this chapter we will examine how to search web content, derive analytical results, and also visualize those results. We will learn how to locate posters of content an visualize the distribution of their locations. Then we will examine how to scrape, model, and visualize the relationships between pages on Wikipedia.

Geocoding an IP address

Geocoding is the process of converting an address into geographic coordinates. These addresses can be actual street addresses, which can be geocoded with various tools such as the Google maps geocoding API (`https://developers.google.com/maps/documentation/geocoding/intro`). IP addresses can be, and often are, geocoded by various applications to determine where computers, and their users, are located. A very common and valuable use is analyzing web server logs to determine the source of users of your website.

This is possible because an IP address does not only represent an address of the computer in terms of being able to communicate with that computer, but often can also be converted into an approximate physical location by looking it up in IP address / location databases. There are many of these databases available, all of which are maintained by various registrars (such as ICANN). There are also other tools that can report geographic locations for public IP addresses.

There are a number of free services for IP geolocation. We will examine one that is quite easy to use, freegeoip.net.

Getting ready

Freegeoip.net is a free geocoding service. If you go to `http://www.freegeoip.net` in your browser, you will be presented with a page similar to the following:

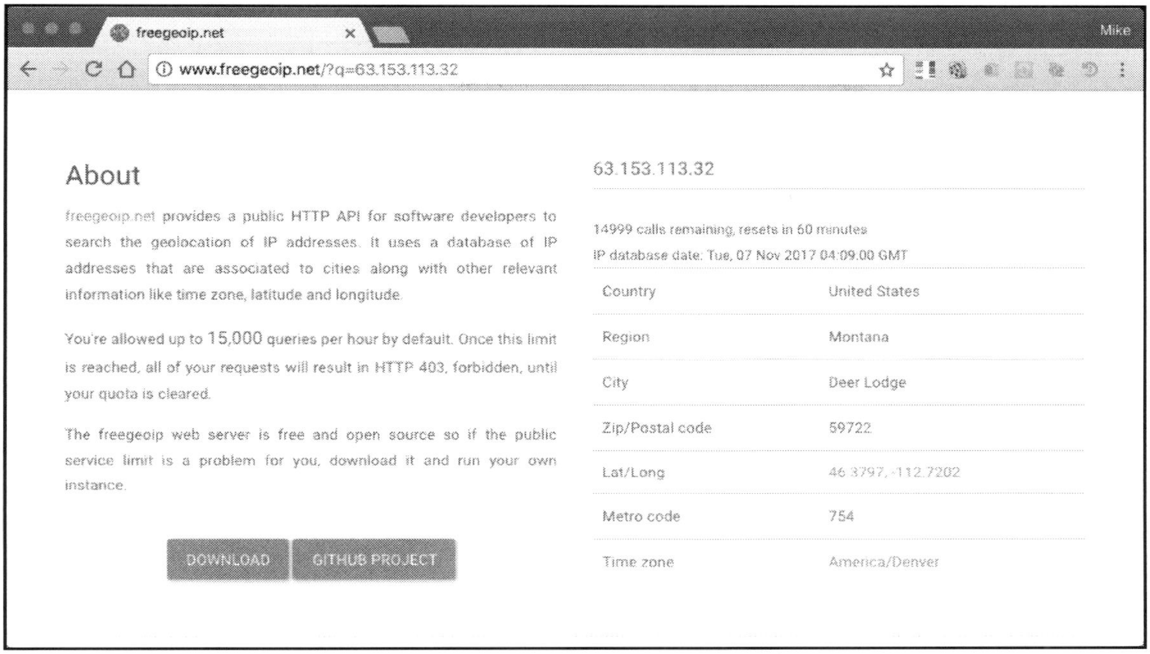

The freegeoip.net home page

The default page reports your public IP address, and also gives you the geolocation of the IP address according to their database. This isn't accurate to the actual address of my house, and is actually quite a few miles off, but the general location in the world is fairly accurate. We can do important things with data that is at this resolution and even lower. Often just knowing the country origin for web requests is enough for many purposes.

Freegeoip lets you make 15000 calls per hour. Each page load counts as one call, and as we will see, each API call also counts as one.

How to do it

We could scrape this page to get this information but fortunately, freegeoip.net gives us a convenient REST API to use. Scrolling further down the page, we can see the API documentation:

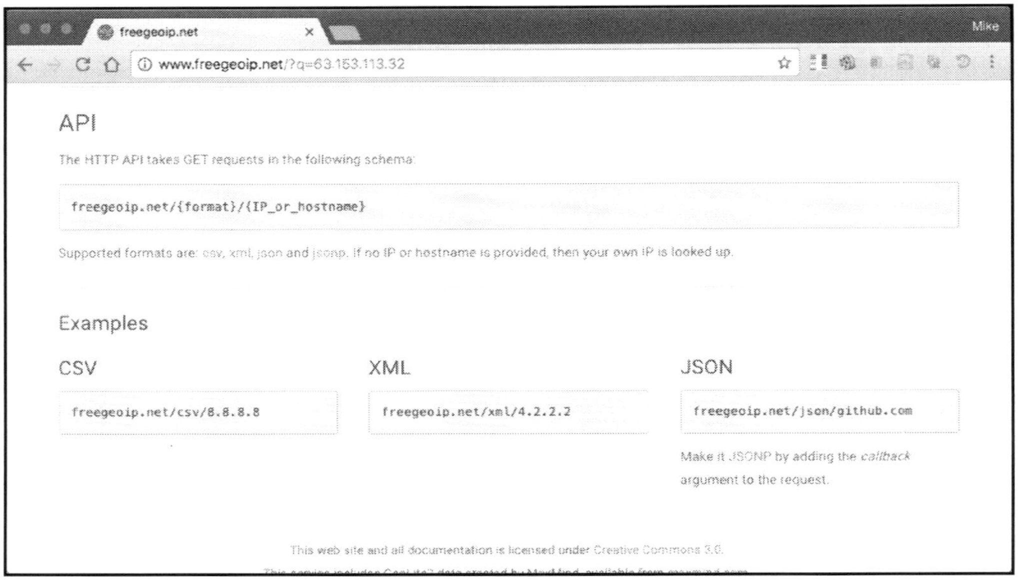

The freegeoio.net API documentation

We can simply use the requests library to make a GET request using the properly formatted URL. As an example, just entering the following URL in the browser returns a JSON representation of the geocoded data for the given IP address:

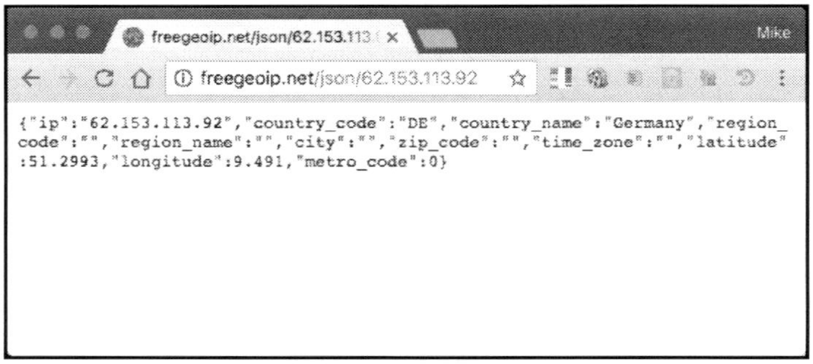

Sample JSON for an IP address

A Python script to demonstrate this is available in `08/01_geocode_address.py`. The is simple and consists of the following:

```
import json
import requests

raw_json = requests.get("http://www.freegeoip.net/json/63.153.113.92").text
parsed = json.loads(raw_json)
print(json.dumps(parsed, indent=4, sort_keys=True))
```

This has the following output:


```
{
    "city": "Deer Lodge",
    "country_code": "US",
    "country_name": "United States",
    "ip": "63.153.113.92",
    "latitude": 46.3797,
    "longitude": -112.7202,
    "metro_code": 754,
    "region_code": "MT",
    "region_name": "Montana",
    "time_zone": "America/Denver",
    "zip_code": "59722"
}
```


Note that your output for this IP address may vary, and surely will with different IP addresses.

How to collect IP addresses of Wikipedia edits

Processing aggregate results of geocoded IP addresses can provide valuable insights. This is very common for server logs and can also be used in many other situations. Many websites include the IP address of contributors of content. Wikipedia provides a history of changes on all of their pages. Edits created by someone that is not a registered user of Wikipedia have their IP address published in the history. We will examine how to create a scraper that will navigate the history of a given Wikipedia topic and collect the IP addresses of unregistered edits.

Getting ready

We will examine the edits made to the **Web scraping** page in Wikipedia. This page is available at: `https://en.wikipedia.org/wiki/Web_scraping`. The following shows a small part of this page:

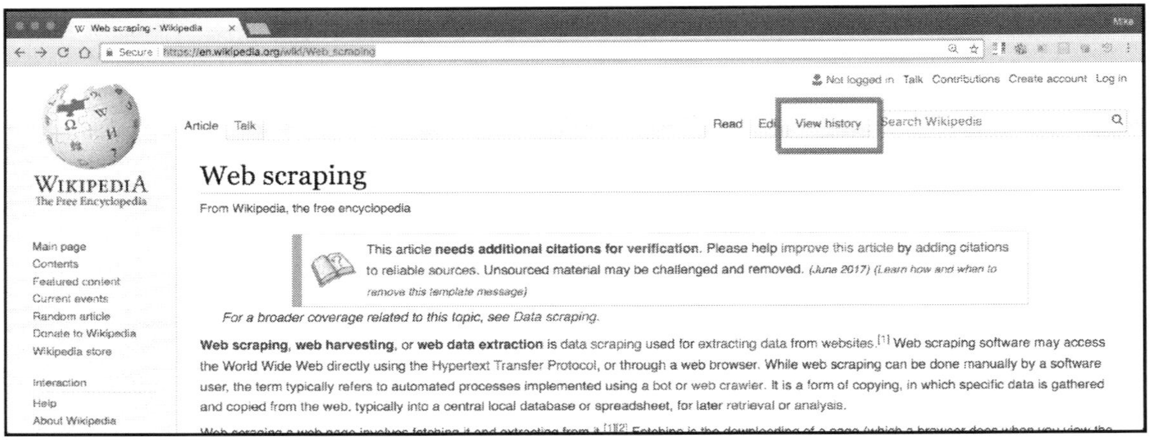

The view history tab

Note **View history** in the upper-right. Clicking on that link gives you access to the history for the edits:

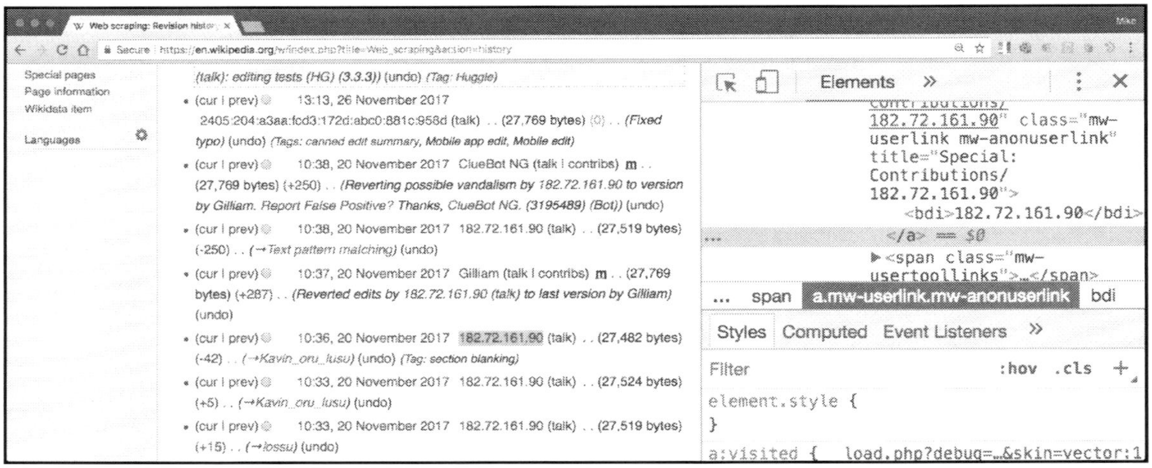

Inspecting an IP address

I've scrolled this down a little bit to highlight an anonymous edit. Note that we can identify these anonymous edit entries using the `mw-userling mw-anonuserlink` class in the source.

Notice also that you can specify the number of edits per page to be listed, which can be specified by adding a parameter to the URL. The following URL will give us the 500 most recent edits:

```
https://en.wikipedia.org/w/index.php?title=Web_scrapingoffset=limit=500action=
history
```

So instead of crawling a number of different pages, walking through them 50 at a time, we'll just do one page of 500.

How to do it

We proceed with the recipe as follows:

1. The code to perform the scraping is in the script file, `08/02_geocode_wikipedia_edits.py`. Running the script produces the following output (truncated to the first few geo IPs):

```
Reading page:
https://en.wikipedia.org/w/index.php?title=Web_scraping&offset=&lim
it=500&action=history
Got 106 ip addresses
{'ip': '2601:647:4a04:86d0:1cdf:8f8a:5ca5:76a0', 'country_code':
'US', 'country_name': 'United States', 'region_code': 'CA',
'region_name': 'California', 'city': 'Sunnyvale', 'zip_code':
'94085', 'time_zone': 'America/Los_Angeles', 'latitude': 37.3887,
'longitude': -122.0188, 'metro_code': 807}
{'ip': '194.171.56.13', 'country_code': 'NL', 'country_name':
'Netherlands', 'region_code': '', 'region_name': '', 'city': '',
'zip_code': '', 'time_zone': 'Europe/Amsterdam', 'latitude':
52.3824, 'longitude': 4.8995, 'metro_code': 0}
{'ip': '109.70.55.226', 'country_code': 'DK', 'country_name':
'Denmark', 'region_code': '85', 'region_name': 'Zealand', 'city':
'Roskilde', 'zip_code': '4000', 'time_zone': 'Europe/Copenhagen',
'latitude': 55.6415, 'longitude': 12.0803, 'metro_code': 0}
{'ip': '101.177.247.131', 'country_code': 'AU', 'country_name':
'Australia', 'region_code': 'TAS', 'region_name': 'Tasmania',
'city': 'Lenah Valley', 'zip_code': '7008', 'time_zone':
'Australia/Hobart', 'latitude': -42.8715, 'longitude': 147.2751,
'metro_code': 0}
```

The script also writes the geo IPs to the `geo_ips.json` file. The next recipe will use this file instead of making all the page requests again.

How it works

The explanation is as follows. The script begins by executing the following code:

```
if __name__ == "__main__":
    geo_ips = collect_geo_ips('Web_scraping', 500)
    for geo_ip in geo_ips:
        print(geo_ip)
    with open('geo_ips.json', 'w') as outfile:
        json.dump(geo_ips, outfile)
```

A call is made to `collect_geo_ips` which will request the page with the specified topic and up to 500 edits. These geo IPs are then printed to the console, and also written to the `geo_ips.json` file.

The code for `collect_geo_ips` is the following:

```
def collect_geo_ips(article_title, limit):
    ip_addresses = get_history_ips(article_title, limit)
    print("Got %s ip addresses" % len(ip_addresses))
    geo_ips = get_geo_ips(ip_addresses)
    return geo_ips
```

This function first makes a call to `get_history_ips`, reports the quantity found, and then makes repeated requests to `get_geo_ips` for each IP address.

The code for `get_history_ips` is the following:

```
def get_history_ips(article_title, limit):
    history_page_url =
"https://en.wikipedia.org/w/index.php?title=%s&offset=&limit=%s&action=hist
ory" % (article_title, limit)
    print("Reading page: " + history_page_url)
    html = requests.get(history_page_url).text
    soup = BeautifulSoup(html, "lxml")

    anon_ip_anchors = soup.findAll("a", {"class": "mw-anonuserlink"})
    addresses = set()
    for ip in anon_ip_anchors:
        addresses.add(ip.get_text())
    return addresses
```

This formulates the URL for the history page, retrieves the page, and then pulls out all distinct IP addresses with the `mw-anonuserlink` class.

`get_geo_ips` then takes this set of IP addresses and calls `freegeoip.net` on each for the data.

```
def get_geo_ips(ip_addresses):
    geo_ips = []
    for ip in ip_addresses:
        raw_json = requests.get("http://www.freegeoip.net/json/%s" %
ip).text
        parsed = json.loads(raw_json)
        geo_ips.append(parsed)
    return geo_ips
```

There's more...

While this data is useful, in our next recipe we will read in the data written to `geo_ips.json` (using pandas) and visualize the distribution of the users by country using a bar chart.

Visualizing contributor location frequency on Wikipedia

We can use the collected data to determine the frequency of edits of Wikipedia articles from countries around the world. This can be done by grouping the captured data by country and counting the number of edits related to each country. Then we will sort the data and create a bar chart to see the results.

How to do it

This is a very simple task to perform with pandas. The code of the example is in `08/03_visualize_wikipedia_edits.py`.

1. The code begins by importing pandas and `matplotlib.pyplot`:

```
>>> import pandas as pd
>>> import matplotlib.pyplot as plt
```

2. The data file we created in the previous recipe is already in a format that can be read directly by pandas. This is one of the benefits of using JSON as a data format; pandas has built-in support for reading and writing data from JSON. The following reads in the data using the `pd.read_json()` function and displays the first five rows on the console:

```
>>> df = pd.read_json("geo_ips.json")
>>> df[:5])

city country_code country_name ip latitude \
0 Hanoi VN Vietnam 118.70.248.17 21.0333
1 Roskilde DK Denmark 109.70.55.226 55.6415
2 Hyderabad IN India 203.217.144.211 17.3753
3 Prague CZ Czechia 84.42.187.252 50.0833
4 US United States 99.124.83.153 37.7510

longitude metro_code region_code region_name time_zone \
0 105.8500 0 HN Thanh Pho Ha Noi Asia/Ho_Chi_Minh
1 12.0803 0 85 Zealand Europe/Copenhagen
2 78.4744 0 TG Telangana Asia/Kolkata
3 14.4667 0 10 Hlavni mesto Praha Europe/Prague
4 -97.8220 0
zip_code
0
1 4000
2
3 130 00
4
```

3. For our immediate purpose we only require the `country_code` column, which we can extract with the following (and shows the first five rows in that result):

```
>>> countries_only = df.country_code
>>> countries_only[:5]

0 VN
1 DK
2 IN
3 CZ
4 US
Name: country_code, dtype:object
```

4. Now we can group the rows in this series using `.groupby('country_code')`, and on the result, `call .count()` will return the number of items in each of those groups. The code also sorts the results from the largest to lowest values by `calling .sort_values()`:

```
>>> counts =
df.groupby('country_code').country_code.count().sort_values(ascendi
ng=False)
>>> counts[:5]

country_code
US 28
IN 12
BR 7
NL 7
RO 6
Name: country_code, dtype: int64
```

We can see from just these results that the US definitely leads in edits, with India being the second most popular.

This data can easily be visualized as a bar graph:

```
counts.plot(kind='bar')
plt.show()
```

This results in the following bar graph showing overall distribution for all of the countries:

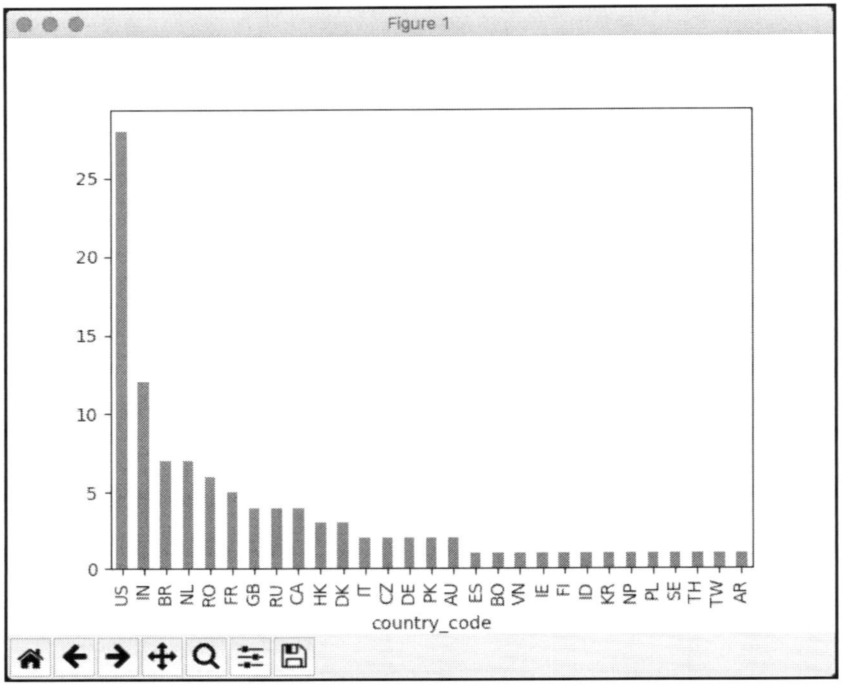

Histogram of the edit frequencies

Creating a word cloud from a StackOverflow job listing

Now lets look at creating a word cloud. Word clouds are an image that demonstrate the frequency of key words within a set of text. The larger the word in the image, the more apparent significance it has in the body of text.

Getting ready

We will use the Word Cloud library to create our word cloud. The source for the library is available at `https://github.com/amueller/word_cloud`. This library can be installed into your Python environment using `pip install wordcloud`.

How to do it

The script to create the word cloud is in the `08/04_so_word_cloud.py` file. This recipe continues on from the stack overflow recipes from chapter 7 to provide a visualization of the data.

1. Start by importing the word cloud and the frequency distribution function from NLTK:

```
from wordcloud import WordCloud
from nltk.probability import FreqDist
```

2. The word cloud is then generated from the probability distribution of the words we collected from the job listing:

```
freq_dist = FreqDist(cleaned)
wordcloud = WordCloud(width=1200,
height=800).generate_from_frequencies(freq_dist)
```

Now we just need to display the word cloud:

```
import matplotlib.pyplot as plt
plt.imshow(wordcloud, interpolation='bilinear')
plt.axis("off")
plt.show()
```

And the resulting word cloud is the following:

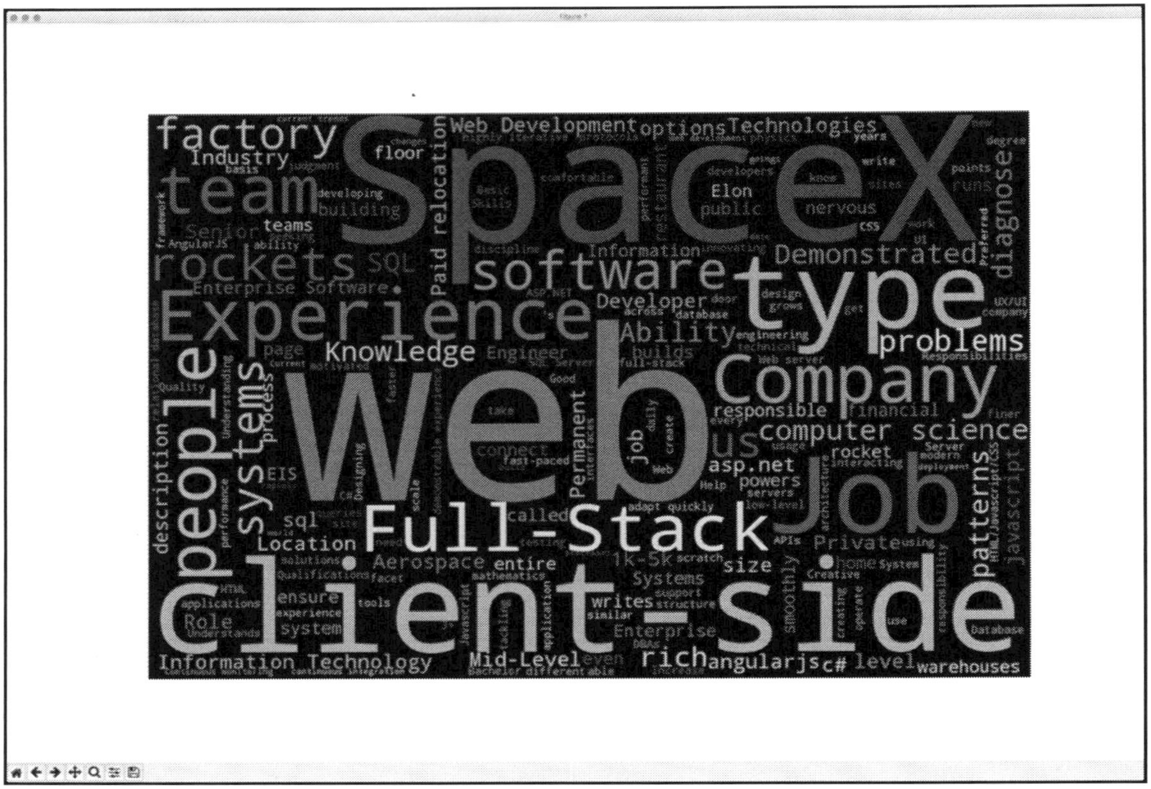

The word cloud for the job listing

The positioning and size have some built-in randomness, so the result you get may differ.

Crawling links on Wikipedia

In this recipe we will write a small program to utilize the crawl the links on a Wikipedia page through several levels of depth. During this crawl we will gather the relationships between the pages and those referenced from each page. During this we will build a relationship amongst these pages the we will ultimately visualize in the next recipe.

Getting ready

The code for this example is in the 08/05_wikipedia_scrapy.py. It references code in a module in the modules/wikipedia folder of the code samples, so make sure that is in your Python path.

How to do it

You can the sample Python script. It will crawl a single Wikipedia page using Scrapy. The page it will crawl is the Python page at https://en.wikipedia.org/wiki/Python_(programming_language), and collect relevant links on that page.

When run you will see the similar output to the following:

```
/Users/michaelheydt/anaconda/bin/python3.6
/Users/michaelheydt/Dropbox/Packt/Books/PyWebScrCookbook/code/py/08/05_wiki
pedia_scrapy.py
parsing: https://en.wikipedia.org/wiki/Python_(programming_language)
parsing: https://en.wikipedia.org/wiki/C_(programming_language)
parsing: https://en.wikipedia.org/wiki/Object-oriented_programming
parsing: https://en.wikipedia.org/wiki/Ruby_(programming_language)
parsing: https://en.wikipedia.org/wiki/Go_(programming_language)
parsing: https://en.wikipedia.org/wiki/Java_(programming_language)
------------------------------------------------------------
0 Python_(programming_language) C_(programming_language)
0 Python_(programming_language) Java_(programming_language)
0 Python_(programming_language) Go_(programming_language)
0 Python_(programming_language) Ruby_(programming_language)
0 Python_(programming_language) Object-oriented_programming
```

The first part of output is from the Scrapy crawler and shows the pages that are passed to the parse method. These are pages that start with our initial page and through the first five most common links from that page.

The second part of this output is a representation of the page that is crawled and the links found on that page that are considered for future processing. The first number is the level of the crawl the crawl that the relationship was found, followed by the parent page and the link found on that page. For every page / link found, there is a separate entry. Since this is a one depth crawl, we just show pages found from the initial page.

How it works

Lets start with the code in them main script file, `08/05_wikipedia_scrapy.py`. This starts with creating a `WikipediaSpider` object and running the crawl:

```
process = CrawlerProcess({
    'LOG_LEVEL': 'ERROR',
    'DEPTH_LIMIT': 1
})

process.crawl(WikipediaSpider)
spider = next(iter(process.crawlers)).spider
process.start()
```

This tells Scrapy that we want to run it for one level of depth, and we get an instance of the crawler as we want to inspect its properties which are the result of the crawl. The results are then printed with the following:

```
print("-"*60)

for pm in spider.linked_pages:
    print(pm.depth, pm.title, pm.child_title)
```

Each result from the crawler is stored in the `linked_pages` property. Each of those objects is represented by several properties including the title of the page (the last portion of the wikipedia URL) and the title of each page found within the content of the HTML of that page.

Now let's walk through how the crawler functions. The code for the spider is in `modules/wikipedia/spiders.py`. The crawler starts off by defining a sub-class of a Scrapy `Spider`:

```
class WikipediaSpider(Spider):
    name = "wikipedia"
    start_urls = [
"https://en.wikipedia.org/wiki/Python_(programming_language)" ]
```

We are starting on the Python page in Wikipedia. Next are the definition of a few class level variable to define how the crawl operates and for the results to be retrieved:

```
page_map = {}
linked_pages = []
max_items_per_page = 5
max_crawl_depth = 1
```

Each page of this crawl will the processed by the parse method of the spider. Let's walk through it. It starts with the following:

```
def parse(self, response):
    print("parsing: " + response.url)

    links = response.xpath("//*/a[starts-with(@href, '/wiki/')]/@href")
    link_counter = {}
```

In each Wikipedia page we look for links what start with `/wiki`. There are other links in the page but these are the ones this this crawl will consider important.

This crawler implements an algorithm where all found links on the page are counted for similarity. There are quite a few repeat links. Some of these are spurious. Others represent a true importance of linking multiple times to other pages.

The `max_items_per_page` defines how many links on the current page we will further investigate. There will be quite a few links on each page, and this algorithm counts all the similar links and puts them into buckets. It then follows the `max_items_per_page` most popular links.

This process is managed though the use of the `links_counter` variable. This is a dictionary of mappings between the current page and all links found on the page. For each link we decide to follow We count the number of times it is referenced on the page. This variable is a map between that URL and and instance of the following object that counts the number of references:

```
class LinkReferenceCount:
    def __init__(self, link):
        self.link = link
        self.count = 0
```

The code then walks through all the identified links:

```
for l in links:
    link = l.root
    if ":" not in link and "International" not in link and link !=
self.start_urls[0]:
        if link not in link_counter:
            link_counter[link] = LinkReferenceCount(link)
        link_counter[link].count += 1
```

This examines every link and only considers them for further crawling based upon the stated rules (no ':' in the link, nor 'International' as it is quite popular so we exclude it, and finally we don't include the start URL). If the link passes this, then a new `LinkReferenceCounter` object is created (if this link as not been seen before), or its reference count is incremented.

Since there are likely repeat links on each page, we want to consider only the `max_items_per_page` most common links. The code does this by the following:

```
references = list(link_counter.values())
s = sorted(references, key=lambda x: x.count, reverse=True)
top = s[:self.max_items_per_page]
```

Out of the `link_counter` dictionary we pull all of the `LinkReferenceCounter` objects and sort them by the count, and then select the top `max_items_per_page` items.

The next step is for each of these qualifying items we recored them in the `linked_pages` field of the class. Each object in this list of the the type `PageToPageMap`. This class has the following definition:

```
class PageToPageMap:
    def __init__(self, link, child_link, depth): #, parent):
        self.link = link
        self.child_link = child_link
        self.title = self.get_page_title(self.link)
        self.child_title = self.get_page_title(self.child_link)
        self.depth = depth

    def get_page_title(self, link):
        parts = link.split("/")
        last = parts[len(parts)-1]
        label = urllib.parse.unquote(last)
        return label
```

Fundamentally this object represents a source page URL to a linked page URL, and it also tracks the current level of the crawl. The title properties are the URL decoded forms of the last part of the Wikipedia URL, and represent a more human-friendly version of the URL.

Finally, the code yields to Scrapy new pages to crawl to.

```
for item in top:
    new_request = Request("https://en.wikipedia.org" + item.link,
                          callback=self.parse, meta={ "parent": pm })
    yield new_request
```

Theres more...

This crawler / algorithm also keeps track of the current level of **depth** in the crawl. If a new link is considered to be beyond the maximum depth of the crawl. While this can be controlled to a point by Scrapy, this code still needs to not include links beyond the maximum depth.

This is controlled by using the depth field of the `PageToPageMap` object. For each page of the crawl, we check to see if the response has meta-data, a property which represents the "`parent`" PageToPageMap object for an given page. We find this with the following code:

```
depth = 0
if "parent" in response.meta:
    parent = response.meta["parent"]
    depth = parent.depth + 1
```

This code in the page parser looks to see if there is a parent object. Only the first page of the crawl does not have a parent page. If there is an instance, the depth of this crawl is considered one higher. When the new `PageToPageMap` object is created, this value is passed to it and stored.

The code passes this object to the next level of the crawl by using the meta property of the request object:

```
meta={ "parent": pm }
```

In this way we can pass data from one level of a crawl in a Scrapy spider to the next.

Visualizing page relationships on Wikipedia

In this recipe we take the data we collected in the previous recipe and create a force-directed network visualization of the page relationships using the NetworkX Python library.

Getting ready

NetworkX is software for modeling, visualizing, and analyzing complex network relationships. You can find more information about it at: `https://networkx.github.io`. It can be installed in your Python environment using `pip install networkx`.

How to do it

The script for this example is in the `08/06_visualizze_wikipedia_links.py` file. When run it produces a graph of the links found on the initial Python page in Wikipedia:

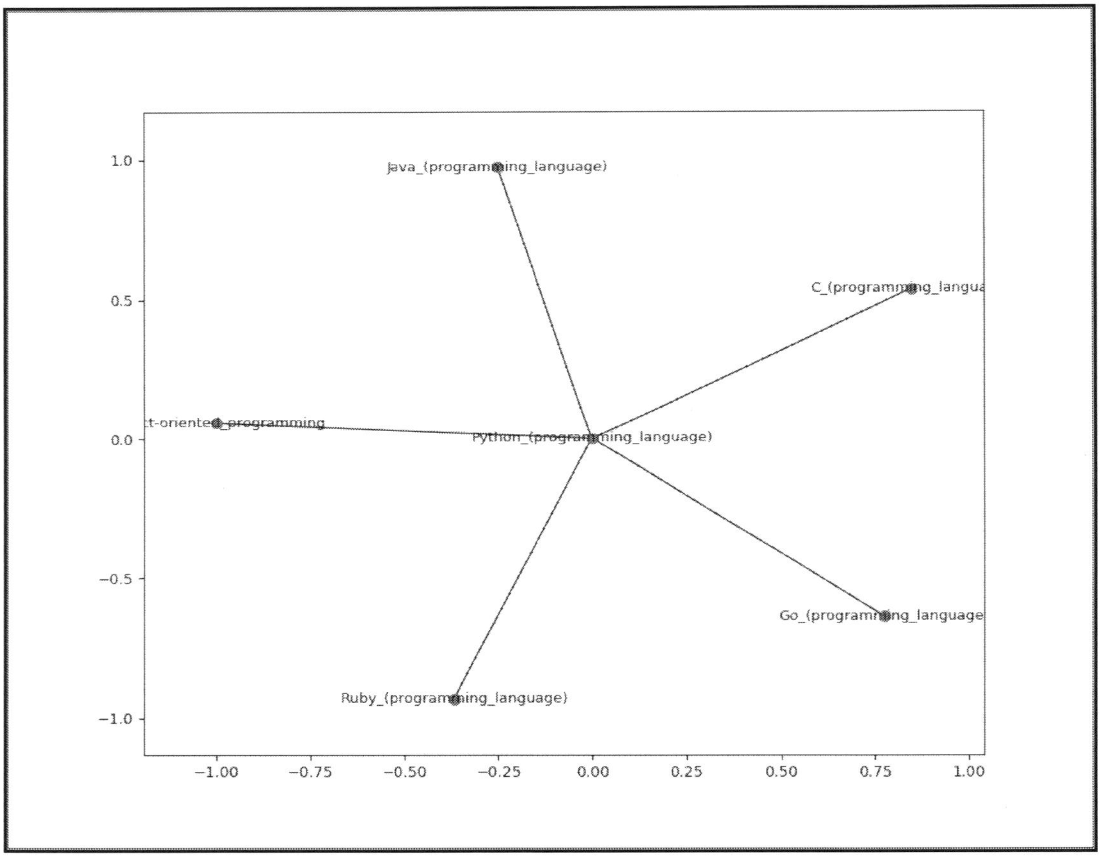

Graph of the links

Now we can see the relationships between the pages!

How it works

The crawl starts with defining a one level of depth crawl:

```
crawl_depth = 1
process = CrawlerProcess({
    'LOG_LEVEL': 'ERROR',
    'DEPTH_LIMIT': crawl_depth
})
process.crawl(WikipediaSpider)
spider = next(iter(process.crawlers)).spider
spider.max_items_per_page = 5
spider.max_crawl_depth = crawl_depth
process.start()

for pm in spider.linked_pages:
    print(pm.depth, pm.link, pm.child_link)
print("-"*80)
```

This information is similar to the previous recipe, and new we need to convert it into a model that NetworkX can use for a graph. This starts with creating a NetworkX graph model:

```
g = nx.Graph()
```

A NetworkX graph consists of nodes and edges. From the data collected we must crate a set of unique nodes (the pages) and the edges (the fact that a page references another page). This performed with the following:

```
nodes = {}
edges = {}

for pm in spider.linked_pages:
    if pm.title not in nodes:
        nodes[pm.title] = pm
        g.add_node(pm.title)

    if pm.child_title not in nodes:
        g.add_node(pm.child_title)

    link_key = pm.title + " ==> " + pm.child_title
    if link_key not in edges:
        edges[link_key] = link_key
        g.add_edge(pm.title, pm.child_title)
```

This iterates through all the results from out crawl and identifies all the unique nodes (the distinct pages), and then all of the links between any pages and other pages. For each node and edge, we register those with NetworkX.

Next we create the plot with Matplotlib and tell NetworkX how to create the visuals in the plot:

```
plt.figure(figsize=(10,8))

node_positions = nx.spring_layout(g)

nx.draw_networkx_nodes(g, node_positions, g.nodes, node_color='green',
node_size=50)
nx.draw_networkx_edges(g, node_positions)

labels = { node: node for node in g.nodes() }
nx.draw_networkx_labels(g, node_positions, labels, font_size=9.5)

plt.show()
```

The important parts of this are first the use of NetworkX to form a spring layout on the nodes. That calculates the actual positions of the nodes but does not render them or the edges. That is the purpose of the next two lines which give NetworkX the instructions on how to render both the nodes and edges. and finally, we need to put labels on the nodes.

There's more...

This crawl only did a single depth crawl. The crawl can be increased with the following change to the code:

```
crawl_depth = 2
process = CrawlerProcess({
    'LOG_LEVEL': 'ERROR',
    'DEPTH_LIMIT': crawl_depth
})
process.crawl(WikipediaSpider)
spider = next(iter(process.crawlers)).spider
spider.max_items_per_page = 5
spider.max_crawl_depth = crawl_depth
process.start()
```

Fundamentally the only change is to increase the depth one level. This then results in the following graph (there is randomization in any spring graph so the actual results have a different layout):

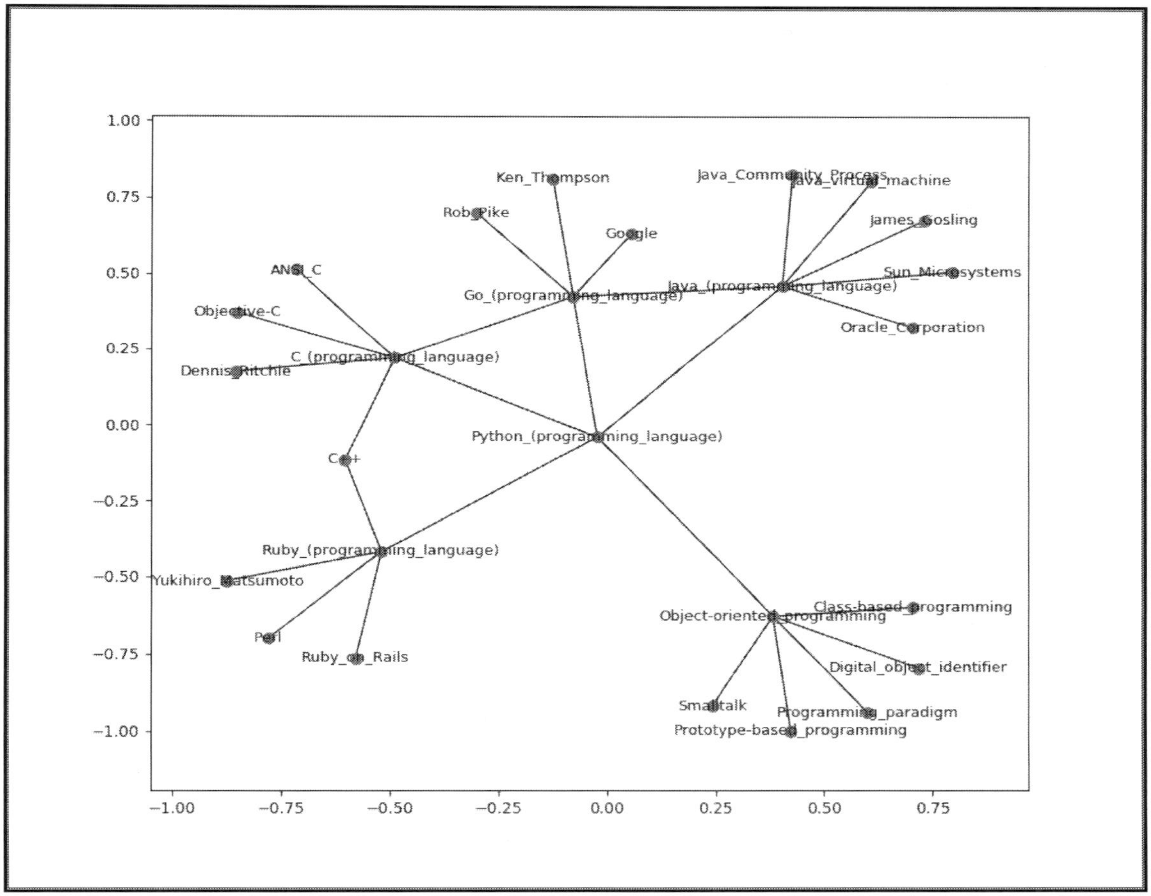

Spider graph of the links

This begins to be interesting as we now start to see inter-relationships and cyclic relationships between pages.

I dare you to further increase the depth and number of links per page.

Calculating degrees of separation

Now let's calculate the degrees of separation between any two pages. This answers the question of how many pages we need to go through from a source page to find another page. This could be a non-trivial graph traversal problem as there can be multiple paths between the two pages. Fortunately for us, NetworkX, using the exact same graph model, has built in function to solve this with the exact same model from the previous recipe.

How to do it

The script for this example is in the `08/07_degrees_of_separation.py`. The code is identical to the previous recipe, with a 2-depth crawl, except that it omits the graph and asks NetworkX to solve the degrees of separation between `Python_(programming_language)` and `Dennis_Ritchie`:

```
Degrees of separation: 1
 Python_(programming_language)
   C_(programming_language)
     Dennis_Ritchie
```

This tells us that to go from `Python_(programming_language)` to `Dennis_Ritchie` we have to go through one other page: `C_(programming_language)`. Hence, one degree of separation. If we went directly to `C_(programming_language)`, it would be 0 degrees of separation.

How it works

The solution of this problem is solved by an algorithm known as **A***. The **A*** algorithm determines the shortest path between two nodes in a graph. Note that this path can be multiple paths of different lengths and that the correct result is the shortest path. A good thing for us is that NetworkX has a built in function to do this for us. It is done with one simple statement:

```
path = nx.astar_path(g, "Python_(programming_language)", "Dennis_Ritchie")
```

From this we report on the actual path:

```
degrees_of_separation = int((len(path) - 1) / 2)
print("Degrees of separation: {}".format(degrees_of_separation))
for i in range(0, len(path)):
    print(" " * i, path[i])
```

There's more...

For more information on the **A*** algorithm check out this page at `https://en.wikipedia.org/A*_search_algorithm`.

9
Creating a Simple Data API

In this chapter, we will cover:

- Creating a REST API with Flask-RESTful
- Integrating the REST API with scraping code
- Adding an API to find the skills for a job listing
- Storing data in Elasticsearch as the result of a scraping request
- Checking Elasticsearch for a listing before scraping

Introduction

We have now reached an exciting inflection point in our learning about scraping. From this point on, we will learn about making scrapers as a service using several APIs, microservice, and container tools, all of which will allow the running of the scraper either locally or in the cloud, and to give access to the scraper through standardized REST APIs.60;

We will start this new journey in this chapter with the creation of a simple REST API using Flask-RESTful which we will eventually use to make requests to the service to scrape pages on demand. We will connect this API to a scraper function implemented in a Python module that reuses the concepts for scraping StackOverflow jobs, as discussed in `Chapter 7`, *Text Wrangling and Analysis*.

The final few recipes will focus on using Elasticsearch as a cache for these results, storing documents we retrieve from the scraper, and then looking for them first within the cache. We will examine more elaborate uses of ElasticCache, such as performing searches for jobs with a given set of skills, later in `Chapter 11`, *Making the Scraper as a Service Real*.

Creating a REST API with Flask-RESTful

We start with the creation of a simple REST API using Flask-RESTful. This initial API will consist of a single method that lets the caller pass an integer value and which returns a JSON blob. In this recipe, the parameters and their values, as well as the return value, are not important at this time as we want to first simply get an API up and running using Flask-RESTful.

Getting ready

Flask is a web microframework that makes creating simple web application functionality incredibly easy. Flask-RESTful is an extension to Flask which does the same for making REST APIs just as simple. You can get Flask and read more about it at `flask.pocoo.org`. Flask-RESTful can be read about at `https://flask-restful.readthedocs.io/en/latest/`. Flask can be installed into your Python environment using `pip install flask`. and Flask-RESTful can also be installed with `pip install flask-restful`.

The remainder of the recipes in the book will be in a subfolder of the chapter's directory. This is because most of these recipes either require multiple files to operate, or use the same filename (ie: `apy.py`).

How to do it

The initial API is implemented in `09/01/api.py`. The API itself and the logic of the API is implemented in this single file: `api.py`. The API can be run in two manners, the first of which is by simply executing the file as a Python script.

The API can then be launched with the following:

```
python api.py
```

When run, you will initially see output similar to the following:

```
Starting the job listing API
 * Running on http://127.0.0.1:5000/ (Press CTRL+C to quit)
 * Restarting with stat
Starting the job listing API
 * Debugger is active!
 * Debugger pin code: 362-310-034
```

This program exposes a REST API on `127.0.0.1:5000`, and we can make requests for job listings using a `GET` request to the path `/joblisting/<joblistingid>`. We can try this with curl:

```
curl localhost:5000/joblisting/1
```

The result of this command will be the following:

```
{
 "YouRequestedJobWithId": "1"
}
```

And just like that, we have a REST API up and running. Now let's see how it is implemented.

How it works

There really isn't a lot of code, which is the beauty of Flask-RESTful. The code begins with importing of `flask` and `flask_restful`.

```
from flask import Flask
from flask_restful import Resource, Api
```

These are followed with code to set up the initial configuration of Flask-RESTful:

```
app = Flask(__name__)
api = Api(app)
```

Next comes a definition of a class which represents the implementation of our API:

```
class JobListing(Resource):
    def get(self, job_listing_id):
        print("Request for job listing with id: " + job_listing_id)
        return {'YouRequestedJobWithId': job_listing_id}
```

What we will have Flask-RESTful do is map HTTP requests to methods in this class. Specifically, by convention `GET` requests will be mapped to member functions named `get`. There will be a mapping of the values passed as part of the URL to the `jobListingId` parameter of the function. This function then returns a Python dictionary, which Flask-RESTful converts to JSON for us.

The next line of code tells Flask-RESTful how to map portions of the URL to our class:

```
api.add_resource(JobListing, '/', '/joblisting/<string:job_listing_id>')
```

This defines that URLs with paths beginning with `/joblisting` will be mapped to our `JobListing` class, and that the next portion of the URL represents a string to be passed to the `jobListingId` parameter of the `get` method. The GET HTTP verb is implied as no other verb has been defined in this mapping.

Finally, we have code that specifies that when the file is run as a script that we simply execute `app.run()` (passing in this case a parameter to give us debug output).

```
if __name__ == '__main__':
    print("Starting the job listing API")
    app.run(debug=True)
```

Flask-RESTful then finds our class and sets of the mappings, starts listening on `127.0.0.1:5000` (the default), and forwarding requests to our class and method.

There's more...

The default for Flask-RESTful is to run on port `5000`. This can be changed using alternate forms of `app.run()`. We will be fine with leaving it at 5000 for our recipes. Ultimately, you would run this service in something like a container and front it with a reverse proxy such as NGINX and perform a public port mapping to the internal service port.

Integrating the REST API with scraping code

In this recipe, we will integrate code that we wrote for scraping and getting a clean job listing from StackOverflow with our API. This will result in a reusable API that can be used to perform on-demand scrapes without the client needing any knowledge of the scraping process. Essentially, we will have created a *scraper as a service,* a concept we will spend much time with in the remaining recipes of the book.

Getting ready

The first part of this process is to create a module out of our preexisting code that was written in `Chapter 7`, *Text Wrangling and Analysis* so that we can reuse it. We will reuse this code in several recipes throughout the remainder of the book. Let's briefly examine the structure and contents of this module before going and integrating it with the API.

The code for the module is in the `sojobs` (for StackOverflow Jobs) module in the project's modules folder.

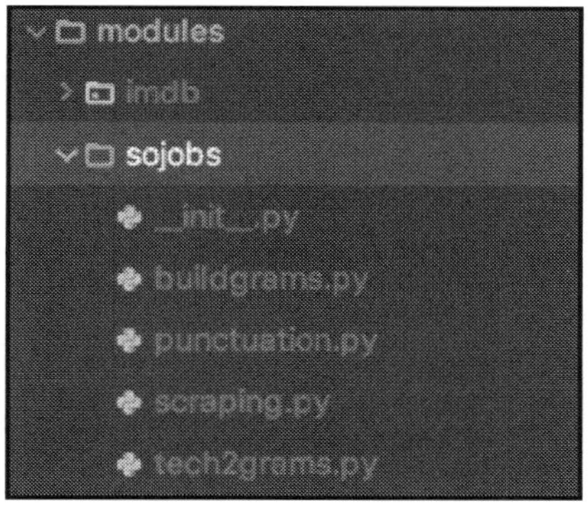

The sojobs folder

For the most part, these files are copied from those used in `Chapter 7`, *Text Wrangling and Analysis*. The primary file for reuse is `scraping.py`, which contains several functions that facilitate scraping. The function that we will use in this recipe is `get_job_listing_info`:

```
def get_job_listing(job_listing_id):
    print("Got a request for a job listing with id: " + job_listing_id)

    req = requests.get("https://stackoverflow.com/jobs/" + job_listing_id)
    content = req.text
```

```
    bs = BeautifulSoup(content, "lxml")
    script_tag = bs.find("script", {"type": "application/ld+json"})

    job_listing_contents = json.loads(script_tag.contents[0])
    desc_bs = BeautifulSoup(job_listing_contents["description"], "lxml")
    just_text = desc_bs.find_all(text=True)

    joined = ' '.join(just_text)
    tokens = word_tokenize(joined)

    stop_list = stopwords.words('english')
    with_no_stops = [word for word in tokens if word.lower() not in
stop_list]
    two_grammed = tech_2grams(with_no_stops)
    cleaned = remove_punctuation(two_grammed)

    result = {
        "ID": job_listing_id,
        "JSON": job_listing_contents,
        "TextOnly": just_text,
        "CleanedWords": cleaned
    }

    return json.dumps(result)
```

Heading back to the code in `Chapter 7`, *Text Wrangling and Analysis*, you can see that this code is reused code that we created in those recipes. A difference is that instead of reading a single local `.html` file, this function is passed the identifier for a job listing, then constructs the URL for that job listing, reads the content with requests, performs several analyses, and then returns the results.

Note that the function returns a Python dictionary that consists of the requested job ID, the original HTML, the text of the listing, and the list of cleaned words. This API is returning to the caller an aggregate of these results, with the `ID` so it is easy to know the requested job, as well as all of the other results that we did to perform various clean ups. Hence, we have created a value-added service for job listings instead of just getting the raw HTML.

Make sure that you either have your PYTHONPATH environment variable pointing to the modules directory, or that you have set up your Python IDE to find modules in this directory. Otherwise, you will get errors that this module cannot be found.

How to do it

We proceed with the recipe as follows:

1. The code of the API for this recipe is in `09/02/api.py`. This extends the code in the previous recipe to make a call to this function in the `sojobs` module. The code for the service is the following:

```
from flask import Flask
from flask_restful import Resource, Api
from sojobs.scraping import get_job_listing_info

app = Flask(__name__)
api = Api(app)

class JobListing(Resource):
    def get(self, job_listing_id):
        print("Request for job listing with id: " + job_listing_id)
        listing = get_job_listing_info(job_listing_id)
        print("Got the following listing as a response: " +
listing)
        return listing

api.add_resource(JobListing, '/',
'/joblisting/<string:job_listing_id>')

if __name__ == '__main__':
    print("Starting the job listing API")
    app.run(debug=True)
```

Note that the main difference is the import of the function from the module, and the call to the function and return of the data from the result.

2. The service is run by executing the script with Python `api.py`. We can then test the API using `curl`. The following requests the SpaceX job listing we have previously examined.

```
curl localhost:5000/joblisting/122517
```

3. This results in quite a bit of output. The following is some of the beginning of the response:


```
"{\"ID\": \"122517\", \"JSON\": {\"@context\":
\"http://schema.org\", \"@type\": \"JobPosting\", \"title\":
\"SpaceX Enterprise Software Engineer, Full Stack\", \"skills\":
[\"c#\", \"sql\", \"javascript\", \"asp.net\", \"angularjs\"],
\"description\": \"<h2>About this job</h2>\\r\\n<p><span>Location
options: <strong>Paid relocation</strong></span><br/><span>Job
type: <strong>Permanent</strong></span><br/><span>Experience level:
<strong>Mid-Level, Senior</strong></span><br/><span>Role:
<strong>Full Stack Developer</strong></span><br/><span>Industry:
<strong>Aerospace, Information Technology, Web
Development</strong></span><br/><span>Company size: <strong>1k-5k
people</strong></span><br/><span>Company type:
<strong>Private</strong></span><br/></p><br/><br/><h2>Technologies<
/h2> <p>c#, sql, javascr
```


Adding an API to find the skills for a job listing

In this recipe, we add an additional operation to our API which will allow us to request the skills associated with a job listing. This demonstrates a means of being able to retrieve only a subset of the data instead of the entire content of the listing. While we will only do this for the skills, the concept can be easily extended to any other subsets of the data, such as the location of the job, title, or almost any other content that makes sense for the user of your API.

Getting ready

The first thing that we will do is add a scraping function to the `sojobs` module. This function will be named `get_job_listing_skills`. The following is the code for this function:

```
def get_job_listing_skills(job_listing_id):
    print("Got a request for a job listing skills with id: " +
job_listing_id)

    req = requests.get("https://stackoverflow.com/jobs/" + job_listing_id)
    content = req.text
```

```
bs = BeautifulSoup(content, "lxml")
script_tag = bs.find("script", {"type": "application/ld+json"})

job_listing_contents = json.loads(script_tag.contents[0])
skills = job_listing_contents['skills']

return json.dumps(skills)
```

This function retrieves the job listing, extracts the JSON provided by StackOverflow, and then only returns the `skills` property of the JSON.

Now, let's see how to add a method to the REST API to call it.

How to do it

We proceed with the recipe as follows:

1. The code of the API for this recipe is in `09/03/api.py`. This script adds an additional class, `JobListingSkills`, with the following implementation:

```
class JobListingSkills(Resource):
    def get(self, job_listing_id):
        print("Request for job listing's skills with id: " +
job_listing_id)
        skills = get_job_listing_skills(job_listing_id)
        print("Got the following skills as a response: " + skills)
        return skills
```

This implementation is similar to that of the previous recipe, except that it calls the new function for getting skills.

2. We still need to add a statement to inform Flask-RESTful how to map URLs to this classes' `get` method. Since we are actually looking at retrieving a sub-property of the larger job listing, we will extend our URL scheme to include an additional segment representing the sub-property of the overall job listing resource.

```
api.add_resource(JobListingSkills, '/',
'/joblisting/<string:job_listing_id>/skills')
```

3. Now we can retrieve just the skills using the following curl:

```
curl localhost:5000/joblisting/122517/skills
```

Which gives us the following result:

```
"[\"c#\", \"sql\", \"javascript\", \"asp.net\", \"angularjs\"]"
```

Storing data in Elasticsearch as the result of a scraping request

In this recipe, we extend our API to save the data we received from the scraper into Elasticsearch. We will use this later (in the next recipe) to be able to optimize requests by using the content in Elasticsearch as a cache so that we do not repeat the scraping process for jobs listings already scraped. Therefore, we can play nice with StackOverflows servers.

Getting ready

Make sure you have Elasticsearch running locally, as the code will access Elasticsearch at `localhost:9200`. There a good quick-start available at `https://www.elastic.co/guide/en/elasticsearch/reference/current/_installation.html`, or you can check out the docker Elasticsearch recipe in `Chapter 10`, *Creating Scraper Microservices with Docker* if you'd like to run it in Docker.

Once installed, you can check proper installation with the following `curl`:

```
curl 127.0.0.1:9200?pretty
```

If installed properly, you will get output similar to the following:

```
{
 "name": "KHhxNlz",
 "cluster_name": "elasticsearch",
 "cluster_uuid": "fA1qyp78TB623C8IKXgT4g",
 "version": {
 "number": "6.1.1",
 "build_hash": "bd92e7f",
 "build_date": "2017-12-17T20:23:25.338Z",
 "build_snapshot": false,
 "lucene_version": "7.1.0",
 "minimum_wire_compatibility_version": "5.6.0",
```

```
    "minimum_index_compatibility_version": "5.0.0"
  },
  "tagline": "You Know, for Search"
}
```

You will also need to have elasticsearch-py installed. This is available at `https://www.elastic.co/guide/en/elasticsearch/client/python-api/current/index.html`, but can be quickly installed using `pip install elasticsearch`.

How to do it

We will make a few small changes to our API code. The code from the previous recipe has been copied into `09/04/api.py`, with the few modifications made.

1. First, we add an import for elasticsearch-py:

```
from elasticsearch import Elasticsearch
```

2. Now we make a quick modification to the `get` method of the `JobListing` class (I've done the same in JobListingSkills, but it's omitted here for brevity):

```
class JobListing(Resource):
    def get(self, job_listing_id):
        print("Request for job listing with id: " + job_listing_id)
        listing = get_job_listing_info(job_listing_id)

        es = Elasticsearch()
        es.index(index='joblistings', doc_type='job-listing',
id=job_listing_id, body=listing)

        print("Got the following listing as a response: " +
listing)
        return listing
```

3. The two new lines create an `Elasticsearch` object, and then insert the resulting document into ElasticSearch. Before the first time of calling the API, we can see that there is no content, nor a `'joblistings'` index, by using the following curl:

```
curl localhost:9200/joblistings
```

4. Given we just installed Elasticsearch, this will result in the following error.


```
{"error":{"root_cause":[{"type":"index_not_found_exception","reason
":"no such
index","resource.type":"index_or_alias","resource.id":"joblistings"
,"index_uuid":"_na_","index":"joblistings"}],"type":"index_not_foun
d_exception","reason":"no such
index","resource.type":"index_or_alias","resource.id":"joblistings"
,"index_uuid":"_na_","index":"joblistings"},"status":404}
```


5. Now start up the API by using `python api.py`. Then issue the `curl` to get the job listing (`curl localhost:5000/joblisting/122517`). This will result in output similar to the previous recipes. The difference now is that this document will be stored in Elasticsearch.
6. Now reissue the previous curl for the index:

```
curl localhost:9200/joblistings
```

7. And now you will get the following result (only the first few lines shown):


```
{
 "joblistings": {
  "aliases": {},
  "mappings": {
   "job-listing": {
     "properties": {
       "CleanedWords" {
         "type": "text",
         "fields": {
           "keyword": {
           "type": "keyword",
           "ignore_above": 256
          }
         }
       },
     "ID": {
       "type": "text",
       "fields": {
         "keyword": {
         "type": "keyword",
         "ignore_above": 256
         }
       }
     },
```

There has been an index created, named `joblistings`, and this result demonstrates the index structure that Elasticsearch has identified by examining the document.

> **TIP:** While Elasticsearch is schema-less, it does examine the documents submitted and build indexes based upon what it finds.

8. The specific document that we just stored can be retrieved by using the following curl:

```
curl localhost:9200/joblistings/job-listing/122517
```

9. Which will give us the following result (again, just the beginning of the content shown):

```
{
 "_index": "joblistings",
 "_type": "job-listing",
 "_id": "122517",
 "_version": 1,
 "found": true,
 "_source": {
  "ID": "122517",
  "JSON": {
   "@context": "http://schema.org",
   "@type": "JobPosting",
   "title": "SpaceX Enterprise Software Engineer, Full Stack",
   "skills": [
    "c#",
    "sql",
    "javascript",
    "asp.net",
    "angularjs"
  ],
  "description": "<h2>About this job</h2>\r\n<p><span>Location
options: <strong>Paid relocation</strong></span><br/><span>Job
type: <strong>Permanent</strong></span><br/><span>Experience level:
<strong>Mid-Level,
```

And just like that, with two lines of code, we have the document stored in our Elasticsearch database. Now let's briefly examine how this worked.

How it works

The storing of the document was performed using the following line:

```
es.index(index='joblistings', doc_type='job-listing', id=job_listing_id,
body=listing)
```

Let's examine what each of these parameters does relative to storing this document.

The `index` parameter specifies which Elasticsearch index we want to store the document within. That is named `joblistings`. This also becomes the first portion of the URL used to retrieve the documents.

Each Elasticsearch index can also have multiple document 'types', which are logical collections of documents that can represent different types of documents within the index. We used `'job-listing'`, and that value also forms the second part of our URL for retrieving a specific document.

Elasticsearch does not require that an indentifier be specified for each document, but if we provide one we can look up specific documents without having to do a search. We will use the job listing ID for the document ID.

The final parameter, body, specifies the actual content of the document. This code simply passed the result received from the scraper.

There's more...

Let's look briefly at a few more facets of what Elasticsearch has done for us by looking at the results of this document retrieval.

First, we can see the index, document type, and ID in the first few lines of the result:

```
{
 "_index": "joblistings",
 "_type": "job-listing",
 "_id": "122517",
```

This makes a retrieval of a document very efficient when using these three values as we did in this query.

There is also a version stored for each document, which in this case is 1.

```
    "_version": 1,
```

If we do this same query with the code remaining as it is, then this document will be stored again with the same index, doc type, and ID, and hence will have the version incremented. Trust me, do the curl on the API again, and you will see this increment to 2.

Now examine the content of the first few properties of the `"JSON"` property. We assigned this property of the result from the API to be the JSON of the job description returned by StackOverflow embedded within the HTML.

```
"JSON": {
 "@context": "http://schema.org",
 "@type": "JobPosting",
 "title": "SpaceX Enterprise Software Engineer, Full Stack",
 "skills": [
  "c#",
  "sql",
  "javascript",
  "asp.net",
  "angularjs"
 ],
```

This is some of the beauty of a web site like StackOverflow giving us structured data, and with using a tools like Elasticsearch as we get nicely structured data. We can, and will, leverage this for great effect with very small amounts of code. We can easily perform queries using Elasticsearch to identify job listing based upon specific skills (we'll do this in an upcoming recipe), industry, job benefits, and other attributes.

The result of our API also returned a property '`CleanedWords`', which was the result of several of our NLP processes extracting high-value words and terms. The following is an excerpt of the values that ended up in Elasticsearch:

```
"CleanedWords": [
 "job",
 "Location",
 "options",
 "Paid relocation",
 "Job",
 "type",
 "Permanent",
 "Experience",
 "level",
```

And again, we will be able to use these to perform rich queries that can help us find specific matches based upon these specific words.

Checking Elasticsearch for a listing before scraping

Now lets leverage Elasticsearch as a cache by checking to see if we already have stored a job listing and hence do not need to hit StackOverflow again. We extend the API for performing a scrape of a job listing to first search Elasticsearch, and if the result is found there we return that data. Hence, we optimize the process by making Elasticsearch a job listings cache.

How to do it

We proceed with the recipe as follows:

The code for this recipe is within `09/05/api.py`. The `JobListing` class now has the following implementation:

```
class JobListing(Resource):
    def get(self, job_listing_id):
        print("Request for job listing with id: " + job_listing_id)

        es = Elasticsearch()
        if (es.exists(index='joblistings', doc_type='job-listing',
id=job_listing_id)):
            print('Found the document in ElasticSearch')
            doc =  es.get(index='joblistings', doc_type='job-listing',
id=job_listing_id)
            return doc['_source']

        listing = get_job_listing_info(job_listing_id)
        es.index(index='joblistings', doc_type='job-listing',
id=job_listing_id, body=listing)

        print("Got the following listing as a response: " + listing)
        return listing
```

Before calling the scraper code, the API checks to see if the document already exists in Elasticsearch. This is performed by the appropriately named '`exists`' method, which we pass the index, doc type and ID we are trying to get.

If that returns true, then the document is retrieved using the `get` method of the Elasticsearch object, which is also given the same parameters. This returns a Python dictionary representing the Elasticsearch document, not the actual data that we stored. That actual data/document is referenced by accessing the `'_source'` key of the dictionary.

There's more...

The `JobListingSkills` API implementation follows a slightly different pattern. The following is its code:

```
class JobListingSkills(Resource):
    def get(self, job_listing_id):
        print("Request for job listing's skills with id: " +
job_listing_id)

        es = Elasticsearch()
        if (es.exists(index='joblistings', doc_type='job-listing',
id=job_listing_id)):
            print('Found the document in ElasticSearch')
            doc =  es.get(index='joblistings', doc_type='job-listing',
id=job_listing_id)
            return doc['_source']['JSON']['skills']

        skills = get_job_listing_skills(job_listing_id)

        print("Got the following skills as a response: " + skills)
        return skills
```

This implementation only uses ElasticSearch to the extent of checking if the document already is in ElasticSearch. It does not try to save a newly retrieved document from the scraper. That is because the result of the `get_job_listing` scraper is only a list of the skills and not the entire document. So, this implementation can use the cache, but it adds no new data. This is one of the design decisions of having different a method for scraping which returns only a subset of the actual document that is scraped.

A potential solution to this is to have this API method call `get_job_listing_info` instead, then save the document, and finally only return the specific subset (in this case the skills). Again, this is ultimately a design consideration around what types of methods your users of the sojobs module need. For purposes of these initial recipes, it was considered better to have two different functions at that level to return the different sets of data.

10
Creating Scraper Microservices with Docker

In this chapter, we will cover:

- Installing Docker
- Installing a RabbitMQ container from Docker Hub
- Running a Docker container (RabbitMQ)
- Stopping and removing a container and image
- Creating an API container
- Creating a generic microservice with Nameko
- Creating a scraping microservice
- Creating a scraper container
- Creating a backend (ElasticCache) container
- Composing and running the scraper containers with Docker Compose

Introduction

In this chapter, we will learn to containerize our scraper, getting it ready for the real world by starting to package it for real, modern, cloud-enabled operations. This will involve packaging the different elements of the scraper (API, scraper, backend storage) as Docker containers that can be run locally or in the cloud. We will also examine implementing the scraper as a microservice that can be independently scaled.

Much of the focus will be upon using Docker to create our containerized scraper. Docker provides us a convenient and easy means of packaging the various components of the scraper as a service (the API, the scraper itself, and other backends such as Elasticsearch and RabbitMQ). By containerizing these components using Docker, we can easily run the containers locally, orchestrate the different containers making up the services, and also conveniently publish to Docker Hub. We can then deploy them easily to cloud providers to create our scraper in the cloud.

One of the great things about Docker (and containers in general) is that we can both easily install pre-packaged containers without all the fuss of having to get an installer for an application and deal with all of the configuration hassle. We can then also package our own software that we wrote into a container, and run that container without having to deal with all those details. Additionally, we can also publish to a private or public repository to share our software.

What is really great about Docker is that the containers are, for the most part, platform-independent. Any Linux-based container can be run on any operating system, including Windows (which uses VirtualBox underneath to virtualize Linux and is mostly transparent to the Windows user). So one benefit is that any Linux-based Docker container can be run on any Docker supported operating system. No more need to create multiple OS versions of your application!

So let's go and learn a little Docker and put our scraper components into containers.

Installing Docker

In this recipe, we look at how to install Docker and verify that it is running.

Getting ready

Docker is supported on Linux, macOS, and Windows, so it has the major platforms covered. The installation process for Docker is different depending on the operating system that you are using, and even differs among the different Linux distributions.

The Docker website has good documentation on the installation processes, so this recipe will quickly walk through the important points of the installation on macOS. Once the install is complete, the user experience for Docker, at least from the CLI, is identical.

For reference, the main page for installation instructions for Docker is found at: `https://docs.docker.com/engine/installation/`

How to do it

We will be proceeding with the recipe as follows:

1. We will be using a variant of Docker known as Docker Community Edition, and walk through the installation on macOS. On the download page for macOS you will see the following section. Click on the download for the Stable channel, unless you are feeling brave and want to use the Edge channel.

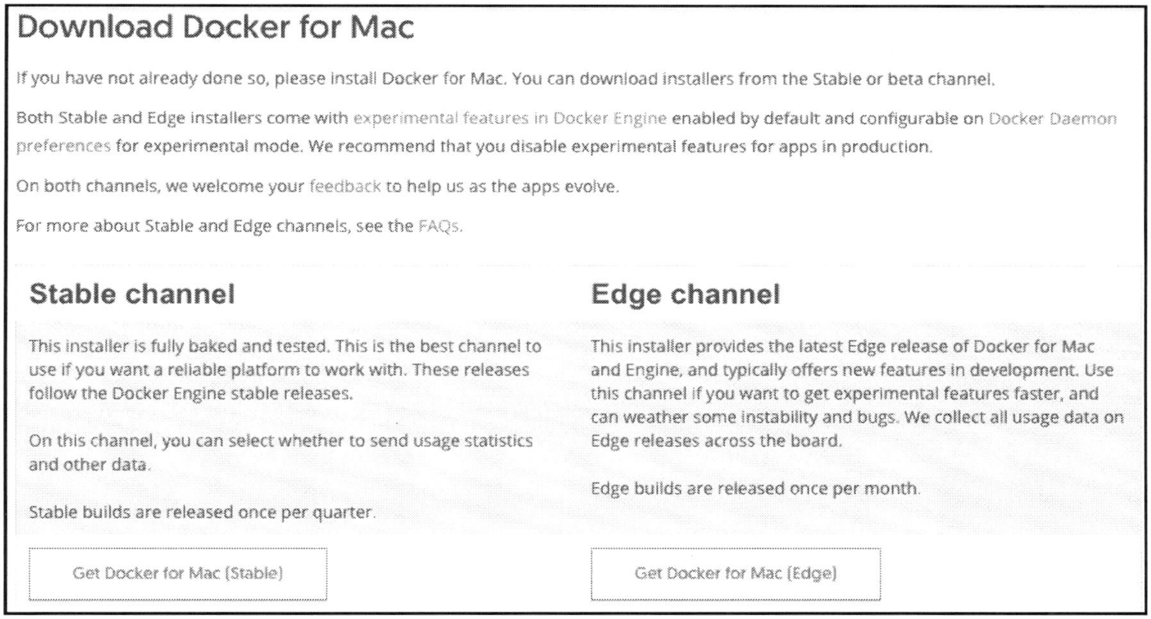
Download Docker for Mac
If you have not already done so, please install Docker for Mac. You can download installers from the Stable or beta channel.
Both Stable and Edge installers come with experimental features in Docker Engine enabled by default and configurable on Docker Daemon preferences for experimental mode. We recommend that you disable experimental features for apps in production.
On both channels, we welcome your feedback to help us as the apps evolve.
For more about Stable and Edge channels, see the FAQs.
Stable channel
This installer is fully baked and tested. This is the best channel to use if you want a reliable platform to work with. These releases follow the Docker Engine stable releases.
On this channel, you can select whether to send usage statistics and other data.
Stable builds are released once per quarter.
Get Docker for Mac (Stable)
Edge channel
This installer provides the latest Edge release of Docker for Mac and Engine, and typically offers new features in development. Use this channel if you want to get experimental features faster, and can weather some instability and bugs. We collect all usage data on Edge releases across the board.
Edge builds are released once per month.
Get Docker for Mac (Edge)

The docker download page

2. This will download a `Docker.dmg` file. Open the DMG and you will be presented with the following window:

The Docker for Mac installer window

3. Drag *Moby* the whale into your applications folder. Then open `Docker.app`. You will be asked to authenticate the installation, so enter your password and the installation will complete. When that is done, you will see Moby in your status bar:

The Moby toolbar icon

4. There are number of configuration settings, statuses, and pieces of information available by clicking on Moby. We will mostly use the command-line tools. To verify things are working from the command line, open a terminal and enter the command, docker info. Docker will give you some information on its configuration and status.

Installing a RabbitMQ container from Docker Hub

Pre-built containers can be obtained from a number of container repositories. Docker is preconfigured with connectivity to Docker Hub, where many software vendors, and also enthusiasts, publish containers with one or more configurations.

In this recipe, we will install RabbitMQ, which will be used by another tool we use in another recipe, Nameko, to function as the messaging bus for our scraping microservice.

Getting ready

Normally, the installation of RabbitMQ is a fairly simple process, but it does require several installers: one for Erlang, and then one for RabbitMQ itself. If management tools, such as the web-based administrative GUI are desired, that is yet one more step (albeit a fairly small one). By using Docker, we can simply get the container with all of this preconfigured. Let's go do that.

How to do it

We proceed with the recipe as follows:

1. Containers can be obtained using the `docker pull` command. This command will check and see if a container is installed locally, and if not, go and fetch it for us. Try the command from the command line, including the `--help flag`. You will get the following, informing you that you need at least one more parameter: the name and possibly tag for the container:

```
$ docker pull --help

Usage: docker pull [OPTIONS] NAME[:TAG|@DIGEST]

Pull an image or a repository from a registry

Options:
  -a, --all-tags Download all tagged images in the repository
      --disable-content-trust Skip image verification (default
true)
      --help Print usage
```

2. We are going to pull the `rabbitmq:3-management` container. The portion before the colon is the container name, and the second part is a tag. Tags often represent a version of the container, or a specific configuration. In this case, we will want to get the RabbitMQ container with tag 3-management. This tag means we want the container version with version 3 of RabbitMQ and with the management tools installed.

Before we do this, you might be thinking where this comes from. It comes from Docker Hub (`hub.docker.com`), from the RabbitMQ repository. The page for this repository is at `https://hub.docker.com/_/rabbitmq/`, and will look like the following:

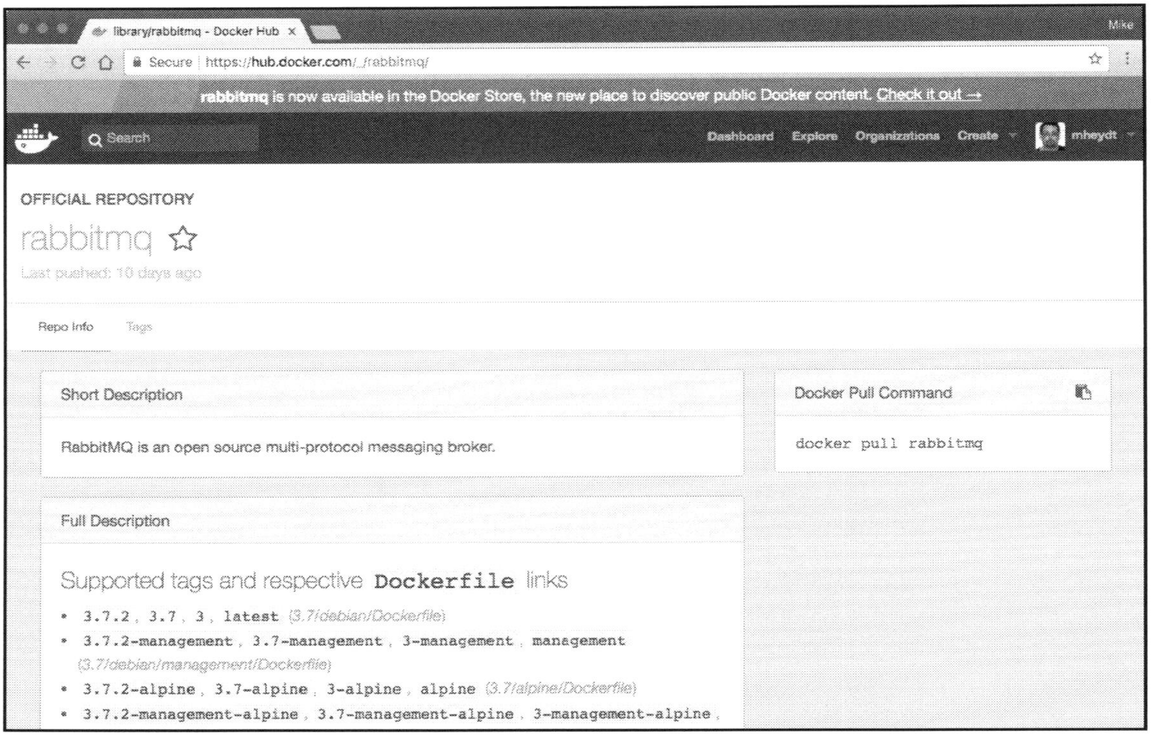

Page for RabbitMQ repository

> Note the section showing tags, and that it has the 3-management tag. If you scroll down, you will also see a lot more information about the container and tags, and what they comprise.

3. Now let's pull this container. Issue the following command from the terminal:

```
$docker pull rabbitmq:3-management
```

4. Docker will go out to Docker Hub and start the download. You'll see this in action with output similar to the following, which will likely run for a few minutes depending on your download speed:

```
3-management: Pulling from library/rabbitmq
e7bb522d92ff: Pull complete
ad90649c4d84: Pull complete
5a318b914d6c: Pull complete
cedd60f70052: Pull complete
f4ec28761801: Pull complete
b8fa44aa9074: Pull complete
e3b16d5314a0: Pull complete
7d93dd9659c8: Pull complete
356c2fc6e036: Pull complete
3f52408394ed: Pull complete
7c89a0fb0219: Pull complete
1e37a15bd7aa: Pull complete
9313c22c63d5: Pull complete
c21bcdaa555d: Pull complete
Digest:
sha256:c7466443efc28846bb0829d0f212c1c32e2b03409996cee38be4402726c5
6a26
Status: Downloaded newer image for rabbitmq:3-management
```

Congratulations! If this is your first time using Docker, you have downloaded your first container image. You can verify it is downloaded and installed using the docker images command.

```
$ docker images
REPOSITORY TAG IMAGE    ID           CREATED     SIZE
rabbitmq   3-management 6cb6e2f951a8 10 days ago 151MB
```

Running a Docker container (RabbitMQ)

In this recipe we learn how to run a docker image, thereby making a container.

Getting ready

We will start the RabbitMQ container image that we downloaded in the previous recipe. This process is representative of how many containers are run, so it makes a good example.

How to do it

We proceed with the recipe as follows:

1. What we have downloaded so far is an image that can be run to create an actual container. A container is an actual instantiation of an image with specific parameters needed to configure the software in the container. We run the container by running an image using docker run and passing the image name/tag, and any other parameters required to run the image (these are specific to the image and normally can be found on the Docker Hub page for the image). The specific command we need to run RabbitMQ using this image is the following:

```
$ docker run -d -p 15672:15672 -p 5672:5672 rabbitmq:3-management
094a138383764f487e5ad0dab45ff64c08fe8019e5b0da79cfb1c36abec69cc8
```

2. `docker run` tells Docker to run an image in a container. The image we want to run is at the end of the statement: `rabbitmq:3-management`. The `-d` option tells Docker to run the container detached, meaning the output of the container is not routed to the terminal. This allows us to retain control of the terminal. The `-p` option maps a host port to a container port. RabbitMQ uses port 5672 for actual commands, and port 15672 for the web UI. This maps an identical port on your actual operating system to the ports used by the software running in the container.

The big hexidecimal value output is an identifier of the container. The first portion, 094a13838376, is the container ID created by Docker (this will be different for every container that is started).

3. We can check which containers are running using docker ps, which gives us the process status of each container:

```
$ docker ps
CONTAINER ID IMAGE COMMAND CREATED STATUS PORTS NAMES
094a13838376 rabbitmq:3-management "docker-entrypoint..." 5 minutes
ago Up 5 minutes 4369/tcp, 5671/tcp, 0.0.0.0:5672->5672/tcp,
15671/tcp, 25672/tcp, 0.0.0.0:15672->15672/tcp dreamy_easley
```

We can see the container ID and other information such as which image it is based on, how long it has been up, which ports the container exposes, the port mappings we defined, and a friendly name made up by Docker for us to refer to the container.

4. The real way to check whether this is running is to open the browser and navigate to `localhost:15672`, the RabbitMQ management UI URL:

The RabbitMQ Admin UI login page

5. The default username and password for this container is guest:guest. Enter those values and you will see the management UI:

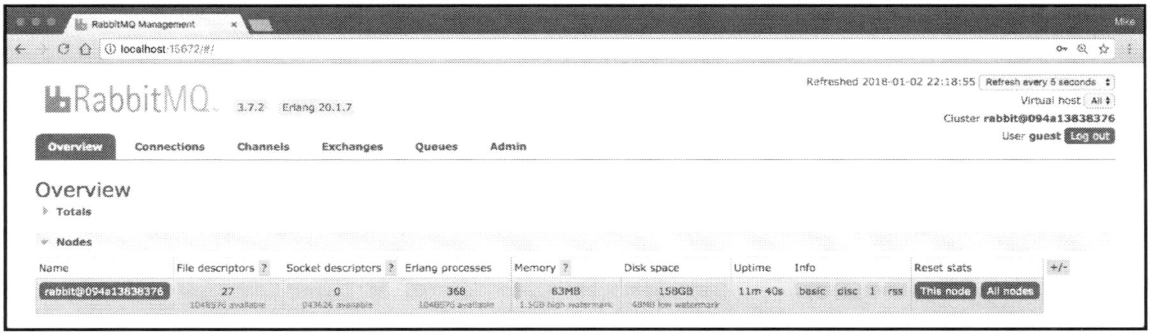

The management UI

There's more...

This is actually as far as we will progress with RabbitMQ. In a later recipe, we will use the Nameko Python microservice framework, which will transparently use RabbitMQ without our knowledge. We first needed to make sure it was installed and running.

Creating and running an Elasticsearch container

While we are looking at pulling container images and starting containers, let's go and run an Elasticsearch container.

How to do it

Like most things Docker, there are a lot of different versions of Elasticsearch containers available. We will use the official Elasticsearch image available in Elastic's own Docker repository:

1. To install the image, enter the following:

```
$docker pull docker.elastic.co/elasticsearch/elasticsearch:6.1.1
```

> Note that we are using another way of specifying the image to pull. Since this is on Elastic's Docker repository, we include the qualified name that includes the URL to the container image instead of just the image name. The :6.1.1 is the tag and specifies a specific version of that image.

2. You will see some output while this is processing, showing the download process. When it is complete, you will have a few lines letting you know it is done:

```
Digest:
sha256:9e6c7d3c370a17736c67b2ac503751702e35a1336724741d00ed9b3d0043
4fcb
Status: Downloaded newer image for
docker.elastic.co/elasticsearch/elasticsearch:6.1.1
```

3. Now let's check that the images are available for Docker:

```
$ docker images
REPOSITORY TAG IMAGE ID CREATED SIZE
rabbitmq 3-management 6cb6e2f951a8 12 days ago 151MB
docker.elastic.co/elasticsearch/elasticsearch 6.1.1 06f0d8328d66 2
weeks ago 539MB
```

4. Now we can run Elasticsearch with the following Docker command:

```
docker run -e ELASTIC_PASSWORD=MagicWord -p 9200:9200 -p 9300:9300
docker.elastic.co/elasticsearch/elasticsearch:6.1.1
```

5. The environment variable, `ELASTIC_PASSWORD` passes in a password, and the two ports map the host ports to the Elasticsearch ports exposed in the container.
6. Next, check that the container is running in Docker:

```
$ docker ps
CONTAINER ID IMAGE COMMAND CREATED STATUS PORTS NAMES
308a02f0e1a5 docker.elastic.co/elasticsearch/elasticsearch:6.1.1
"/usr/local/bin/do..." 7 seconds ago Up 6 seconds
0.0.0.0:9200->9200/tcp, 0.0.0.0:9300->9300/tcp romantic_kowalevski
094a13838376 rabbitmq:3-management "docker-entrypoint..." 47 hours
ago Up 47 hours 4369/tcp, 5671/tcp, 0.0.0.0:5672->5672/tcp,
15671/tcp, 25672/tcp, 0.0.0.0:15672->15672/tcp dreamy_easley
```

7. And finally, perform the following curl. If Elasticsearch is running you will get the `You Know, for Search` message:

```
$ curl localhost:9200
{
 "name" : "8LaZfMY",
 "cluster_name" : "docker-cluster",
 "cluster_uuid" : "CFgPERC8TMm5KaBAvuumvg",
 "version" : {
 "number" : "6.1.1",
 "build_hash" : "bd92e7f",
 "build_date" : "2017-12-17T20:23:25.338Z",
 "build_snapshot" : false,
 "lucene_version" : "7.1.0",
 "minimum_wire_compatibility_version" : "5.6.0",
 "minimum_index_compatibility_version" : "5.0.0"
 },
 "tagline" : "You Know, for Search"
}
```

Stopping/restarting a container and removing the image

Let's look at how to stop and remove a container, and then also its image.

How to do it

We proceed with the recipe as follows:

1. First query Docker for running containers:

```
$ docker ps
CONTAINER ID IMAGE COMMAND CREATED STATUS PORTS NAMES
308a02f0e1a5 docker.elastic.co/elasticsearch/elasticsearch:6.1.1
"/usr/local/bin/do..." 7 seconds ago Up 6 seconds
0.0.0.0:9200->9200/tcp, 0.0.0.0:9300->9300/tcp romantic_kowalevski
094a13838376 rabbitmq:3-management "docker-entrypoint..." 47 hours
ago Up 47 hours 4369/tcp, 5671/tcp, 0.0.0.0:5672->5672/tcp,
15671/tcp, 25672/tcp, 0.0.0.0:15672->15672/tcp dreamy_easley
```

2. Let's stop the Elasticsearch container. To stop a container, we use `docker stop <container-id>`. Elasticsearch has a container ID of 308a02f0e1a5. The following stops the container

```
$ docker stop 30
30
```

To acknowledge the container is stopped, Docker will echo the container ID you told it to stop

> Note that I didn't have to enter the full container ID and only entered 30. You only have to enter the first digits of the container ID until what you have entered is unique among all containers. It's a nice shortcut!.

3. Checking the running container status, Docker only reports the other container:

```
$ docker ps
CONTAINER ID IMAGE COMMAND CREATED STATUS PORTS NAMES
094a13838376 rabbitmq:3-management "docker-entrypoint..." 2 days
ago Up 2 days 4369/tcp, 5671/tcp, 0.0.0.0:5672->5672/tcp,
15671/tcp, 25672/tcp, 0.0.0.0:15672->15672/tcp dreamy_easley
```

4. The container is not running, but it is also not deleted. Let's look at using `docker ps -a` command:

```
$ docker ps -a
CONTAINER ID IMAGE COMMAND CREATED STATUS PORTS NAMES
308a02f0e1a5 docker.elastic.co/elasticsearch/elasticsearch:6.1.1
"/usr/local/bin/do..." 11 minutes ago Exited (143) 5 minutes ago
romantic_kowalevski
548fc19e8b8d docker.elastic.co/elasticsearch/elasticsearch:6.1.1
"/usr/local/bin/do..." 12 minutes ago Exited (130) 12 minutes ago
competent_keller
15c83ca72108 docker.elastic.co/elasticsearch/elasticsearch:6.1.1
"/usr/local/bin/do..." 15 minutes ago Exited (130) 14 minutes ago
peaceful_jennings
3191f204c661 docker.elastic.co/elasticsearch/elasticsearch:6.1.1
"/usr/local/bin/do..." 18 minutes ago Exited (130) 16 minutes ago
thirsty_hermann
b44f1da7613f docker.elastic.co/elasticsearch/elasticsearch:6.1.1
"/usr/local/bin/do..." 25 minutes ago Exited (130) 19 minutes ago
```

This lists all containers currently on the system. I actually truncated my listing by quite a bit as I have a lot of these!

5. We can restart our Elasticsearch container using `docker restart`:

```
$ docker restart 30
30
```

6. If you check `docker ps` you will see the container is operational again.

This is important as this container is storing the Elasticsearch data within the file system of the container. By stopping and restarting, this data is not lost. So, you can stop to reclaim the resources (CPU and memory) used by the container, and then restart without loss at a later time.

7. Running or stopped, a container takes up disk space. A container can be removed to reclaim disk space. This can be done using `docker container rm <container-id>`, however a container can only be removed if it is not running. Let's try and remove the running container:

```
$ docker container rm 30
Error response from daemon: You cannot remove a running container
308a02f0e1a52fe8051d1d98fa19f8ac01ff52ec66737029caa07a8358740bce.
Stop the container before attempting removal or force remove
```

8. We got a warning about the container running. We can force it with a flag, but it's best to stop it first. Stopping ensures the application inside shuts down cleanly:

```
$ docker stop 30
30
$ docker rm 30
30
```

9. Now if you go back to docker `ps -a`, the Elasticsearch container is no longer in the list and disk space for the container is reclaimed.

> Note that we have now lost any data that was stored in that container! It's beyond the scope of this book, but most containers can be told to store data on the host's file system, and therefore we don't lost data.

10. The disk space for the container has been removed, but the image for the container is still on the disk. That's good if we want to make another container. But if you also want to free that space, you can use `docker images rm <image-id>`. Going back to the Docker images result, we can see the image had an ID of `06f0d8328d66`. The following deletes that image and we get that space back (in this case 539MB):

```
$ docker image rm 06
Untagged: docker.elastic.co/elasticsearch/elasticsearch:6.1.1
Untagged:
docker.elastic.co/elasticsearch/elasticsearch@sha256:9e6c7d3c370a17
736c67b2ac503751702e35a1336724741d00ed9b3d00434fcb
Deleted:
sha256:06f0d8328d66a0f620075ee689ddb2f7535c31fb643de6c785deac8ba6db
6a4c
Deleted:
sha256:133d33f65d5a512c5fa8dc9eb8d34693a69bdb1a696006628395b07d5af0
8109
```

```
Deleted:
sha256:ae2e02ab7e50b5275428840fd68fced2f63c70ca998a493d200416026c68
4a69
Deleted:
sha256:7b6abb7badf2f74f1ee787fe0545025abcffe0bf2020a4e9f30e437a715c
6d6a
```

And now the image is gone and we have that space reclaimed also.

> Note that if there are any containers that have been run off that image that still exist, then this will fail and those containers can be either running or stopped. Just doing a `docker ps -a` may not show the offending container, so you may have to use `docker ps -a` to find the stopped containers and delete them first.

There's more...

At this point you know enough about Docker to become very dangerous! So let's move on to examining how we can create our own containers with our own applications installed. First, let's go and look at making the crawler into a microservice that can be run in a container.

Creating a generic microservice with Nameko

In the next few recipes, we are going to create a scraper that can be run as a microservice within a Docker container. But before jumping right into the fire, let's first look at creating a basic microservice using a Python framework known as Nameko.

Getting ready

We will use a Python framework known as Nameko (pronounced [nah-meh-koh] to implement microservices. As with Flask-RESTful, a microservice implemented with Nameko is simply a class. We will instruct Nameko how to run the class as a service, and Nameko will wire up a messaging bus implementation to allow clients to communicate with the actual microservice.

Nameko, by default, uses RabbitMQ as a messaging bus. RabbitMQ is a high-performance messaging bus that is great for performing the type of messaging service used between microservices. It's a similar model to what we saw earlier with SQS, but designed more for services located in the same data center instead of across that cloud. That's actually a great use for RabbitMQ, as we tend to cluster/scale microservices in the same environment these days, particularly within a containerized cluster such as Docker or Kubernetes.

Therefore, we will need to have a local instance of RabbitMQ running. Make sure that you have a RabbitMQ container running as show in the earlier recipe.

Also make sure you have Nameko installed:

```
pip install Nameko
```

How to do it

We proceed with the recipe as follows:

1. The sample microservice is implemented in 10/01/hello_microservice.py. This is a very simple service that can be passed a name for which the microservice replies Hello, <name>!.
2. To run the microservice, we need to simply execute the following command from the terminal (while in the directory for the script):

```
$nameko run hello_microservice
```

3. Nameko opens the Python file matching the specified microservices name and starts up the microservice. When starting, we will see a few lines of output:

```
starting services: hello_microservice
Connected to amqp://guest:**@127.0.0.1:5672//
```

4. This states that Nameko has found our microservice, and that it has connected to an AMQP server (RabbitMQ) on port 5672 (RabbitMQ's default port). The microservice is now up and running and awaiting requests.

If you go into the RabbitMQ API and go into the queues tab, you will see that Nameko has automatically created a queue for the microservice.

5. Now we have to do something to make a request of the microservice. We will look at two ways of doing this. First, Nameko comes with an interactive shell that lets us interactively make requests to Nameko microservices. You can start the shell with the following command in a separate terminal window to the one running the microservice:

   ```
   nameko shell
   ```

6. You will see an interactive Python session start, with output similar to the following:

   ```
   Nameko Python 3.6.1 |Anaconda custom (x86_64)| (default, Mar 22
   2017, 19:25:17)
   [GCC 4.2.1 Compatible Apple LLVM 6.0 (clang-600.0.57)] shell on
   darwin
   Broker: pyamqp://guest:guest@localhost
   In [1]:
   ```

7. In this shell, we can simply refer to Nameko as 'n'. To talk to our service we issue the following statement:

   ```
   n.rpc.hello_microservice.hello(name='Mike')
   ```

8. This tells Nameko that we want to make an rpc call to the `hello` method of `hello_microservice`. When pressing *Enter* you will get the following result back:

   ```
   Out[1]: 'Hello, Mike!'
   ```

9. If you check in the terminal window running the service you should see an additional line of output:

   ```
   Received a request from: Mike
   ```

10. It is also possible to call the microservice from within Python code. There is an implementation of this available in `10/01/say_hi.py`. Executing this script with Python has the following output:

    ```
    $python say_hi.py
    Hello, Micro-service Client!
    ```

So let's go and see how these are implemented.

How it works

Let's first look at the implementation of the microservice in `hello_microservice.py`. There really isn't a lot of code, so here it all is:

```
from nameko.rpc import rpc

class HelloMicroService:
    name = "hello_microservice"

    @rpc
    def hello(self, name):
        print('Received a request from: ' + name)
        return "Hello, {}!".format(name)
```

There are two thing to point out about this class. The first is the declaration of `name = "hello_microservice"`. This is a declaration of the actual name of the microservice. This member variable is used instead of the class name.

The second is the use of the `@rpc` attribute on the `hello` method. This is a Nameko attribute that specifies that this method should be exposed as an `rpc` style method by the microservice. Hence, the caller is suspended until the reply is received from the microservice. There are other implementations, but for our purposes this is the only one we will use.

When run with the nameko run command, that module will interrogate the file for methods with Nameko attributes and wire them up to the underlying bus.

The implementation in `say_hi.py` constructs a dynamic proxy that can call the service. The code for that is the following:

```
from nameko.standalone.rpc import ClusterRpcProxy

CONFIG = {'AMQP_URI': "amqp://guest:guest@localhost"}

with ClusterRpcProxy(CONFIG) as rpc:
    result = rpc.hello_microservice.hello("Micro-service Client")
    print(result)
```

The dynamic proxy is implemented by the `ClusterRpcProxy` class. When creating the class, we pass it a configuration object, which in this case specifies the address of the AMQP server that the service is located on, and we refer to this instance as the variable `rpc`. Nameko then dynamically identifies the next portion, `.hello_microservice`, as the name of the microservice (as specified earlier with the name field on the microservice class).

The next section, `.hello` then represents the method to call. Combined together, Nameko makes a call to the `hello` method of `hello_microservice`, passing it the specified string, and since this is an RPC proxy, waits until the reply is received.

> Remote procedure calls, RPC for short, block until the result comes back from the other system. In contrast with a publish model, where the message is sent off and the sending app continues along.

There's more...

There is quite a lot of good stuff in Nameko that we have not even seen. One very useful factor is that Nameko runs listeners for multiple instances of your microservice. The default at the time of writing is 10. Under the covers, Nameko sends requests from the clients of the microservice to a RabbitMQ queue, of which there will be 10 simultaneous request processors listening to that queue. If there are too many requests to be handled at once, RabbitMQ will hold the message until Nameko recycles an existing microservice instance to process the queued message. To increase the scalability of the microservice, we can simply increase the number of workers through the configuration of the microservice, or run a separate Nameko microservice container in another Docker container or on another computer system.

Creating a scraping microservice

Now let's take our scraper and make it into a Nameko microservice. This scraper microservice will be able to be run independently of the implementation of the API. This will allow the scraper to be operated, maintained, and scaled independently of the API's implementation.

How to do it

We proceed with the recipe as follows:

1. The code for the microservice is straightforward. The code for it is in `10/02/call_scraper_microservice.py` and is shown here:

```
from nameko.rpc import rpc
import sojobs.scraping
```

```
class ScrapeStackOverflowJobListingsMicroService:
    name = "stack_overflow_job_listings_scraping_microservice"

    @rpc
    def get_job_listing_info(self, job_listing_id):
        listing =
sojobs.scraping.get_job_listing_info(job_listing_id)
        print(listing)
        return listing

if __name__ == "__main__":
    print(ScrapeStackOverflowJobListingsMicroService("122517"))
```

2. We have created a class to implement the microservice and given it a single method, `get_job_listing_info`. This method simply wraps the implementation in the `sojobs.scraping` module, but gives it an `@rpc` attribute so that Nameko exposes that method on the microservice bus. This can be run by opening a terminal and running the service with Nameko:

```
$ nameko run scraper_microservice
 starting services:
stack_overflow_job_listings_scraping_microservice
 Connected to amqp://guest:**@127.0.0.1:5672//
```

3. Now we can run the scraper with the code in the `10/02/call_scraper_microservice.py` script. The code in the files is the following:

```
from nameko.standalone.rpc import ClusterRpcProxy

CONFIG = {'AMQP_URI': "amqp://guest:guest@localhost"}

with ClusterRpcProxy(CONFIG) as rpc:
    result =
rpc.stack_overflow_job_listings_scraping_microservice.get_job_listi
ng_info("122517")
    print(result)
```

4. It's basically the same as the code for the client in the previous recipe, but changing the microservice and method names, and of course passing the specific job listing ID. When run, you will see the following output (truncated):

```
{"ID": "122517", "JSON": {"@context": "http://schema.org", "@type":
"JobPosting", "title": "SpaceX Enterprise Software Engineer, Full
Stack", "skills": ["c#", "sql", "javascript", "asp.net",
"angularjs"],

...
```

5. And just like that, we have created a microservice to get job listings from StackOverflow!

There's more...

This microservice is only callable using the `ClusterRpcProxy` class and is not open to being called by anyone on the internet or even locally using REST. We'll solve this issue in an upcoming recipe, where we create a REST API in a container that will talk to this microservice, which will be running in another container.

Creating a scraper container

Now we create a container for our scraper microservice. We will learn about Dockerfiles and how to instruct Docker on how to build a container. We will also examine giving our Docker container hostnames so that they can find each other through Docker's integrated DNS system. Last but not least, we will learn how to configure our Nameko microservice to talk to RabbitMQ in another container instead of just on localhost.

Getting ready

The first thing we want to do is make sure that RabbitMQ is running in a container and assigned to a custom Docker network, where various containers connected to that network will talk to each other. Among many other features, it also provides software defined network (SDN) capabilities to provide various types of integration between containers, hosts, and other systems.

Docker comes with several predefined networks built. You can see the networks currently installed by using the `docker network ls` command:

```
$ docker network ls
NETWORK ID     NAME                                        DRIVER   SCOPE
bc3bed092eff   bridge                                      bridge   local
26022f784cc1   docker_gwbridge                             bridge   local
448d8ce7f441   dockercompose2942991694582470787_default    bridge   local
4e549ce87572   dockerelkxpack_elk                          bridge   local
ad399a431801   host                                        host     local
rbultxlnlhfb   ingress                                     overlay  swarm
389586bebcf2   none                                        null     local
806ff3ec2421   stackdockermaster_stack                     bridge   local
```

To get our containers to communicate with each other, let's create a new bridge network named `scraper-net`.

```
$ docker network create --driver bridge scraper-net
e4ea1c48395a60f44ec580c2bde7959641c4e1942cea5db7065189a1249cd4f1
```

Now when we start a container, we attach it to `scraper-net` using the `--network` parameter:

```
$docker run -d --name rabbitmq --network scrape-rnet -p 15672:15672 -p
5672:5672 rabbitmq:3-management
```

This container is now connected to both the scraper-net network and to the host network. Because it is also connected to host, it is still possible to connect to it from the host system.

Note also that we used `--name rabbitmq` as an option. This gives this container the name, `rabbitmq`, but Docker will also resolve DNS queries from other containers attached to `scraper-net` so that they can find this container!

Now let's go and put the scraper in a container.

How to do it

We proceed with the recipe as follows:

1. The way that we create a container is by creating a `dockerfile` and then using that to tell Docker to create a container. I've included a Dockerfile in the `10/03` folder. The contents are the following (we will examine what this means in the *How it works* section):

```
FROM python:3
WORKDIR /usr/src/app

RUN pip install nameko BeautifulSoup4 nltk lxml
RUN python -m nltk.downloader punkt -d /usr/share/nltk_data all

COPY 10/02/scraper_microservice.py .
COPY modules/sojobs sojobs

CMD ["nameko", "run", "--broker", "amqp://guest:guest@rabbitmq",
"scraper_microservice"]
```

2. To create an image/container from this Dockerfile, from a terminal, and within the `10/03` folder, run the following command:

```
$docker build ../.. -f Dockerfile  -t scraping-microservice
```

3. This tells Docker that we want to *build* a container based upon the instructions in the given Dockerfile (specified with -f). The image that is created is specified by `-t scraping-microservice`. The `../..` after build specifies the context of the build. When building, we will copy files into the container. This context specifies the home directory that copies are relative to. When you run this command, you will see output similar to the following:

```
Sending build context to Docker daemon 2.128MB
Step 1/8 : FROM python:3
 ---> c1e459c00dc3
Step 2/8 : WORKDIR /usr/src/app
 ---> Using cache
 ---> bf047017017b
Step 3/8 : RUN pip install nameko BeautifulSoup4 nltk lxml
 ---> Using cache
 ---> a30ce09e2f66
Step 4/8 : RUN python -m nltk.downloader punkt -d
/usr/share/nltk_data all
 ---> Using cache
```

```
 ---> 108b063908f5
Step 5/8 : COPY 10/07/. .
 ---> Using cache
 ---> 800a205d5283
Step 6/8 : COPY modules/sojobs sojobs
 ---> Using cache
 ---> 241add5458a5
Step 7/8 : EXPOSE 5672
 ---> Using cache
 ---> a9be801d87af
Step 8/8 : CMD nameko run --broker amqp://guest:guest@rabbitmq
scraper_microservice
 ---> Using cache
 ---> 0e1409911ac9
Successfully built 0e1409911ac9
Successfully tagged scraping-microservice:latest
```

4. This will likely take a while as the build process needs to download all of the NLTK files into the container. To check that the image is created we can run the following command:

```
$ docker images | head -n 2
REPOSITORY            TAG    IMAGE ID     CREATED     SIZE
scraping-microservice latest 0e1409911ac9 3 hours ago 4.16GB
```

5. Note that this container is 4.16GB in size. This image is based on the `Python:3` container, which can be seen to be `692MB` in size:

```
$ docker images | grep python
 python 3 c1e459c00dc3 2 weeks ago 692MB
```

TIP: Most of the size of this container is because of the inclusion of the NTLK data files.

6. We can now run this image as a container using the following command:

```
03 $ docker run --network scraper-net scraping-microservice
starting services:
stack_overflow_job_listings_scraping_microservice
Connected to amqp://guest:**@rabbitmq:5672//
```

The scraper that we put together is now running in this container, and this output shows that it has connected to an AMQP server located on a system named `rabbitmq`.

7. Now let's test that this is working. In another terminal window run the Nameko shell:

```
03 $ nameko shell
Nameko Python 3.6.1 |Anaconda custom (x86_64)| (default, Mar 22
2017, 19:25:17)
[GCC 4.2.1 Compatible Apple LLVM 6.0 (clang-600.0.57)] shell on
darwin
Broker: pyamqp://guest:guest@localhost
In [1]:
```

8. Now, enter the following in the prompt to call the microservice:

```
n.rpc.stack_overflow_job_listings_scraping_microservice.get_job_lis
ting_info("122517")
```

9. You will see quite a bit of output as a result of the scrape (the following is truncated):

```
Out[1]: '{"ID": "122517", "JSON": {"@context": "http://schema.org",
"@type": "JobPosting", "title": "SpaceX Enterprise Software
Engineer, Full Stack", "skills": ["c#", "sql", "javascript",
"asp.net"
```

Congratulations! We now have successfully called our scraper microservice. Now, let's discuss how this works, and how the Dockerfile constructed the Docker image for the microservice.

How it works

Let's first discuss the Dockerfile by walking through what it told Docker to do during the build process. The first line:

```
FROM python:3
```

This informs Docker that we want to build our container image based on the `Python:3` image found on Docker Hub. This is a prebuilt Linux image with Python 3 installed. The next line informs Docker that we want all of our file operations to be relative to the `/usr/src/app` folder.

```
WORKDIR /usr/src/app
```

At this point in building the image we have a base Python 3 install in place. We need to then install the various libraries that our scraper uses, so the following tells Docker to run pip to install them:

```
RUN pip install nameko BeautifulSoup4 nltk lxml
```

We also need to install the NLTK data files:

```
RUN python -m nltk.downloader punkt -d /usr/share/nltk_data all
```

Next, we copy in the implementation of our scraper. The following copies the `scraper_microservice.py` file from the previous recipe's folder into the container image.

```
COPY 10/02/scraper_microservice.py .
```

This also depends on the `sojobs` module, so we copy that also:

```
COPY modules/sojobs sojobs
```

The final line informs Docker of the command to run when the container is started:

```
CMD ["nameko", "run", "--broker", "amqp://guest:guest@rabbitmq",
"scraper_microservice"]
```

This tells Nameko to run the microservices in `scraper_microservice.py`, and to also talk to the RabbitMQ message broker located on a system with the name, `rabbitmq`. Since we attached our scraper container to the scraper-net network, and also did the same for the RabbitMQ container, Docker connects these two up for us!

Finally, we ran the Nameko shell from the Docker host system. When it started, it reported that it would communicate with the AMQP server (RabbitMQ) at `pyamqp://guest:guest@localhost`. When we executed the command in the shell, the Nameko shell sent that message to localhost.

So how does it talk to the RabbitMQ instance in that container? When we started the RabbitMQ container, we told it to connect to the `scraper-net` network. It is still also connected to the host network, so we can still talk to the RabbitMQ broker as long as we mapped the `5672` port when we started it.

Our microservice in the other container is listening for messages in the RabbitMQ container, and then responds to that container, which is then picked up by the Nameko shell. Isn't that cool?

Creating an API container

At this point, we can only talk to our microservice using AMQP, or by using the Nameko shell or a Nameko `ClusterRPCProxy` class. So let's put our Flask-RESTful API into another container, run that alongside the other containers, and make REST calls. This will also require that we run an Elasticsearch container, as that API code also communicates with Elasticsearch.

Getting ready

First let's start up Elasticsearch in a container that is attached to the `scraper-net` network. We can kick that off with the following command:

```
$ docker run -e ELASTIC_PASSWORD=MagicWord --name=elastic --network
scraper-net  -p 9200:9200 -p 9300:9300
docker.elastic.co/elasticsearch/elasticsearch:6.1.1
```

Elasticsearch is now up and running on our `scarper-net` network. It can be reached by apps in other containers using the name elastic. Now let's move onto creating the container for the API.

How to do it

We proceed with the recipe as follows:

1. In the `10/04` folder is an `api.py` file that implements a modified Flask-RESTful API from earlier, but with several modifications. Let's examine the code of the API:

```
from flask import Flask
from flask_restful import Resource, Api
from elasticsearch import Elasticsearch
from nameko.standalone.rpc import ClusterRpcProxy

app = Flask(__name__)
api = Api(app)

CONFIG = {'AMQP_URI': "amqp://guest:guest@rabbitmq"}

class JobListing(Resource):
    def get(self, job_listing_id):
        print("Request for job listing with id: " + job_listing_id)
```

```
        es = Elasticsearch(hosts=["elastic"])
        if (es.exists(index='joblistings', doc_type='job-listing',
id=job_listing_id)):
            print('Found the document in Elasticsearch')
            doc =  es.get(index='joblistings', doc_type='job-
listing', id=job_listing_id)
            return doc['_source']

        print('Not found in Elasticsearch, trying a scrape')
        with ClusterRpcProxy(CONFIG) as rpc:
            listing =
rpc.stack_overflow_job_listings_scraping_microservice.get_job_listi
ng_info(job_listing_id)
            print("Microservice returned with a result - storing in
Elasticsearch")
            es.index(index='joblistings', doc_type='job-listing',
id=job_listing_id, body=listing)
            return listing

api.add_resource(JobListing, '/',
'/joblisting/<string:job_listing_id>')

if __name__ == '__main__':
    print("Starting the job listing API ...")
    app.run(host='0.0.0.0', port=8080, debug=True)
```

2. The first change is that there is only one method on the API. We'll focus on the `JobListing` method for now. Within that method, we now make the following call to create the Elasticsearch object:

```
es = Elasticsearch(hosts=["elastic"])
```

3. The default constructor assumes that the Elasticsearch server is on localhost. This change now points to the host with the name elastic on our scraper-net network.
4. The second change is the removal of the calls to the functions in the sojobs module. Instead, we use a `Nameko ClusterRpcProxy` object to make the call to the scraper microservice running within our scraper container. This object is passed a configuration that points the RPC proxy to the rabbitmq container.
5. The final change is to the startup of the Flask application:

```
app.run(host='0.0.0.0', port=8080, debug=True)
```

6. The default connects to localhost, or 127.0.0.1. Within a container, this doesn't bind to our `scraper-net` network or even on the host network. Using `0.0.0.0` binds the service to all network interfaces, and hence we can communicate with it via port mapping on the container. The port has also been moved to `8080`, a more common port for REST APIs than 5000.
7. With the API modified to run within a container, and to talk to the scraper microservice, we can now construct the container. In the `10/04` folder is a Dockerfile to configure the container. Its content is the following:

```
FROM python:3
WORKDIR /usr/src/app

RUN pip install Flask-RESTful Elasticsearch Nameko

COPY 10/04/api.py .

CMD ["python", "api.py"]
```

This is simpler than the Dockerfile for the previous container. This container doesn't have all the weight of NTLK. Finally, the startup simply executes the `api.py` files.

8. The container is built using the following:

```
$docker build ../.. -f Dockerfile -t scraper-rest-api
```

9. And then we can run the container using the following:

```
$docker run -d -p 8080:8080 --network scraper-net scraper-rest-api
```

10. Let's now check that all of our containers are running:

```
$ docker ps
CONTAINER ID IMAGE COMMAND CREATED STATUS PORTS NAMES
55e438b4afcd scraper-rest-api "python -u api.py" 46 seconds ago Up
45 seconds 0.0.0.0:8080->8080/tcp vibrant_sammet
bb8aac5b7518 docker.elastic.co/elasticsearch/elasticsearch:6.1.1
"/usr/local/bin/do..." 3 hours ago Up 3 hours
0.0.0.0:9200->9200/tcp, 0.0.0.0:9300->9300/tcp elastic
ac4f51c1abdc scraping-microservice "nameko run --brok..." 3 hours
ago Up 3 hours thirsty_ritchie
18c2f01f58c7 rabbitmq:3-management "docker-entrypoint..." 3 hours
ago Up 3 hours 4369/tcp, 5671/tcp, 0.0.0.0:5672->5672/tcp,
15671/tcp, 25672/tcp, 0.0.0.0:15672->15672/tcp rabbitmq
```

11. Now, from the terminal on the host we can issue a curl to the REST endpoint (output truncated):

```
$ curl localhost:8080/joblisting/122517
"{\"ID\": \"122517\", \"JSON\": {\"@context\":
\"http://schema.org\", \"@type\": \"JobPosting\", \"title\":
\"SpaceX Enterprise Software Engineer, Full Stack\", \"skills\":
[\"c#\", \"sql\", \"javas
```

And there we have it. We have containerized the API and the functionality, and also run RabbitMQ and Elasticsearch in containers.

There's more...

This type of containerization is a great boon to the design and deployment of operations but still, we needed to create a number of Dockerfiles, containers, and a network to connect them, and run them all independently. Fortunately, we can simplify this with docker-compose. We'll see this in the next recipe.

Composing and running the scraper locally with docker-compose

Compose is a tool for defining and running multi-container Docker applications. With Compose, you use a YAML file to configure your application's services. Then, with a single command and a simple configuration file, you create and start all the services from your configuration.

Getting ready

The first thing that needs to be done to use Compose is to make sure it is installed. Compose is automatically installed with Docker for macOS. On other platforms, it may or not be installed. You can find the instructions at the following URL: `https://docs.docker.com/compose/install/#prerequisites`.

Also, make sure all of the existing containers that we created earlier are not running, as we will create new ones.

How to do it

We proceed with the recipe as follows:

1. Docker Compose uses a `docker-compose.yml` file that tells Docker how to compose containers as `services`. In the `10/05` folder there is a `docker-compose.yml` file to start up all the parts of our scraper as a service. The following is the file's contents:

```
version: '3'
services:
  api:
    image: scraper-rest-api
    ports:
      - "8080:8080"
    networks:
      - scraper-compose-net

  scraper:
    image: scraping-microservice
    depends_on:
      - rabbitmq
    networks:
      - scraper-compose-net

  elastic:
    image: docker.elastic.co/elasticsearch/elasticsearch:6.1.1
    ports:
      - "9200:9200"
      - "9300:9300"
    networks:
      - scraper-compose-net

  rabbitmq:
    image: rabbitmq:3-management
    ports:
      - "15672:15672"
    networks:
      - scraper-compose-net

networks:
  scraper-compose-net:
    driver: bridge
```

With Docker Compose we move away from thinking in terms of containers and toward working with services. In this file, we described four services (api, scraper, elastic, and rabbitmq) and how they are created. The image tag for each tells Compose which Docker image to use for that service. If we need to map ports, then we can use the `ports` tag. The `network` tag specifies a network to connect the service to, in this case the network is also declared in the file to be a `bridged` network. One last thing to point out is the use of the `depends_on` tag for the scraper service. This service requires the `rabbitmq` service to be running beforehand, and this tells docker compose to make sure that this happens in the specified sequence.

2. Now to bring everything up, open a terminal and from that folder run the following command:

```
$ docker-compose up
```

3. There will be pause while Compose reads the configuration and figures out what to do, and then there will be quite a bit of output as every container's output will be streamed into this one console. At the beginning of the output you will see something similar to the following:

```
Starting 10_api_1 ...
 Recreating elastic ...
 Starting rabbitmq ...
 Starting rabbitmq
 Recreating elastic
 Starting rabbitmq ... done
 Starting 10_scraper_1 ...
 Recreating elastic ... done
 Attaching to rabbitmq, 10_api_1, 10_scraper_1, 10_elastic_1
```

4. In another terminal, you can issue a `docker ps` to see the containers that have started:

```
$ docker ps
 CONTAINER ID IMAGE COMMAND CREATED STATUS PORTS NAMES
 2ed0d456ffa0 docker.elastic.co/elasticsearch/elasticsearch:6.1.1
"/usr/local/bin/do..." 3 minutes ago Up 2 minutes
0.0.0.0:9200->9200/tcp, 0.0.0.0:9300->9300/tcp 10_elastic_1
 8395989fac8d scraping-microservice "nameko run --brok..." 26
minutes ago Up 3 minutes 10_scraper_1
 4e9fe8479db5 rabbitmq:3-management "docker-entrypoint..." 26
minutes ago Up 3 minutes 4369/tcp, 5671-5672/tcp, 15671/tcp,
25672/tcp, 0.0.0.0:15672->15672/tcp rabbitmq
 0b0df48a7201 scraper-rest-api "python -u api.py" 26 minutes ago Up
```

```
3 minutes 0.0.0.0:8080->8080/tcp 10_api_1
```

Note the names of the service containers. They are wrapped with two different identifiers. The prefix is simply the folder that the composition is run from, in this case 10 (for a '10_' prefix). You can change this using the -p option to docker-compose up to specify something different. The trailing number is the instance number of the container for that service. In this scenario, we only started one container per service, so these are all _1 at this point. In a little while, we will see this change when we do scaling.

You might ask then: if my service is named `rabbitmq`, and Docker creates a container with the name `10_rabbitmq_1`, how does the microservice, which uses `rabbitmq` as a hostname, still connect to the RabbitMQ instance? Docker Compose has you covered in this situation, as it knows that `rabbitmq` needs to be translated to `10_rabbitmq_1`. Nice!

5. As part of bringing this environment up, Compose has also created the specified network:

```
$ docker network ls | head -n 2
 NETWORK ID NAME DRIVER SCOPE
 0e27be3e30f2 10_scraper-compose-net bridge local
```

If we didn't specify a network, then Compose would have made a default network and wired everything to that. In this case that would work fine. But in more complicated scenarios this default may not be correct.

6. Now, at this point everything is up and running. Let's check things are working well by making a call to the REST scraping API:

```
$ curl localhost:8080/joblisting/122517
 "{\"ID\": \"122517\", \"JSON\": {\"@context\":
\"http://schema.org\", \"@type\": \"JobPosting\", \"title\":
\"SpaceX Enterprise Software Engineer, Full Stack\", \"
...
```

7. And let's also check that Elasticsearch is running by examining the index for the job listings now that we have requested one:

```
$ curl localhost:9200/joblisting
{"error":{"root_cause":[{"type":"index_not_found_exception","reason
":"no such
index","resource.type":"index_or_alias","resource.id":"joblisting",
"index_uuid":"_na_","index":"j
...
```

8. We can also use docker-compose to scale the services. If we want to add more microservice containers to increase the amount of requests that can be handled, we can tell Compose to increase the number of scraper service containers. The following increases the number of scraper containers to 3:

```
docker-compose up --scale scraper=3
```

9. Compose will go and think about this request for a bit and then emit the following, stating that it is starting up two more scraper service containers (and this will be followed with a lot of output from those containers initializing):

```
10_api_1 is up-to-date
10_elastic_1 is up-to-date
10_rabbitmq_1 is up-to-date
Starting 10_scraper_1 ... done
Creating 10_scraper_2 ...
Creating 10_scraper_3 ...
Creating 10_scraper_2 ... done
Creating 10_scraper_3 ... done
Attaching to 10_api_1, 10_elastic_1, 10_rabbitmq_1, 10_scraper_1,
10_scraper_3, 10_scraper_2
```

10. A `docker ps` will now show three scraper containers running:

```
Michaels-iMac-2:09 michaelheydt$ docker ps
CONTAINER ID IMAGE COMMAND CREATED STATUS PORTS NAMES
b9c2da0c9008 scraping-microservice "nameko run --brok..." About a
minute ago Up About a minute 10_scraper_2
643221f85364 scraping-microservice "nameko run --brok..." About a
minute ago Up About a minute 10_scraper_3
73dc31fb3d92 scraping-microservice "nameko run --brok..." 6 minutes
ago Up 6 minutes 10_scraper_1
5dd0db072483 scraper-rest-api "python api.py" 7 minutes ago Up 7
minutes 0.0.0.0:8080->8080/tcp 10_api_1
d8e25b6ce69a rabbitmq:3-management "docker-entrypoint..." 7 minutes
ago Up 7 minutes 4369/tcp, 5671-5672/tcp, 15671/tcp, 25672/tcp,
0.0.0.0:15672->15672/tcp 10_rabbitmq_1
f305f81ae2a3 docker.elastic.co/elasticsearch/elasticsearch:6.1.1
"/usr/local/bin/do..." 7 minutes ago Up 7 minutes
0.0.0.0:9200->9200/tcp, 0.0.0.0:9300->9300/tcp 10_elastic_1
```

11. Now we can see that we have three containers named `10_scraper_1`, `10_scraper_2`, and `10_scraper_3`. Cool! And if you go into the RabbitMQ admin UI, you can see that there are three connections:

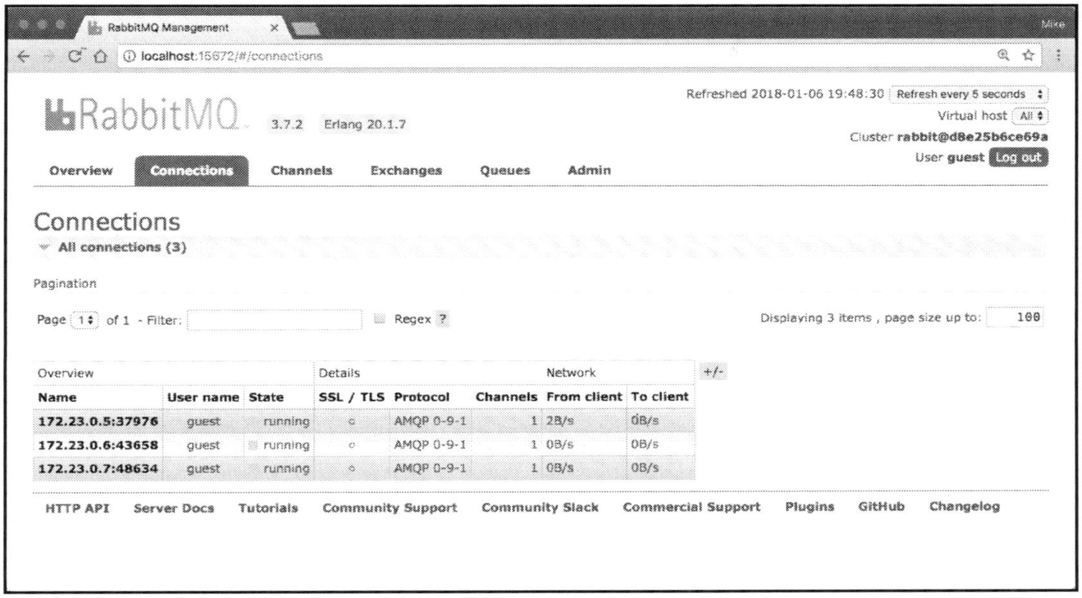

The Nameko queues in RabbitMQ

Note that each has a different IP address. On a bridged network like the one we have created, Compose allocates the IP addresses on the `172.23.0` network, starting at `.2`.

Operationally, all incoming scraping requests from the API will be routed to the rabbitmq container, and the actual RabbitMQ service would then spread the messages across all of the active connections and hence across all three containers, helping us to scale out processing.

Service instances can also be scaled down by issuing a scale value with a smaller number of containers, which Compose will respond to by removing containers until the value is achieved.

And when we are all done, we can tell Docker Compose to bring everything down:

```
$ docker-compose down
Stopping 10_scraper_1 ... done
Stopping 10_rabbitmq_1 ... done
Stopping 10_api_1 ... done
Stopping 10_elastic_1 ... done
Removing 10_scraper_1 ... done
Removing 10_rabbitmq_1 ... done
Removing 10_api_1 ... done
Removing 10_elastic_1 ... done
Removing network 10_scraper-compose-net
```

Executing a docker ps will now show that all of the containers have been removed.

There's more...

We have barely touched many of the capabilities of Docker and Docker Compose, and we have not even yet got into looking at using services such as Docker swarm. While docker Compose is convenient, it only runs the containers on a single host, which ultimately has scalability limitations. Docker swarm will perform similar things to Docker Compose, but work that magic across multiple systems within a cluster, allowing much greater scalability. But hopefully this has given you a feel for the value of Docker and Docker Compose, and how they can be of value when creating a flexible scraping service.

11
Making the Scraper as a Service Real

In this chapter, we will cover:

- Creating and configuring an Elastic Cloud trial account
- Accessing the Elastic Cloud cluster with curl
- Connecting to the Elastic Cloud cluster with Python
- Performing an Elasticsearch query with the Python API
- Using Elasticsearch to query for jobs with specific skills
- Modifying the API to search for jobs by skill
- Storing configuration in the environment
  Creating an AWS IAM user and a key pair for ECS
- Configuring Docker to authenticate with ECR
- Pushing containers into ECR
- Creating an ECS cluster
- Creating a task to run our containers
- Starting and accessing the containers in AWS

Introduction

In this chapter, we will first add a feature to search job listings using Elasticsearch and extend the API for this capability. Then will move Elasticsearch functions to Elastic Cloud, a first step in cloud-enabling our cloud based scraper. Then, we will move our Docker containers to Amazon **Elastic Container Repository** (**ECR**), and finally run our containers (and scraper) in Amazon **Elastic Container Service** (**ECS**).

Creating and configuring an Elastic Cloud trial account

In this recipe we will create and configure an Elastic Cloud trial account so that we can use Elasticsearch as a hosted service. Elastic Cloud is a cloud service offered by the creators of Elasticsearch, and provides a completely managed implementation of Elasticsearch.

> While we have examined putting Elasticsearch in a Docker container, actually running a container with Elasticsearch within AWS is very difficult due to a number of memory requirements and other system configurations that are complicated to get working within ECS. Therefore, for a cloud solution, we will use Elastic Cloud.

How to do it

We'll proceed with the recipe as follows:

1. Open your browser and navigate to `https://www.elastic.co/cloud/as-a-service/signup`. You will see a page similar to the following:

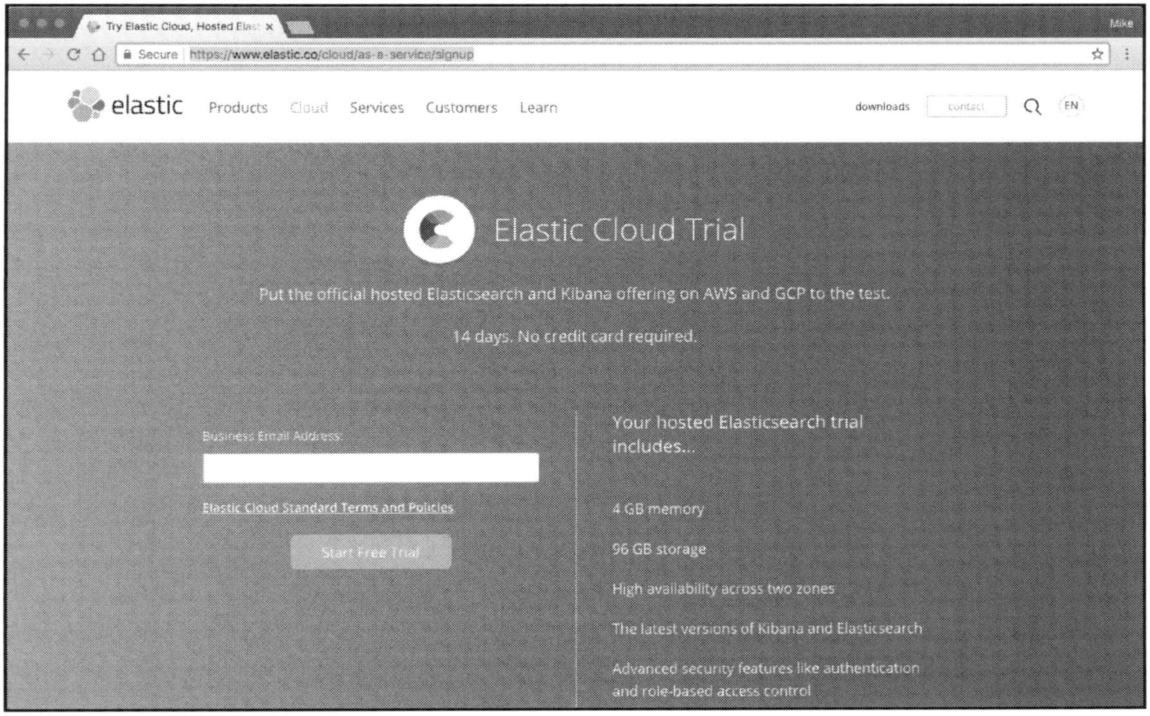

The Elastic Cloud signup page

2. Enter your email and press the **Start Free Trial** button. When the email arrives, verify yourself. You will be taken to a page to create your cluster:

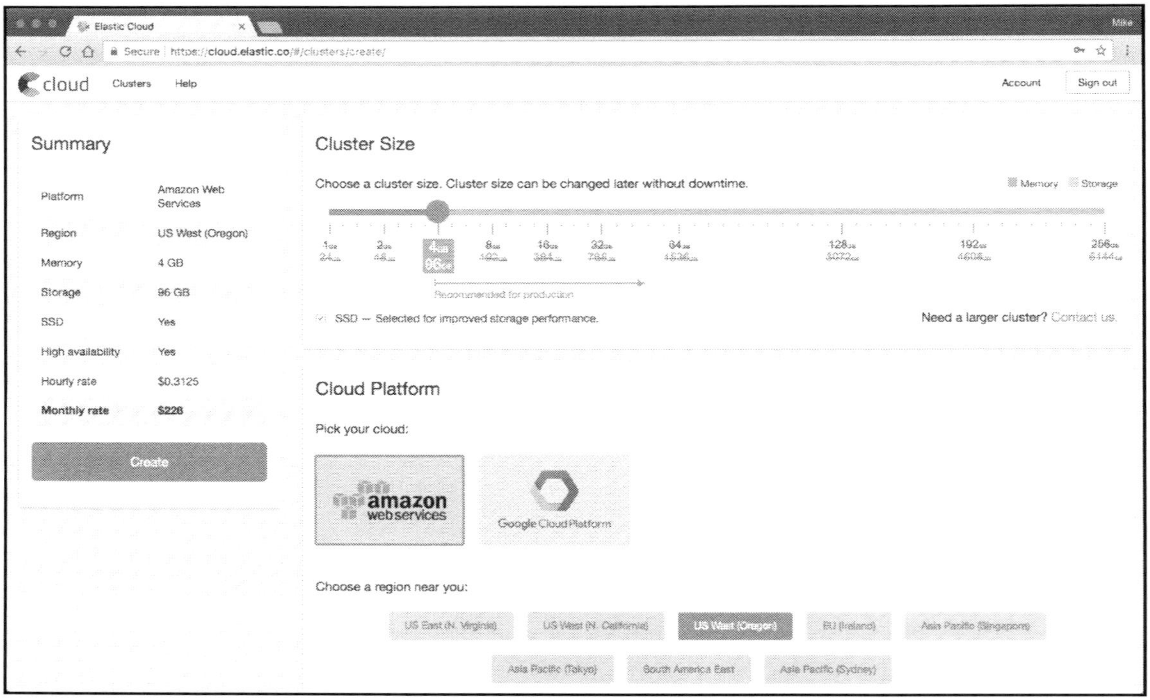

Cluster creation page

3. I'll be using AWS (not Google) in the Oregon (us-west-2) region in other examples, so I'll pick both of those for this cluster. You can pick a cloud and region that works for you. You can leave the other options as it is, and just press create. You will then be presented with your username and password. Jot those down. The following screenshot gives an idea of how it displays the username and password:

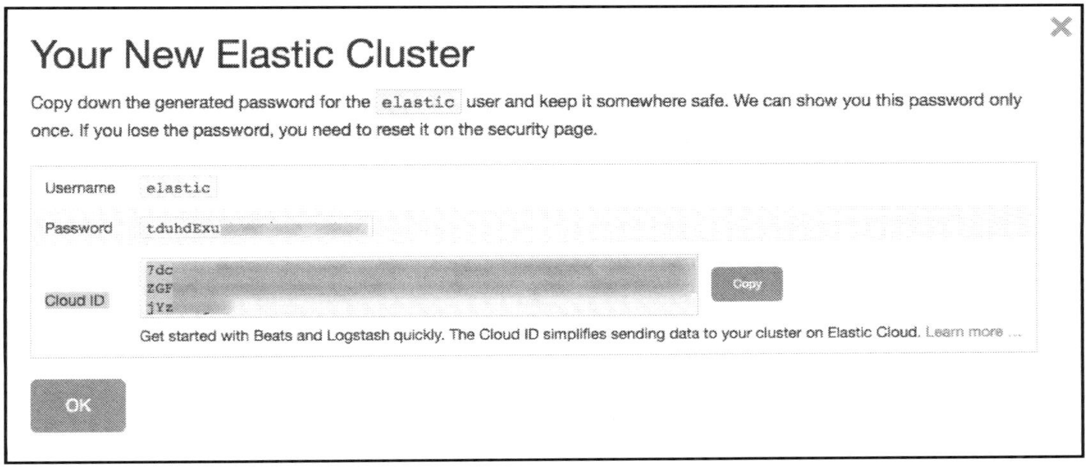

The credentials info for the Elastic Cloud account

> We won't use the Cloud ID in any recipes.

4. Next, you will be presented with your endpoints. The Elasticsearch URL is what's important to us:

5. And that's it - you are ready to go (at least for 14 days)!

Accessing the Elastic Cloud cluster with curl

Elasticsearch is fundamentally accessed via a REST API. Elastic Cloud is no different and is actually an identical API. We just need to be able to know how to construct the URL properly to connect. Let's look at that.

How to do it

We proceed with the recipe as follows:

1. When you signed up for Elastic Cloud, you were given various endpoints and variables, such as username and password. The URL was similar to the following:

```
https://<account-id>.us-west-2.aws.found.io:9243
```

> TIP: Depending on the cloud and region, the rest of the domain name, as well as the port, may differ.

2. We'll use a slight variant of the following URL to communicate and authenticate with Elastic Cloud:

```
https://<username>:<password>@<account-id>.us-west-2.aws.found.io:9
243
```

3. Currently, mine is (it will be disabled by the time you read this):

```
https://elastic:tduhdExunhEWPjSuH73O6yLS@d7c72d3327076cc4daf5528103
c46a27.us-west-2.aws.found.io:9243
```

4. Basic authentication and connectivity can be checked with curl:

```
$ curl
https://elastic:tduhdExunhEWPjSuH73O6yLS@7dc72d3327076cc4daf5528103
c46a27.us-west-2.aws.found.io:9243
{
  "name": "instance-0000000001",
  "cluster_name": "7dc72d3327076cc4daf5528103c46a27",
  "cluster_uuid": "g9UMPEo-QRaZdIlgmOA7hg",
  "version": {
    "number": "6.1.1",
    "build_hash": "bd92e7f",
```

```
        "build_date": "2017-12-17T20:23:25.338Z",
        "build_snapshot": false,
        "lucene_version": "7.1.0",
        "minimum_wire_compatibility_version": "5.6.0",
        "minimum_index_compatibility_version": "5.0.0"
      },
      "tagline": "You Know, for Search"
    }
    Michaels-iMac-2:pems michaelheydt$
```

And we are up and talking!

Connecting to the Elastic Cloud cluster with Python

Now let's look at how to connect to Elastic Cloud using the Elasticsearch Python library.

Getting ready

The code for this recipe is in the `11/01/elasticcloud_starwars.py` script. This script will scrape Star Wars character data from the swapi.co API/website and put it into the Elastic Cloud.

How to do it

We proceed with the recipe as follows:

1. Execute the file as a Python script:

```
$ python elasticcloud_starwars.py
```

2. This will loop through up to 20 characters and drop them into the `sw` index with a document type of `people`. The code is straightforward (replace the URL with yours):

```
from elasticsearch import Elasticsearch
import requests
import json

if __name__ == '__main__':
```

```
    es = Elasticsearch(
        [
"https://elastic:tduhdExunhEWPjSuH73O6yLS@d7c72d3327076cc4daf552810
3c46a27.us-west-2.aws.found.io:9243"
        ])

i = 1
while i<20:
    r = requests.get('http://swapi.co/api/people/' + str(i))
    if r.status_code is not 200:
        print("Got a " + str(r.status_code) + " so stopping")
        break
 j = json.loads(r.content)
 print(i, j)
 #es.index(index='sw', doc_type='people', id=i,
body=json.loads(r.content))
 i = i + 1
```

3. The connection is made using the URL with the username and password added to it. The data is pulled from swapi.co using a GET request and then with a call to `.index()` on the Elasticsearch object. You'll see output similar to the following:

```
1 Luke Skywalker
2 C-3PO
3 R2-D2
4 Darth Vader
5 Leia Organa
6 Owen Lars
7 Beru Whitesun lars
8 R5-D4
9 Biggs Darklighter
10 Obi-Wan Kenobi
11 Anakin Skywalker
12 Wilhuff Tarkin
13 Chewbacca
14 Han Solo
15 Greedo
16 Jabba Desilijic Tiure
Got a 404 so stopping
```

There's more...

When you signed up for Elastic Cloud, you were also given a URL to Kibana. Kibana is a powerful graphical frontend to Elasticsearch:

1. Open the URL in your browser. You'll see see a login page:

The Kibana login page

2. Enter your username and password and you'll be taken to the main dashboard:

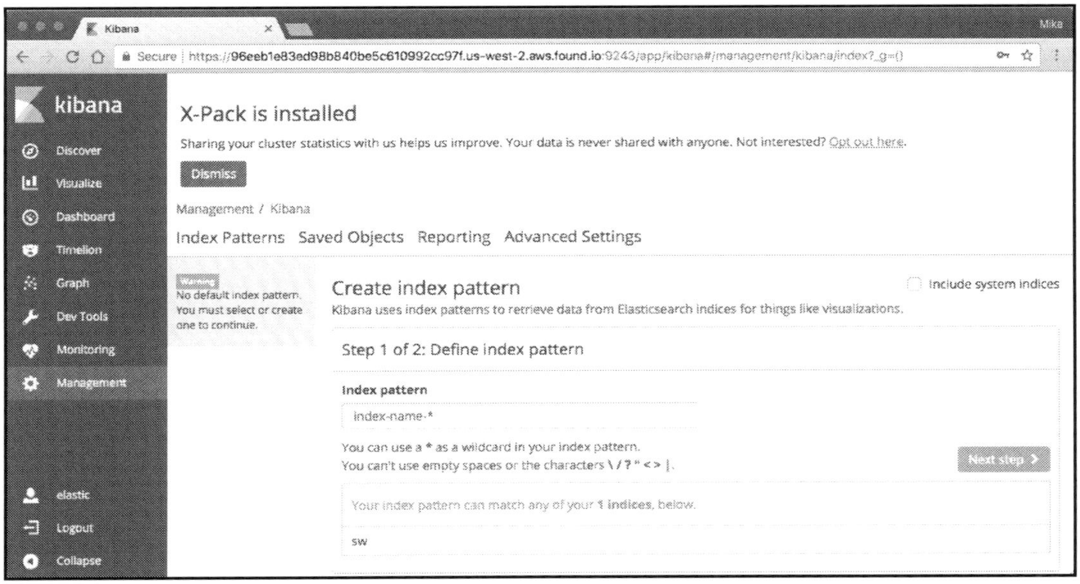

Creating an index pattern

We're being asked to create an index pattern for the one index that was created by our app: **sw**. In the index pattern textbox, enter `sw*` and then press **Next step**.

3. We'll be asked to select a time filter field name. Select **I don't want to use the Time Filter** and press the **Create Index Pattern** button. A few moments later, you will see a confirmation of the index that was created:

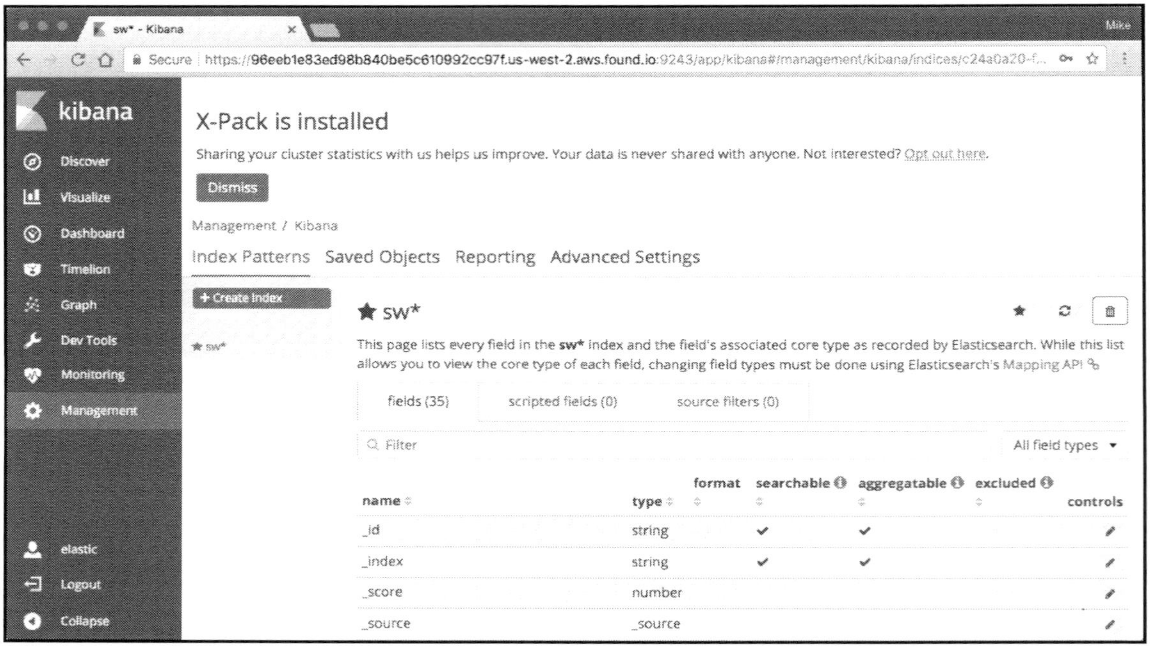

The index that was created

4. Now click the **Discover** menu item, and you'll be taken to the interactive data explorer, where you will see the data we just entered:

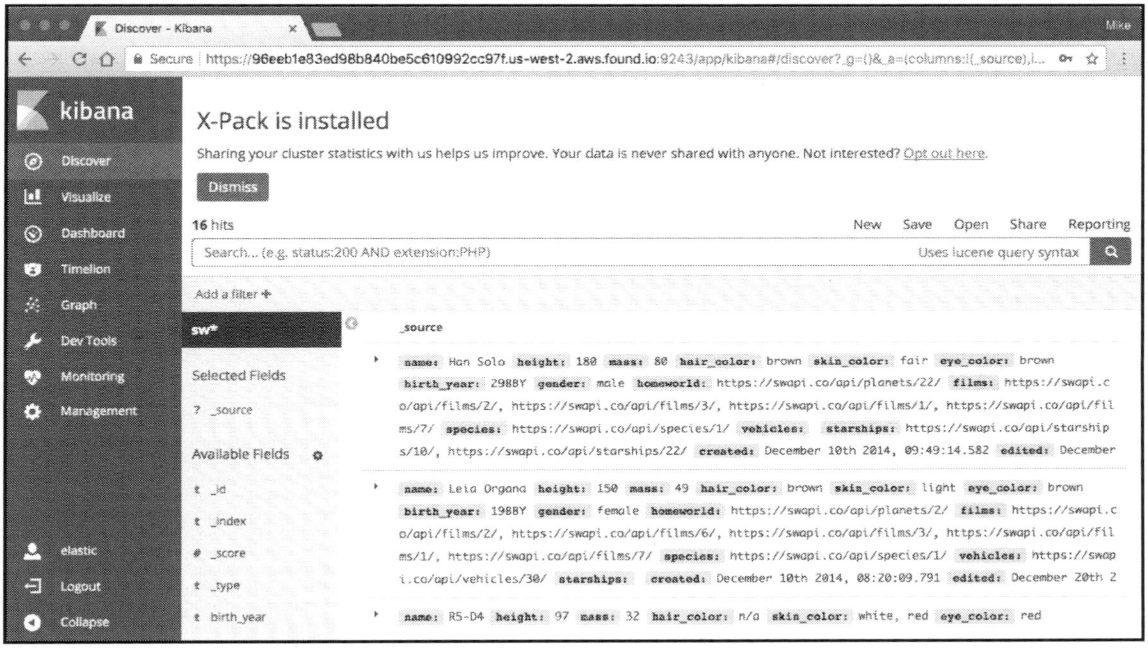

The data added to our index

Here you can navigate through the data and see just how effectively Elasticsearch stored and organized this data.

Performing an Elasticsearch query with the Python API

Now let's look at how we can search Elasticsearch using the Elasticsearch Python library. We will perform a simple search on the Star Wars index.

Getting ready

Make sure to modify the connection URL in the samples to your URL.

How to do it

The code for the search is in the `11/02/search_starwars_by_haircolor.py` script, and can be run by simply executing the script. This is a fairly simple search to find the characters whose hair color is `blond`:

1. The main portion of the code is:

```
es = Elasticsearch(
    [
"https://elastic:tduhdExunhEWPjSuH73O6yLS@7dc72d3327076cc4daf552810
3c46a27.us-west-2.aws.found.io:9243"
    ])

search_definition = {
    "query":{
        "match": {
            "hair_color": "blond"
        }
    }
}

result = es.search(index="sw", doc_type="people",
body=search_definition)
print(json.dumps(result, indent=4))
```

2. A search is performed by constructing a dictionary that expresses an Elasticsearch DSL query. In this case, our query asks for all documents where the `"hair_color"` property is `"blond"`. This object is then passed as the body parameter of the `.search` method. The result of this method is a diction describing what was found (or not). In this case:

```
{
  "took": 2,
  "timed_out": false,
  "_shards": {
    "total": 5,
    "successful": 5,
    "skipped": 0,
    "failed": 0
```

```
},
"hits": {
  "total": 2,
  "max_score": 1.3112576,
  "hits": [
    {
      "_index": "sw",
      "_type": "people",
      "_id": "1",
      "_score": 1.3112576,
      "_source": {
        "name": "Luke Skywalker",
        "height": "172",
        "mass": "77",
        "hair_color": "blond",
        "skin_color": "fair",
        "eye_color": "blue",
        "birth_year": "19BBY",
        "gender": "male",
        "homeworld": "https://swapi.co/api/planets/1/",
        "films": [
          "https://swapi.co/api/films/2/",
          "https://swapi.co/api/films/6/",
          "https://swapi.co/api/films/3/",
          "https://swapi.co/api/films/1/",
          "https://swapi.co/api/films/7/"
        ],
        "species": [
          "https://swapi.co/api/species/1/"
        ],
        "vehicles": [
          "https://swapi.co/api/vehicles/14/",
          "https://swapi.co/api/vehicles/30/"
        ],
        "starships": [
          "https://swapi.co/api/starships/12/",
          "https://swapi.co/api/starships/22/"
        ],
        "created": "2014-12-09T13:50:51.644000Z",
        "edited": "2014-12-20T21:17:56.891000Z",
        "url": "https://swapi.co/api/people/1/"
      }
    },
    {
      "_index": "sw",
      "_type": "people",
      "_id": "11",
      "_score": 0.80259144,
```

```
                    "_source": {
                      "name": "Anakin Skywalker",
                      "height": "188",
                      "mass": "84",
                      "hair_color": "blond",
                      "skin_color": "fair",
                      "eye_color": "blue",
                      "birth_year": "41.9BBY",
                      "gender": "male",
                      "homeworld": "https://swapi.co/api/planets/1/",
                      "films": [
                        "https://swapi.co/api/films/5/",
                        "https://swapi.co/api/films/4/",
                        "https://swapi.co/api/films/6/"
                      ],
                      "species": [
                        "https://swapi.co/api/species/1/"
                      ],
                      "vehicles": [
                        "https://swapi.co/api/vehicles/44/",
                        "https://swapi.co/api/vehicles/46/"
                      ],
                      "starships": [
                        "https://swapi.co/api/starships/59/",
                        "https://swapi.co/api/starships/65/",
                        "https://swapi.co/api/starships/39/"
                      ],
                      "created": "2014-12-10T16:20:44.310000Z",
                      "edited": "2014-12-20T21:17:50.327000Z",
                      "url": "https://swapi.co/api/people/11/"
                    }
                  }
                ]
              }
            }
```

The results give us some metadata about the search execution and then the results in the `hits` property. Each hit returns the actual document as well as the index name, document type, document ID, and a score. The score is a lucene calculation of the relevance of the document to the search query. While this query uses an exact match of a property to a value, you can see that these two documents still have different scores. I'm not sure why in this case, but searching can also be less exact and based on various built-in heuristics to find items "like" a certain sentence, that is, such as when you enter text into a Google search box.

There's more...

The Elasticsearch search DSL, and the search engine itself, is very powerful and expressive. We'll only look at this example and one more in the next recipe, so we don't go into it in much detail. To find out more about the DSL, you can start with the official documentation at `https://www.elastic.co/guide/en/elasticsearch/reference/current/query-dsl.html`.

Using Elasticsearch to query for jobs with specific skills

In this recipe, we move back to using the crawler that we created to scrape and store job listings from StackOverflow in Elasticsearch. We then extend this capability to query Elasticsearch to find job listings that contain one or more specified skills.

Getting ready

The example we will use is coded to use a local Elastic Cloud engine and not a local Elasticsearch engine. You can change that if you want. For now, we will perform this process within a single python script that is run locally and not inside a container or behind an API.

How to do it

We proceed with the recipe as follows:

1. The code for the recipe is in the `11/03/search_jobs_by_skills.py` file:

```
from sojobs.scraping import get_job_listing_info
from elasticsearch import Elasticsearch
import json

if __name__ == "__main__":

    es = Elasticsearch()

    job_ids = ["122517", "163854", "138222", "164641"]

    for job_id in job_ids:
```

```
        if not es.exists(index='joblistings', doc_type='job-
listing', id=job_id):
            listing = get_job_listing_info(job_id)
            es.index(index='joblistings', doc_type='job-listing',
id=job_id, body=listing)

    search_definition = {
        "query": {
            "match": {
                "JSON.skills": {
                    "query": "c#"
                }
            }
        }
    }

    result = es.search(index="joblistings", doc_type="job-listing",
body=search_definition)
    print(json.dumps(result, indent=4))
```

The first part of this code defines four job listings to be put into Elasticsearch, if they already are not available. It iterates through this job's ID, and if not already available, retrieves them and puts them in Elasticsearch.

The remainder of this defines a query to be executed against Elasticsearch, and follows the same pattern for executing the search. The only difference is in the definition of the search criteria. Ultimately, we want to match a list of job skills to those in the job listings.

This query simply matches a single skill to those in the skills field in our job listings documents. The sample specifies that we want to match to the JSON.skills property in the target documents. The skills in those documents are just beneath the root of the document, so in this syntax we preface it with JSON.

This property in Elasticsearch is an array, and the query value we have will match the document if any of the values in that property array are `"c#"`.

2. Running this search with just those four documents in Elasticsearch results in the following (the output here just shows the results and not the complete contents of the four documents returned):

```
{
  "took": 4,
  "timed_out": false,
```

```
  "_shards": {
    "total": 5,
    "successful": 5,
    "skipped": 0,
    "failed": 0
  },
  "hits": {
    "total": 2,
    "max_score": 1.031828,
    "hits": [
```

Each of the jobs placed in Elasticsearch has C# for a skill (I randomly picked these documents, so this is a little bit of a coincidence).

3. The results of these searches return the entire contents of each of the documents that are identified. If we don't want the entire document returned for each hit, we can change the query to make this happen. Let's modify the query to only return the ID in the hits. Change the `search_definition` variable to the following:

```
search_definition = {
    "query": {
        "match": {
            "JSON.skills": {
                "query": "c# sql"
            }
        }
    },
    "_source": ["ID"]
}
```

4. Including the `"_source"` property tells Elasticsearch to return the specified document properties in the result. Executing this query results in the following output:

```
{
  "took": 4,
  "timed_out": false,
  "_shards": {
    "total": 5,
    "successful": 5,
    "skipped": 0,
    "failed": 0
  },
  "hits": {
    "total": 2,
```

```
        "max_score": 1.031828,
        "hits": [
          {
            "_index": "joblistings",
            "_type": "job-listing",
            "_id": "164641",
            "_score": 1.031828,
            "_source": {
              "ID": "164641"
            }
          },
          {
            "_index": "joblistings",
            "_type": "job-listing",
            "_id": "122517",
            "_score": 0.9092852,
            "_source": {
              "ID": "122517"
            }
          }
        ]
      }
    }
```

TIP: Each of the hits now only returns the ID property of the document. This will help control the size of the result if there are a lot of hits.

5. Let's get to the ultimate goal of this recipe, identifying documents that have multiple skills. This is actually a very simple change to `search_defintion`:

```
search_definition={
  "query": {
    "match": {
      "JSON.skills": {
        "query": "c# sql",
        "operator": "AND"
      }
    }
  },
  "_source": [
    "ID"
  ]
}
```

This states that we only want documents where the skills contain both `"c#"` and `"sql"`. The result from running the script is then the following:

```
{
  "took": 4,
  "timed_out": false,
  "_shards": {
    "total": 5,
    "successful": 5,
    "skipped": 0,
    "failed": 0
  },
  "hits": {
    "total": 2,
    "max_score": 1.031828,
    "hits": [
      {
        "_index": "joblistings",
        "_type": "job-listing",
        "_id": "164641",
        "_score": 1.031828,
        "_source": {
          "ID": "164641"
        }
      },
      {
        "_index": "joblistings",
        "_type": "job-listing",
        "_id": "122517",
        "_score": 0.9092852,
        "_source": {
          "ID": "122517"
        }
      }
    ]
  }
}
```

The result set is now cut down to two hits, and if you check, these are the only two with those values in the skills.

Modifying the API to search for jobs by skill

In this recipe, we will modify our existing API to add a method to enable searching for jobs with a set of skills.

How to do it

We will be extending the API code. We will make two fundamental changes to the implementation of the API. The first is that we will add an additional Flask-RESTful API implementation for the search capability, and the second is that we will make addresses for both Elasticsearch and our own microservice configurable by environment variables.

The API implementation is in `11/04_scraper_api.py`. By default, the implementation attempts to connect to Elasticsearch on the local system. If you are using Elastic Cloud, make sure to change the URL (and make sure you have documents in the index):

1. The API can be started by simply executing the script:

```
$ python scraper_api.py
Starting the job listing API ...
 * Running on http://0.0.0.0:8080/ (Press CTRL+C to quit)
 * Restarting with stat
Starting the job listing API ...
 * Debugger is active!
 * Debugger pin code: 449-370-213
```

2. To make a search request, we make a POST to the `/joblistings/search` endpoint, passing data in the form of `"skills=<skills separated with a space>"`. The following performs a search for jobs with C# and SQL:

```
$ curl localhost:8080/joblistings/search -d "skills=c# sql"
{
  "took": 4,
  "timed_out": false,
  "_shards": {
    "total": 5,
    "successful": 5,
    "skipped": 0,
    "failed": 0
  },
  "hits": {
    "total": 2,
    "max_score": 1.031828,
    "hits": [
      {
        "_index": "joblistings",
        "_type": "job-listing",
        "_id": "164641",
        "_score": 1.031828,
        "_source": {
          "ID": "164641"
```

```
                }
            },
            {
                "_index": "joblistings",
                "_type": "job-listing",
                "_id": "122517",
                "_score": 0.9092852,
                "_source": {
                  "ID": "122517"
                }
            }
        ]
    }
}
```

And we get the results that we saw in the previous recipe. We've now made our search capabilities accessible over the internet with REST!

How it works

This works by adding another Flask-RESTful class implementation:

```
class JobSearch(Resource):
    def post(self):
        skills = request.form['skills']
        print("Request for jobs with the following skills: " + skills)

        host = 'localhost'
        if os.environ.get('ES_HOST'):
            host = os.environ.get('ES_HOST')
        print("ElasticSearch host: " + host)

        es = Elasticsearch(hosts=[host])
        search_definition = {
            "query": {
                "match": {
                    "JSON.skills": {
                        "query": skills,
                        "operator": "AND"
                    }
                }
            },
            "_source": ["ID"]
        }

        try:
```

```
            result = es.search(index="joblistings", doc_type="job-listing",
body=search_definition)
            print(result)
            return result

        except:
            return sys.exc_info()[0]

api.add_resource(JobSearch, '/', '/joblistings/search')
```

This class implements a post method as a resource mapped to `/joblistings/search`. The reason for the POST operation is that we are passing a string consisting of multiple words. While this could be URL-encoded in a GET operation, a POST allows us to pass this in as a keyed value. And while we only have the one key, skills, future expansion to other keys to support other search parameters can be simply added.

There's more...

The decision to perform the search from within the API implementation is one that should be considered as a system evolves. It is my opinion, and just mine (but I think others would agree), that like how the API calls a microservice for the actual scraping, it should also call a microservice that handles the search (and that microservice would then interface with Elasticsearch). This would also be the case for storing the document returned from the scraping microservice, as well as accessing Elasticsearch to check for a cached document. But for our purposes here, we'll try and keep it simple.

Storing configuration in the environment

This recipe points out a change made in the code of the API in the previous recipe to support one of the *factors* of a **12-Factor** application. A 12-Factor app is defined as an app that is designed to be run as a software as a service. We have been moving our scraper in this direction for a while now, breaking it into components that can be run independently, as scripts, or in containers, and as we will see soon, in the cloud. You can learn all about 12-Factor apps at `https://12factor.net/`.

Factor-3 states that we should pass in configuration to our application through environment variables. While we definitely don't want to hardcode things, such as URLs, to external services, it also isn't best practice to use configuration files. When deploying to various environments, such as containers or the cloud, a config file will often get fixed in an image and not be able to be changed on-demand as the application is dynamically deployed to different environments.

The best way to fix this is to always look in environment variables for configuration settings that can change based on how the application is run. Most tools for running 12-Factor apps allow the setting of environment variables based on how and where the environment decides the app should be run.

How to do it

In our job listings implementation, we used the following code to determine the host for Elasticsearch:

```
host = 'localhost'
if os.environ.get('ES_HOST'):
    host = os.environ.get('ES_HOST')
print("ElasticSearch host: " + host)

es = Elasticsearch(hosts=[host])
```

It's a straightforward and simple thing to do, but it's very important for making our app incredibly portable to different environments. This defaults to using localhost, but lets us define a different host with the `ES_HOST` environment variable.

The implementation of the skills search also makes a similar change to allow us to change a default of localhost for our scraping microservice:

```
CONFIG = {'AMQP_URI': "amqp://guest:guest@localhost"}
if os.environ.get('JOBS_AMQP_URL'):
    CONFIG['AMQP_URI'] = os.environ.get('JOBS_AMQP_URL')
print("AMQP_URI: " + CONFIG["AMQP_URI"])

with ClusterRpcProxy(CONFIG) as rpc:
```

We will see Factor-3 in use in the upcoming recipes, as we move this code to AWS's Elastic Container Service.

Creating an AWS IAM user and a key pair for ECS

In this recipe, we will create an Identity and Access Management (IAM) user account to allow us to access the AWS Elastic Container Service (ECS). We need this as we are going to package our scraper and API up in Docker containers (we've done this already), but now we are going to move these containers into and run them from AWS ECS, making our scraper a true cloud service.

Getting ready

This assumes that you have already created an AWS account, which we used earlier in the book when we looked at SQS and S3. You don't need a different account, but we need to create a non-root user that has permissions to use ECS.

How to do it

Instructions for creating an IAM user with ECS permissions and a key pair can be found at `https://docs.aws.amazon.com/AmazonECS/latest/developerguide/get-set-up-for-amazon-ecs.html`.

There are a lot of instructions on this page, such as setting up a VPC and security groups. Just focus now on creating the user, assigning permissions, and creating the key pair.

One thing I want to highlight are the permissions for the IAM account you create. There are detailed instructions on doing this at `https://docs.aws.amazon.com/AmazonECS/latest/developerguide/instance_IAM_role.html`. I've seen this not done properly. Just make sure that when you examine the permissions for the user you just created that the following permissions are assigned:

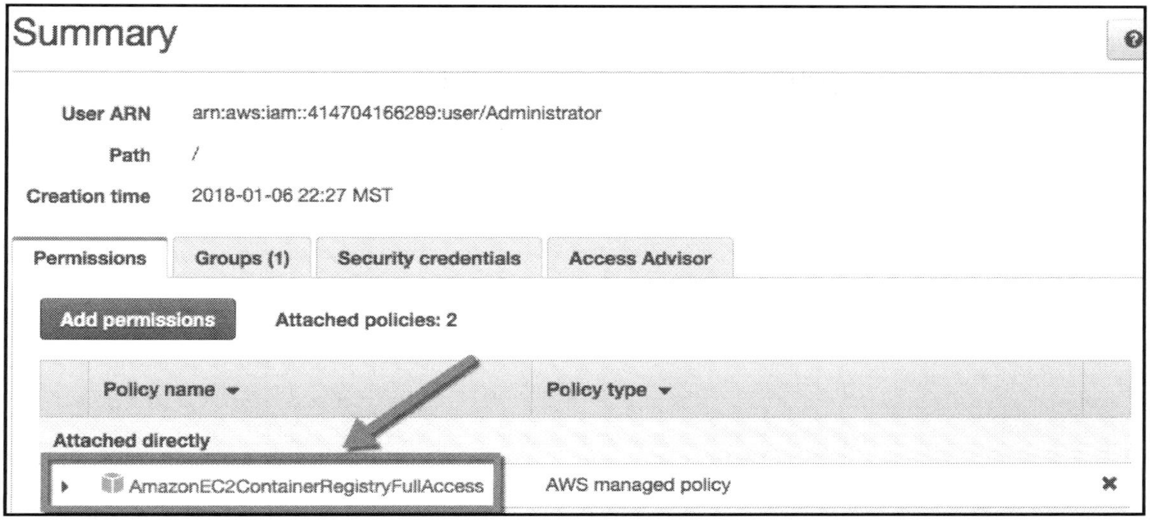

AWS IAM credentials

I attached these directly to the account I use for ECS instead of through the group. If this isn't assigned, you will get cryptic authentication errors when pushing containers to ECR.

One more thing: we will need the access key ID and the associated secret key. This will be presented to you during the creation of the user. If you didn't record it, you can create another one in the security credentials tab of the user's account page:

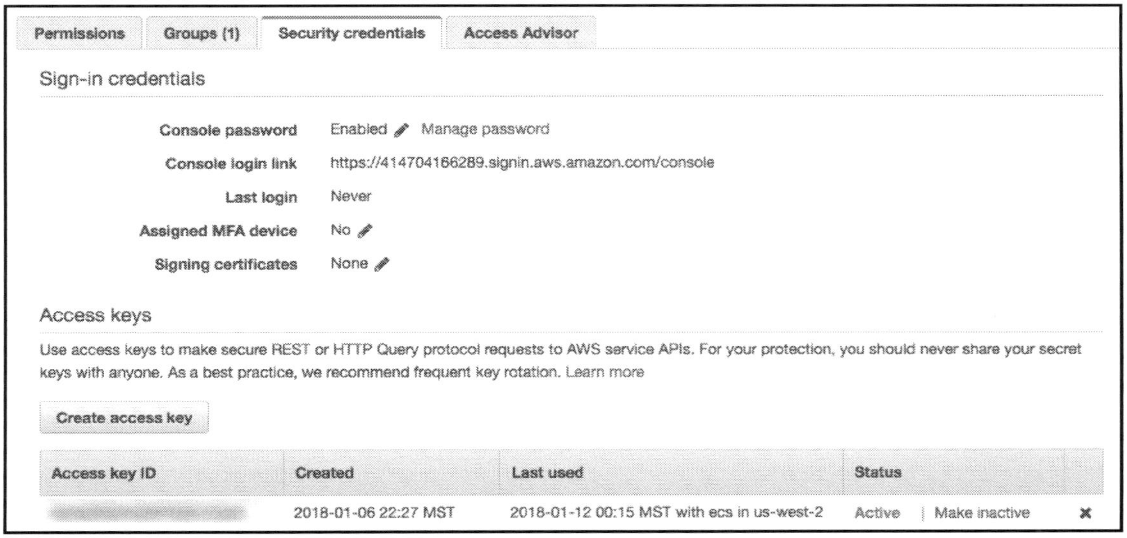

Note that you can't get the secret for an already existing access key ID. You will have to make another.

Configuring Docker to authenticate with ECR

In this recipe, we will configure docker to be able to push our containers to the Elastic Container Repository (ECR).

Getting ready

A key element of Docker is docker container repositories. We have previously used Docker Hub to pull containers. But we can also push our containers to Docker Hub, or any Docker-compatible container repository, such as ECR. But this is not without its troubles. The docker CLI does not naturally know how to authenticate with ECR, so we have to jump through a few hoops to get it to work.

Make sure that the AWS command line tools are installed. These are required to get Docker authenticated to work with ECR. Good instructions are found at `https://docs.aws.amazon.com/cli/latest/userguide/installing.html`. Once the install is verified, you will need to configure the CLI to use the account created in the previous recipe. This can be done using the `aws configure` command, which will prompt you for four items:

```
$ aws configure
AWS Access Key ID [None]: AKIA---------QKCVQAA
AWS Secret Access Key [None]: KEuSaLgn4dpyXe-------------VmEKdhV
Default region name [None]: us-west-2
Default output format [None]: json
```

Swap the keys to be the ones you retrieved earlier, and set your default region and data type.

How to do it

We proceed with the recipe as follows:

1. Execute the following command. This returns a command to authenticate Docker with ECR:

```
$ aws ecr get-login --no-include-email --region us-west-2
docker login -u AWS -p
```

```
eyJwYXlsb2FkIjoiN3BZVWY4Q2JoZkFwYUNKOUp6c1BkRy80VmRYN0Y2LzQ0Y2pVNFJ
KZTA5alBrUEdSMHlNUk9TMytsTFVURGtxb3Q5VTZqV0xxNmRCVHJnL1FIb2lGbEF0dV
ZhNFpEOUkxb1FxUTNwcUluaVhqS1FCZmU2WTRLNlQrbjE4VHdiOEpqbmtwWjJJek8xR
lR2Y2Y5S3NGRlQrbDZhcktUNXZJbjNkb1czVGQ2TXZPUlg5cE5Ea2w4S29vamt6SE10
Ym8rOW5mLzBvVkRRSDlaY3hqRG45d0FzNVA5Z1BPVUU5OVFrTEZGeENNPUHJRZmlTeHF
qaEVPcGo3ZVAxL3pCNnFTdjVXUEozaUNtV0I0b1lFNEcyVzA4M2hKQmpESUFTV1VMZ1
B0MFI2YUlHSHJxTlRvTGZOR1R5clJ2VUZKcnFWZGptMkZlR0ppK3I5emFrdGFKeDJBN
VRCUzBzZDZaOG1yeW1Nd0dBVi81NDZDeU1XYVliby9reWtaNUNuZE8zVXFHdHFKSnJm
QVRKakhlVU1jTXQ1RjE0Tk83OWR0ckNnYmZmUHdtS1hXOVh6MklWUG5VUlJsekRaUjR
MMVFKT2NjNlE0NWFaNkR2enlDRWw1SzVwOEcvK3lSMXFPYzdKUWpxaUErdDZyaCtDNX
JCWHlJQndKRm5mcUJhaVhBMVhNMFNocmlNd0FUTXFjZ0NtZTEyUGhOMmM2c0pNTU5hZ
0JMNEhXSkwyNXZpQzMyOVI2MytBUWhPNkVaajVMdG9iMVRreFFjbjNGamVNdThPM0pp
ZnM5WGxPSVJsOHlsUUh0LzFlQ2ZYelQ1cVFOU2g1NjFiVWZtOXNhNFRRWlhZUlNLVVF
rd3JFK09EUXh3NUVnTXFTbS9FRm1PbHkxdEpncXNzVFljeUE4Y1VYczFnOFBHL2VwVG
tVTG1ReFYwa0p5MzdxUmlIdHU1OWdjMDRmZWFSVGdSekhQcXl0WExxdFpXcTVCeVRZT
nhMeVVpZW0yN3JkQWhmaStpUHpMTXV1NGZJa3JjdmlBZFF3dGwrdEVORTNZSVBhUnZJ
MFN0Q1djN2J2blI2Njg3OEhQZHJKdXlYaTN0czhDYlBXNExxOamVCRm8waUt0SktCckJ
jN0tUZzJEY1d4NlN4b1Vkc2ErdnN4V0N5NWFzeWdMUlBHYVdoNzFwOVhFZWpPZTczNE
80Z0l5RklBU0pHR3o1SVRzYVkwbFB6ajNEYW9QMVhOT3dhcDYwcC9Gb0pQMG1ITjNsb
202eW1EaDA0WEoxWnZ0K0lkMFJ4bE9lVUt3bzRFZFVMaHJ2enBMOUR4SGI5WFFCMEdN
WjFJRlI0MitSb3NMaDVQa0g1RHh1bDJZU0pQMXc0UnVoNUpzUm5rcmF3dHZzSG5PSGd
2YVZTeWl5bFR0cFlQY1haVk51NE5iWnkxSzQwOG5XTVhiMFBNQzJ5OHJuNlpVTDA9Ii
wiZGF0YWtleSI6IkFRRUJBSGo2bGM0WElKdy83bG4wSGMwMERNZWs2R0V4SENiWTRSSS
XBUTUNJNThJblV3QUFBSDR3ZkFZSktvWklodmNOQVFjR29HOHdiUUlCQURCb0Jna3Fo
a2lHOXcwQkJ3RXdIZ1lKWUlaSUFXVURCQUV1TUJFRURQdTFQVXQwRDFkN3c3Rys3Z0l
CRUlBN21Xay9EZnNOM3R5MS9iRFdRYlZtZjdOOURST2xhQWFFbTBFQVFndy9JYlBjTz
hLc0RlNDBCLzhOVnR0YmlFK1FXSDBCaTZmemtCbzNxTkE9IiwidmVyc2lvbiI6IjIiL
CJ0eXBlIjoiREFUQV9LRVkiLCJleHBpcmF0aW9uIjoxNTE1NjA2NzM0fQ==
https://270157190882.dkr.ecr.us-west-2.amazonaws.com
```

This output is a command that you need to execute to get your docker CLI to authenticate with ECR! This secret is only valid for a few hours (twelve I believe). You can copy all this from the where it starts with `docker login` through the end of the URL at the end of the secret.

2. On a Mac (and Linux), I generally shorten this to the following:

```
$(aws ecr get-login --no-include-email --region us-west-2)
WARNING! Using --password via the CLI is insecure. Use --password-
stdin.
Login Succeeded
```

Much easier. At this point, we can use the docker command to push containers to ECR.

This is an area where I've seen a couple of problems. I've found the URL at the end of the secret can still be the root user and not the user you created for ECR (this login HAS to be for that user). If that is the case, later commands will get weird authentication issues. The fix is to delete all the AWS CLI configuration files and reconfigure. This fix doesn't always work. Sometimes, I've had to use a fresh system/VM, go through the AWS CLI install/ config, and then generate this secret to get it to work.

Pushing containers into ECR

In this recipe we will rebuild our API and microservice containers and push them to ECR. We will also push a RabbitMQ container to ECR.

Getting ready

Bear with this, as this can get tricky. In addition to our container images, we also need to push our RabbitMQ container to ECR. ECS doesn't talk to Docker Hub and and can't pull that image. it would be immensely convenient, but at the same time it's probably also a security issue.

Pushing these containers to ECR from a home internet connection can take a long time. I create a Linux image in EC2 in the same region as my ECR, pulled down the code from github, build the containers on that EC2 system, and then push to ECR. The push takes a matter of minutes, if not seconds.

First, let's rebuild our API and microservice containers on our local system. I've included the Python files, two docker files, and a configuration file for the microservice in the `11/05` recipe folder.

Let's start with the build of the API container:

```
$ docker build ../.. -f Dockerfile-api -t scraper-rest-api:latest
```

This docker file is similar to the previous API Docker file with the modification to copy files from the `11/05` folder.

```
FROM python:3
WORKDIR /usr/src/app

RUN pip install Flask-RESTful Elasticsearch Nameko
COPY 11/11/scraper_api.py .

CMD ["python", "scraper_api.py"]
```

Then build the container for the scraper microservice:

```
$ docker build ../.. -f Dockerfile-microservice -t scraper-
microservice:latest
```

This Dockerfile is slightly different from the one for the microservice. Its contents are the following:

```
FROM python:3
WORKDIR /usr/src/app

RUN pip install nameko BeautifulSoup4 nltk lxml
RUN python -m nltk.downloader punkt -d /usr/share/nltk_data all

COPY 11/05/scraper_microservice.py .
COPY modules/sojobs sojobs

CMD ["python", "-u", "scraper_microservice.py"]
```

Now we are ready to work with configuring ECR to store our containers for use by ECS.

> We now run the microservice using python and not with the "nameko run" command. This is due to an issue with sequencing the launch of containers in ECS. The "nameko run" command does not perform well if the RabbitMQ server is not already running, which is not guaranteed in ECS. So, we start this with python. Because of this, the implementation has a startup that essentially copies the code for "nameko run" and wraps it with a while loop and exception handlers as it retries connections until the container is stopped.

How to do it

We proceed with the recipe as follows:

1. When signed in to the account that we created for ECS, we get access to the Elastic Container Repository. This service can hold our containers for use by ECS. There are a number of AWS CLI commands that you can use to work with ECR. Let's start with the following that lists the existing repositories:

```
$ aws ecr describe-repositories
{
    "repositories": []
}
```

2. Right now we don't have any repositories, so let's create some. We will create three repositories, one for each of the different containers: scraper-rest-api, scraper-microservice, and one for a RabbitMQ container, which we will call `rabbitmq`. Each repository maps to one container by its name, but can have multiple tags (up to 1,000 different versions/tags for each). Let's create the three repositories:

```
$ aws ecr create-repository --repository-name scraper-rest-api
{
  "repository": {
    "repositoryArn": "arn:aws:ecr:us-
west-2:414704166289:repository/scraper-rest-api",
    "repositoryUri": "414704166289.dkr.ecr.us-
west-2.amazonaws.com/scraper-rest-api",
    "repositoryName": "scraper-rest-api",
    "registryId": "414704166289",
    "createdAt": 1515632756.0
  }
}

05 $ aws ecr create-repository --repository-name scraper-
microservice
{
  "repository": {
    "repositoryArn": "arn:aws:ecr:us-
west-2:414704166289:repository/scraper-microservice",
    "registryId": "414704166289",
    "repositoryName": "scraper-microservice",
    "repositoryUri": "414704166289.dkr.ecr.us-
west-2.amazonaws.com/scraper-microservice",
    "createdAt": 1515632772.0
  }
```

```
}

05 $ aws ecr create-repository --repository-name rabbitmq
{
  "repository": {
    "repositoryArn": "arn:aws:ecr:us-
west-2:414704166289:repository/rabbitmq",
    "repositoryName": "rabbitmq",
    "registryId": "414704166289",
    "createdAt": 1515632780.0,
    "repositoryUri": "414704166289.dkr.ecr.us-
west-2.amazonaws.com/rabbitmq"
  }
}
```

TIP: Note the data returned. We will need the repository URL for each in the following step(s).

3. We need to *tag* our local container images so their docker knows that when we *push* them, they should go to a specific repository in our ECR. At this point, you should have the following images in docker:

```
$ docker images
REPOSITORY           TAG          IMAGE ID     CREATED        SIZE
scraper-rest-api     latest       b82653e11635 29 seconds ago 717MB
scraper-microservice latest       efe19d7b5279 11 minutes ago
4.16GB
rabbitmq             3-management 6cb6e2f951a8 2 weeks ago    151MB
python               3            c1e459c00dc3 3 weeks ago    692MB
```

4. Tag using the `<image-id> <ECR-repository-uri>` docker tag. Let's tag all three (we don't need to do the python image):

```
$ docker tag b8 414704166289.dkr.ecr.us-
west-2.amazonaws.com/scraper-rest-api

$ docker tag ef 414704166289.dkr.ecr.us-
west-2.amazonaws.com/scraper-microservice

$ docker tag 6c 414704166289.dkr.ecr.us-
west-2.amazonaws.com/rabbitmq
```

5. The list of docker images now shows the tagged images along with the originals:

```
$ docker images
REPOSITORY TAG IMAGE ID CREATED SIZE
414704166289.dkr.ecr.us-west-2.amazonaws.com/scraper-rest-api
latest b82653e11635 4 minutes ago 717MB
scraper-rest-api latest b82653e11635 4 minutes ago 717MB
414704166289.dkr.ecr.us-west-2.amazonaws.com/scraper-microservice
latest efe19d7b5279 15 minutes ago 4.16GB
scraper-microservice latest efe19d7b5279 15 minutes ago 4.16GB
414704166289.dkr.ecr.us-west-2.amazonaws.com/rabbitmq latest
6cb6e2f951a8 2 weeks ago 151MB
rabbitmq 3-management 6cb6e2f951a8 2 weeks ago 151MB
python 3 c1e459c00dc3 3 weeks ago 692MB
```

6. Now we finally push the images into ECR:

```
$ docker push 414704166289.dkr.ecr.us-west-2.amazonaws.com/scraper-
rest-api
The push refers to repository [414704166289.dkr.ecr.us-
west-2.amazonaws.com/scraper-rest-api]
7117db0da9a9: Pushed
8eb1be67ed26: Pushed
5fcc76c4c6c0: Pushed
6dce5c484bde: Pushed
057c34df1f1a: Pushed
3d358bf2f209: Pushed
0870b36b7599: Pushed
8fe6d5dcea45: Pushed
06b8d020c11b: Pushed
b9914afd042f: Pushed
4bcdffd70da2: Pushed
latest: digest:
sha256:2fa2ccc0f4141a1473386d3592b751527eaccb37f035aa08ed0c4b6d7abc
9139 size: 2634

$ docker push 414704166289.dkr.ecr.us-west-2.amazonaws.com/scraper-
microservice
The push refers to repository [414704166289.dkr.ecr.us-
west-2.amazonaws.com/scraper-microservice]
3765fccaf6a6: Pushed
4bde7a8212e1: Pushed
d0aa245987b4: Pushed
5657283a8f79: Pushed
4f33694fe63a: Pushed
5fcc76c4c6c0: Pushed
6dce5c484bde: Pushed
```

```
057c34df1f1a: Pushed
3d358bf2f209: Pushed
0870b36b7599: Pushed
8fe6d5dcea45: Pushed
06b8d020c11b: Pushed
b9914afd042f: Pushed
4bcdffd70da2: Pushed
latest: digest:
sha256:02c1089689fff7175603c86d6ef8dc21ff6aaffadf45735ef754f606f2cf
6182 size: 3262

$ docker push 414704166289.dkr.ecr.us-west-2.amazonaws.com/rabbitmq
The push refers to repository [414704166289.dkr.ecr.us-
west-2.amazonaws.com/rabbitmq]
e38187f05202: Pushed
ea37471972cd: Pushed
2f1d47e88a53: Pushed
e8c84964de08: Pushed
d0537ac3fb13: Pushed
9f345d60d035: Pushed
b45610229549: Pushed
773afacc96cc: Pushed
5eb8d21fccbb: Pushed
10699a5bd960: Pushed
27be686b9e1f: Pushed
96bfbdb03e1c: Pushed
1709335ba200: Pushed
2ec5c0a4cb57: Pushed
latest: digest:
sha256:74308ef1dabc1a0b9615f756d80f5faf388f4fb038660ae42f437be45866
b65e size: 3245
```

7. Now check that the images made it to the repository The following shows this for `scraper-rest-api`:

```
$ aws ecr list-images --repository-name scraper-rest-api
{
  "imageIds": [
    {
      "imageTag": "latest",
      "imageDigest":
"sha256:2fa2ccc0f4141a1473386d3592b751527eaccb37f035aa08ed0c4b6d7ab
c9139"
    }
  ]
}
```

With our containers now stored in ECR, we can go on and create a cluster to run our containers.

Creating an ECS cluster

Elastic Container Service (ECS) is an AWS service that runs your Docker containers in the cloud. There is a lot of power (and detail) in using ECS. We will look at a simple deployment that runs our containers on a single EC2 virtual machine. Our goal is to get our scraper to the cloud. Extensive detail on using ECS to scale out the scraper is for another time (and book).

How to do it

We start by creating an ECR cluster using the AWS CLI. The we will create one EC2 virtual machine in the cluster to run our containers.

> TIP: I've included a shell file, in the `11/06` folder, names `create-cluster-complete.sh`, which runs through all of these commands in one run.

There are number of steps to getting this configured but they are all fairly simple. Let's walk through them:

1. The following creates an ECR cluster named scraper-cluster:

```
$ aws ecs create-cluster --cluster-name scraper-cluster
{
  "cluster": {
    "clusterName": "scraper-cluster",
    "registeredContainerInstancesCount": 0,
    "clusterArn": "arn:aws:ecs:us-
west-2:414704166289:cluster/scraper-cluster",
    "status": "ACTIVE",
    "activeServicesCount": 0,
    "pendingTasksCount": 0,
    "runningTasksCount": 0
  }
}
```

Wow, that was easy! Well, there's a bit of detail to take care of yet. At this point, we don't have any EC2 instances to run the containers. We also need to set up key pairs, security groups, IAM policies, phew! It seems like a lot, but we'll get through it quickly and easily.

2. Create a key pair. Every EC2 instance needs one to launch, and it is needed to remote into the instance (if you want to). The following creates a key pair, puts it in a local file, and then confirms with AWS that it was created:

```
$ aws ec2 create-key-pair --key-name ScraperClusterKP --query
'KeyMaterial' --output text > ScraperClusterKP.pem

$ aws ec2 describe-key-pairs --key-name ScraperClusterKP
{
  "KeyPairs": [
    {
      "KeyFingerprint":
"4a:8a:22:fa:53:a7:87:df:c5:17:d9:4f:b1:df:4e:22:48:90:27:2d",
      "KeyName": "ScraperClusterKP"
    }
  ]
}
```

3. Now we create security groups. A security group allows us to open ports to the cluster instance from the Internet, and hence allows us to access the apps running in our containers. We will create a security group with ports 22 (ssh) and 80 (http), and the two ports for RabbitMQ (5672 and 15672) opened. We need 80 open to talk to the REST API (we'll map 80 to the 8080 containers in the next recipe). We don't need 15672 and 5672 open, but they help with debugging the process by allowing you to connect into RabbitMQ from outside AWS. The following four commands create the security group and the rules in that group:

```
$ aws ec2 create-security-group --group-name ScraperClusterSG --
description "Scraper Cluster SG”
{
  "GroupId": "sg-5e724022"
}

$ aws ec2 authorize-security-group-ingress --group-name
ScraperClusterSG --protocol tcp --port 22 --cidr 0.0.0.0/0

$ aws ec2 authorize-security-group-ingress --group-name
ScraperClusterSG --protocol tcp --port 80 --cidr 0.0.0.0/0

$ aws ec2 authorize-security-group-ingress --group-name
```

```
ScraperClusterSG --protocol tcp --port 5672 --cidr 0.0.0.0/0

$ aws ec2 authorize-security-group-ingress --group-name
ScraperClusterSG --protocol tcp --port 15672 --cidr 0.0.0.0/0
```

You can confirm the contents of the security group using the aws ec2 describe-security-groups --group-names ScraperClusterSG command. This will output a JSON representation of the group.

4. To launch an EC2 instance into an ECS cluster, it needs to have an IAM policy put in place to allow it to connect. It also needs to have various abilities with ECR, such as pulling containers. These are defined in the two files included in the recipe directory, `ecsPolicy.json` and `rolePolicy.json`. The following commands will register these policies with IAM (output is omitted):

```
$ aws iam create-role --role-name ecsRole --assume-role-policy-
document file://ecsPolicy.json

$ aws iam put-role-policy --role-name ecsRole --policy-name
ecsRolePolicy --policy-document file://rolePolicy.json

$ aws iam create-instance-profile --instance-profile-name ecsRole

$ aws iam add-role-to-instance-profile --instance-profile-name
ecsRole --role-name ecsRole
```

We need to do one more thing before we launch the instance. We need to have a file to pass user data to the instance that tells the instance which cluster to connect to. If we don't do this, it will connect to a cluster named `default` instead of `scraper-cluster`. This file is `userData.txt` in the recipe directory. There is no real action here as I provided the file.

5. New we launch an instance in our cluster. We need to use an ECS-optimized AMI or create an AMI with the ECS container agent. We will use a prebuilt AMI with this agent. The following kicks off the instance:

```
$ aws ec2 run-instances --image-id ami-c9c87cb1 --count 1 --
instance-type m4.large --key-name ScraperClusterKP --iam-instance-
profile "Name= ecsRole" --security-groups ScraperClusterSG --user-
data file://userdata.txt
```

This will spit out a bit of JSON describing your instance.

6. After a few minutes, you can check that this instance is running in the container:

```
$ aws ecs list-container-instances --cluster scraper-cluster
{
  "containerInstanceArns": [
    "arn:aws:ecs:us-west-2:414704166289:container-
instance/263d9416-305f-46ff-a344-9e7076ca352a"
  ]
}
```

Awesome! Now we need to define tasks to run on the container instances.

This is an m4.large instance. It's a bit larger than the t2.micro that fits within the free-tier. So, make sure you don't leave this running if you want to keep things cheap.

Creating a task to run our containers

In this recipe, we will create an ECS task. A task tells the ECR cluster manager which containers to run. A task is a description of which containers in ECR to run and the parameters required for each. The task description will feel a lot like that which we have done with Docker Compose.

Getting ready

The task definition can be built with the GUI or started by submitting a task definition JSON file. We will use the latter technique and examine the structure of the file, `td.json`, which describes how to run our containers together. This file is in the `11/07` recipe folder.

How to do it

The following command registers the task with ECS:

```
$ aws ecs register-task-definition --cli-input-json file://td.json
{
  "taskDefinition": {
    "volumes": [
    ],
    "family": "scraper",
```

```
        "memory": "4096",
        "placementConstraints": [
        ]
      ],
      "cpu": "1024",
      "containerDefinitions": [
        {
          "name": "rabbitmq",
          "cpu": 0,
          "volumesFrom": [
          ],
          "mountPoints": [
          ],
          "portMappings": [
            {
              "hostPort": 15672,
              "protocol": "tcp",
              "containerPort": 15672
            },
            {
              "hostPort": 5672,
              "protocol": "tcp",
              "containerPort": 5672
            }
          ],
          "environment": [
          ],
          "image": "414704166289.dkr.ecr.us-west-2.amazonaws.com/rabbitmq",
          "memory": 256,
          "essential": true
        },
        {
          "name": "scraper-microservice",
          "cpu": 0,
          "essential": true,
          "volumesFrom": [
          ],
          "mountPoints": [
          ],
          "portMappings": [
          ],
          "environment": [
            {
              "name": "AMQP_URI",
              "value": "pyamqp://guest:guest@rabbitmq"
            }
          ],
          "image": "414704166289.dkr.ecr.us-west-2.amazonaws.com/scraper-
```

```
microservice",
       "memory": 256,
       "links": [
         "rabbitmq"
       ]
     },
     {
       "name": "api",
       "cpu": 0,
       "essential": true,
       "volumesFrom": [
       ],
       "mountPoints": [
       ],
       "portMappings": [
         {
           "hostPort": 80,
           "protocol": "tcp",
           "containerPort": 8080
         }
       ],
       "environment": [
         {
           "name": "AMQP_URI",
           "value": "pyamqp://guest:guest@rabbitmq"
         },
         {
           "name": "ES_HOST",
           "value":
"https://elastic:tduhdExunhEWPjSuH73O6yLS@7dc72d3327076cc4daf5528103c46a27.
us-west-2.aws.found.io:9243"
         }
       ],
       "image": "414704166289.dkr.ecr.us-west-2.amazonaws.com/scraper-rest-
api",
       "memory": 128,
       "links": [
         "rabbitmq"
       ]
     }
   ],
   "requiresCompatibilities": [
     "EC2"
   ],
   "status": "ACTIVE",
   "taskDefinitionArn": "arn:aws:ecs:us-west-2:414704166289:task-
definition/scraper:7",
   "requiresAttributes": [
```

```
        {
          "name": "com.amazonaws.ecs.capability.ecr-auth"
        }
      ],
      "revision": 7,
      "compatibilities": [
        "EC2"
      ]
    }
```

The output is the definition as filled out by ECS and acknowledges receipt of the task definition.

How it works

The task definition consists of two primary sections. The first gives some general information about the tasks as a whole, such as how much memory and CPU is allowed for the containers as a whole. It then consists of a section that defines the three containers we will run.

The file begins with a few lines that define the overall settings:

```
    {
        "family": "scraper-as-a-service",
        "requiresCompatibilities": [
            "EC2"
        ],
        "cpu": "1024",
        "memory": "4096",
        "volumes": [],
```

The actual name of the task is defined by the `"family"` property. We state the our containers require EC2 (tasks can be run without EC2 - ours needs it). Then we state that we want to constrain the entire task to the specified amount of CPU and memory, and we are not attaching any volumes.

Now let's look at the section where the containers are defined. It starts with the following:

```
    "containerDefinitions": [
```

Now let's examine each container definition. The following is the definition for the `rabbitmq` container:

```
{
    "name": "rabbitmq",
    "image": "414704166289.dkr.ecr.us-west-2.amazonaws.com/rabbitmq",
    "cpu": 0,
    "memory": 256,
    "portMappings": [
        {
            "containerPort": 15672,
            "hostPort": 15672,
            "protocol": "tcp"
        },
        {
            "containerPort": 5672,
            "hostPort": 5672,
            "protocol": "tcp"
        }
    ],
    "essential": true
},
```

The first line defines the name of the container, and this name also participates in DNS resolution of the name of this container by the API and scraper containers. The image tag defines the ECR repository URI to pull for the container.

> Make sure to change the image URL for this and the other two containers to that of your repositories.

Next are a definition of maximum CPU (0 is unlimited) and memory to be allowed for this container. The port mapping defines the mappings between the container host (the EC2 instance we created in the cluster) and the container. We map the two RabbitMQ ports.

> The essential tag states that this container must remain running. If it fails, the entire task will be stopped.

The next container defined is the scraper microservice:

```
{
    "name": "scraper-microservice",
    "image": "414704166289.dkr.ecr.us-west-2.amazonaws.com/scraper-
microservice",
    "cpu": 0,
    "memory": 256,
    "essential": true,
    "environment": [
        {
            "name": "AMQP_URI",
            "value": "pyamqp://guest:guest@rabbitmq"
        }
    ],
    "links": [
        "rabbitmq"
    ]
},
```

This differs in that it has an environment variable and links defined. The environment variable is the URL for the `rabbitmq` container. ECS will ensure that the environment variable is set to this value within this container (implementing Factor-3). While this is the same URL as when we ran this locally on docker compose, it could be a different URL if the `rabbitmq` container was named differently or on another cluster.

The links settings needs a little explanation. Links are a deprecated feature of Docker but still used in ECS. They are required in ECS to have the container resolve DNS names for other containers in the same cluster network. This tells ECS that when this container tries to resolve the `rabbitmq` hostname (as defined in the environment variable), it should return the IP address assigned to that container.

The remainder of the file defines the API container:

```
{
  "name": "api",
  "image": "414704166289.dkr.ecr.us-west-2.amazonaws.com/scraper-rest-api",
  "cpu": 0,
  "memory": 128,
  "essential": true,
  "portMappings": [
    {
      "containerPort": 8080,
      "hostPort": 80,
      "protocol": "tcp"
    }
```

```
    ],
    "environment": [
      {
        "name": "AMQP_URI",
        "value": "pyamqp://guest:guest@rabbitmq"
      },
      {
        "name": "ES_HOST",
        "value":
"https://elastic:tduhdExunhEWPjSuH73O6yLS@7dc72d3327076cc4daf5528103c46a27.
us-west-2.aws.found.io:9243"
      }
    ],
    "links": [
      "rabbitmq"
    ]
}
      ]
}
```

In this definition, we define the port mapping to allow HTTP into the container, and set the environment variables for the API to use to talk to Elastic Cloud and the `rabbitmq` server (which passed the requests to the `scraper-microservice` container). This also defines a link to `rabbitmq` as that needs to also be resolved.

Starting and accessing the containers in AWS

In this recipe, we will start our scraper as a service by telling ECS to run our task definition. Then we will check hat it is running by issuing a curl to get contents of a job listing.

Getting ready

We need to do one quick thing before running the task. Tasks in ECS go through revisions. Each time you register a task definition with the same name ("family"), ECS defines a new revision number. You can run any of the revisions.

To run the most recent one, we need to list the task definitions for that family and find the most recent revision number. The following lists all of the task definitions in the cluster. At this point we only have one:

```
$ aws ecs list-task-definitions
{
  "taskDefinitionArns": [
    "arn:aws:ecs:us-west-2:414704166289:task-definition/scraper-as-a-
service:17"
  ]
}
```

Notice my revision number is at 17. While this is my only currently registered version of this task, I have registered (and unregistered) 16 previous revisions.

How to do it

We proceed with the recipe as follows:

1. Now we can run our task. We do this with the following command:

```
$ aws ecs run-task --cluster scraper-cluster --task-definition
scraper-as-a-service:17 --count 1
{
  "tasks": [
    {
      "taskArn": "arn:aws:ecs:us-
west-2:414704166289:task/00d7b868-1b99-4b54-9f2a-0d5d0ae75197",
      "version": 1,
      "group": "family:scraper-as-a-service",
      "containerInstanceArn": "arn:aws:ecs:us-
west-2:414704166289:container-instance/5959fd63-7fd6-4f0e-92aa-
ea136dabd762",
      "taskDefinitionArn": "arn:aws:ecs:us-
west-2:414704166289:task-definition/scraper-as-a-service:17",
      "containers": [
        {
          "name": "rabbitmq",
          "containerArn": "arn:aws:ecs:us-
west-2:414704166289:container/4b14d4d5-422c-4ffa-
a64c-476a983ec43b",
          "lastStatus": "PENDING",
          "taskArn": "arn:aws:ecs:us-
west-2:414704166289:task/00d7b868-1b99-4b54-9f2a-0d5d0ae75197",
          "networkInterfaces": [
```

```
          ]
        },
        {
          "name": "scraper-microservice",
          "containerArn": "arn:aws:ecs:us-
west-2:414704166289:container/511b39d2-5104-4962-
a859-86fdd46568a9",
          "lastStatus": "PENDING",
          "taskArn": "arn:aws:ecs:us-
west-2:414704166289:task/00d7b868-1b99-4b54-9f2a-0d5d0ae75197",
          "networkInterfaces": [
          ]
        },
        {
          "name": "api",
          "containerArn": "arn:aws:ecs:us-
west-2:414704166289:container/0e660af7-e2e8-4707-b04b-
b8df18bc335b",
          "lastStatus": "PENDING",
          "taskArn": "arn:aws:ecs:us-
west-2:414704166289:task/00d7b868-1b99-4b54-9f2a-0d5d0ae75197",
          "networkInterfaces": [
          ]
        }
      ],
      "launchType": "EC2",
      "overrides": {
        "containerOverrides": [
          {
            "name": "rabbitmq"
          },
          {
            "name": "scraper-microservice"
          },
          {
            "name": "api"
          }
        ]
      },
      "lastStatus": "PENDING",
      "createdAt": 1515739041.287,
      "clusterArn": "arn:aws:ecs:us-
west-2:414704166289:cluster/scraper-cluster",
      "memory": "4096",
      "cpu": "1024",
      "desiredStatus": "RUNNING",
      "attachments": [
      ]
```

```
    }
  ],
  "failures": [
  ]
}
```

The output gives us a current status of the task. The very first time this is run, it will take a little time to get going, as the containers are being copied over to the EC2 instance. The main culprit of that delayu is the `scraper-microservice` container with all of the NLTK data.

2. You can check the status of the task with the following command:

```
$ aws ecs describe-tasks --cluster scraper-cluster --task
00d7b868-1b99-4b54-9f2a-0d5d0ae75197
```

You will need to change the task GUID to match guid in the `"taskArn"` property of the output from running the task. When all the containers are running, we are ready to test the API.

3. To call our service, we will need to find the IP address or DNS name for our cluster instance. you can get this from the output when we created the cluster, through the portal, or with the following commands. First, describe the cluster instances:

```
$ aws ecs list-container-instances --cluster scraper-cluster
{
  "containerInstanceArns": [
    "arn:aws:ecs:us-west-2:414704166289:container-
instance/5959fd63-7fd6-4f0e-92aa-ea136dabd762"
  ]
}
```

4. With the GUID for our EC2 instance, we can query its info and pull the EC2 instance ID with the following:

```
$ aws ecs describe-container-instances --cluster scraper-cluster --
container-instances 5959fd63-7fd6-4f0e-92aa-ea136dabd762 | grep
"ec2InstanceId"
            "ec2InstanceId": "i-08614daf41a9ab8a2",
```

5. With that instance ID, we can get the DNS name:

```
$ aws ec2 describe-instances --instance-ids i-08614daf41a9ab8a2 |
grep "PublicDnsName"
                    "PublicDnsName": "ec2-52-27-26-220.us-
west-2.compute.amazonaws.com",
                                        "PublicDnsName":
"ec2-52-27-26-220.us-west-2.compute.amazonaws.com"
                                "PublicDnsName":
"ec2-52-27-26-220.us-west-2.compute.amazonaws.com"
```

6. And with that DNS name, we can make a curl to get a job listing:

```
$ curl ec2-52-27-26-220.us-
west-2.compute.amazonaws.com/joblisting/122517 | head -n 6
```

And we get the following familiar result!

```
{
  "ID": "122517",
  "JSON": {
    "@context": "http://schema.org",
    "@type": "JobPosting",
    "title": "SpaceX Enterprise Software Engineer, Full Stack",
```

Our scraper is now running in the cloud!

There's more...

Our scraper is running on an `m4.large` instance, so we would like to shut it down to we don't exceed our free-tier usage. This is a two-step process. First, the EC2 instances in the cluster need to be terminated, and the cluster deleted. Note that deleting the cluster DOES NOT terminate the EC2 instances.

We can terminate the EC2 instance using the following (and the instance ID we just got from interrogating the cluster):

```
$ aws ec2 terminate-instances --instance-ids i-08614daf41a9ab8a2
{
  "TerminatingInstances": [
    {
      "CurrentState": {
        "Name": "shutting-down",
        "Code": 32
      },
```

```
        "PreviousState": {
          "Name": "running",
          "Code": 16
        },
        "InstanceId": "i-08614daf41a9ab8a2"
      }
    ]
  }
```

And the cluster can be deleted with:

```
$ aws ecs delete-cluster --cluster scraper-cluster
{
  "cluster": {
    "activeServicesCount": 0,
    "pendingTasksCount": 0,
    "clusterArn": "arn:aws:ecs:us-west-2:414704166289:cluster/scraper-
cluster",
    "runningTasksCount": 0,
    "clusterName": "scraper-cluster",
    "registeredContainerInstancesCount": 0,
    "status": "INACTIVE"
  }
}
```

Other Books You May Enjoy

If you enjoyed this book, you may be interested in these other books by Packt:

Learning Data Mining with Python - Second Edition
Robert Layton

ISBN: 9781787126787

- Apply data mining concepts to real-world problems
- Predict the outcome of sports matches based on past results
- Determine the author of a document based on their writing style
- Use APIs to download datasets from social media and other online services
- Find and extract good features from difficult datasets
- Create models that solve real-world problems
- Design and develop data mining applications using a variety of datasets
- Perform object detection in images using Deep Neural Networks
- Find meaningful insights from your data through intuitive visualizations
- Compute on big data, including real-time data from the internet

Python Social Media Analytics
Siddhartha Chatterjee, Michal Krystyanczuk

ISBN: 9781787121485

- Understand the basics of social media mining
- Use PyMongo to clean, store, and access data in MongoDB
- Understand user reactions and emotion detection on Facebook
- Perform Twitter sentiment analysis and entity recognition using Python
- Analyze video and campaign performance on YouTube
- Mine popular trends on GitHub and predict the next big technology
- Extract conversational topics on public internet forums
- Analyze user interests on Pinterest
- Perform large-scale social media analytics on the cloud

Leave a review - let other readers know what you think

Please share your thoughts on this book with others by leaving a review on the site that you bought it from. If you purchased the book from Amazon, please leave us an honest review on this book's Amazon page. This is vital so that other potential readers can see and use your unbiased opinion to make purchasing decisions, we can understand what our customers think about our products, and our authors can see your feedback on the title that they have worked with Packt to create. It will only take a few minutes of your time, but is valuable to other potential customers, our authors, and Packt. Thank you!

Index

1

12-Factor application
  about 310
  reference 310

A

API container
  creating 279, 282
API
  modifying, for job search 307
auto throttling
  reference 143
  using 142
AWS containers
  accessing 331, 335
  starting 331, 335
AWS queue
  messages, posting to 86
AWS S3
  reference 70
  used, for data storage 65, 70
AWS SQS
  used, for building robust ETL pipelines 85
axis 39

B

bans
  prevention, by scraping via proxies 171
basic authorization
  handling 170
Beautiful Soup
  Python.org, scraping 13, 17, 19

C

caching responses 174, 175
concurrent requests per domain count
  setting 141
container
  image, removing 264
  pushing, into ECR 316
  stopping/restarting 264
contributor location frequency
  visualizing, on Wikipedia 217
crawl depth
  controlling 159
crawl length
  controlling 162
CSS selectors
  reference 48
  used, for querying data 46
CSV
  reference 65
  working with 56, 62
curl
  used, for accessing Elastic Cloud cluster 294

D

degrees of separation
  calculating 232
Docker container (RabbitMQ)
  running 259
Docker Hub
  RabbitMQ container, installing 256
docker-compose
  reference 282
  used, for local composing of scraper 282, 288
Docker
  configuring, for authentication with ECR 314
  installing 254, 256

reference 254
document object model (DOM)
navigating, BeautifulSoup used 30, 35
searching with Beautiful Soup's find methods 35
DSL
reference 303

E

ECR
containers, pushing 316
ECS cluster
creating 322
ECS task
creating 325, 330
ECS
AWS IAM user and key pair, creating 312
Elastic Cloud cluster
accessing, with curl 294
connecting, with Python 295, 299
Elastic Cloud trial account
configuring 290
creating 290
Elasticsearch container
executing 262
Elasticsearch query
performing, with Python 303
performing, with Python API 299
Elasticsearch
data, storing 244, 249
reference 244
stored job listing, checking 250
used, for data storage 81, 84
used, for querying for jobs with specific skills 303, 307
elements
used, for querying data 46
environment
configuration, storing 311

F

failed page downloads
strategies, retrying 146
file extension
determining, from content type 98
find method, Beautiful Soup
used, for searching DOM 35
Flask-RESTful
used, for creating REST API 236
forms authorization
handling 166, 169
forms-based authorization
handling 166, 169
freegeoip.net
reference 210
frequency distributions, words
calculating 188

G

generic microservice
creating, with Nameko 267, 271
Google maps geocoding API
reference 210

H

HTTP cache for development
using 143

I

IAM user
reference 312
identifiable user agents
using 140, 141
images
OCR, perfpytesseract 115
thumbnails, generating 103
infinitely scrolling pages
processing 153, 158
IP address
geocoding 210

J

job listing
description, cleaning 203
description, reading 203
scraping, from StackOverflow 198, 202
skill search, by adding API 242
JSON data
working with 56, 62

JSON
reference 65

L

legality
scraping 123
lemmatization
performing 184
links
crawling, in Wikipedia 223
lxml
reference 39
used, for querying DOM 38, 45

M

media content
downloading, from web 92
media
downloading, to local file system 99
saving, to local file system 99
messages
processing 89
reading 88
MP4 video
ripping, to MP3 120
MySQL
used, for data storage 70, 75

N

n-grams
attaching 194
Nameko
used, for creating generic microservice 267, 271
NLTK
installing 178

P

page redirects 147
page relationships
visualizing, on Wikipedia 227, 231
paginated websites
handling 163, 166
PhantomJS
used, for scraping Python.org 25, 28
Pillow
reference 103
PostgreSQL
used, for data storage 76, 80
punctuation marks
removing 193
pytesseract
reference 115
used, for performing OCR on image 115
Python API
Elasticsearch query, performing with 299
Elasticsearch, performing with 303
Python development environment
setting up 8, 9, 12
Python events
reference 13
Python.org
scraping, in urllib3 19
scraping, with Beautiful Soup 13, 18, 19
scraping, with PhantomJS 25
scraping, with Requests 13, 18
scraping, with Scrapy 21, 24
scraping, with Selenium 25, 28
Python
connecting, with Elastic Cloud cluster 295, 299
page link 223

R

RabbitMQ container
installing, from Docker Hub 257
rare words
identifying 190, 192
removing 190, 192
Requests
Python.org, scraping 13, 17
REST API
integrating, with scraper code 239
robots.txt
reference 126, 129
using, with reppy library 125, 129
robust ETL pipelines
building, with AWS SQS 85

S

S3
  images, downloading 101
  images, saving 101
scraper code
  REST API , integrating with 239
scraper container
  creating 273, 278
scraper
  using, considerations 123
scraping microservice
  creating 271
Scrapy selectors
  reference 50
  using 48
Scrapy
  about 21
  examining, with delays 137, 139
  used, for scraping Python.org 21, 24
screenshot API
  reference 109
screenshot, website
  capturing 106
  capturing, with external service 109
Selenium
  content, awaiting 149
  used, for scraping Python.org 25, 28
sentence splitting
  performing 179, 181
single domain
  crawling, limiting 152
sitemap
  about 129
  used, for crawling 130, 135
StackOverflow job listing
  scraping 198
  word cloud, creating 220
StackOverflow
  job listing , scraping 201
stemming
  performing 183
stop words
  determining 186
  removing 186

T

thumbnails
  generating, for images 103
tokenization
  performing 181

U

unicode / UTF-8
  data, loading 50, 53
URL
  content type, determining 96
  parsing, with urllib 94
urllib3
  Python.org, scraping 19
urllib
  used, for parsing URL 94
user agents
  randomization 172

V

video thumbnail
  creating 117, 120

W

Web scraping page
  reference 214
web
  media content, downloading 92
  screenshot, capturing 106
  screenshot, capturing with external service 109
websites
  parsing 30, 35
Wikipedia edits
  addresses, collecting 213, 217
Wikipedia
  contributor location frequency, visualizing 217
  links, crawling 222, 227
  page relationships, visualizing 227, 231
word cloud
  creating, from StackOverflow job listing 220

X

XPath
  reference 45
  used, for querying CSS selectors 46
  used, for querying DOM 38, 44
XSLT (eXtensible Stylesheet Language Transformation) 45

Printed in Great Britain
by Amazon

82062819R00208